PANZER
COMMANDER
HERMANN
BALCK

STEPHEN ROBINSON studied Asian history and politics at the University of Western Sydney, graduating with First Class Honours. He has worked at the Department of Veterans' Affairs researching British atomic weapons tests and as a policy officer in the Department of Defence. He is also an officer in the Australian Army Reserve and has served as an instructor at the Royal Military College. He also graduated from Australian Command and Staff College. His book *False Flags: Disguised German Raiders of World War II* was published in 2016, and *The Blind Strategist: John Boyd and the American Art of War* was published in early 2021, both by Exisle Publishing.

PANZER
COMMANDER
HERMANN BALCK
GERMANY'S MASTER
TACTICIAN

STEPHEN ROBINSON

EXISLE
PUBLISHING

First published 2019
This edition published 2022

Exisle Publishing Pty Ltd
PO Box 864, Chatswood, NSW 2057, Australia
226 High Street, Dunedin, 9016, New Zealand
www.exislepublishing.com

A CiP record for this book is available from the National Library of Australia.

ISBN 978-1-922539-11-3

Designed by Nick Turzynski, redinc. Book Design, www.redinc.co.nz
Typeset in Baskerville 11/15
Printed in China

This book uses paper sourced under ISO 14001 guidelines from well-managed forests and
other controlled sources.

10 9 8 7 6 5 4 3 2 1

To my brother James

CONTENTS

Hermann Balck.
(Bundesarchiv, Bild 101I-732-0118-03)

INTRODUCTION

Although Germany produced a number of truly outstanding Panzer commanders during World War II, few were more successful or more accomplished than Hermann Balck.[1]

Carlo D'Este

Perhaps the most brilliant field commander on either side in World War II was Hermann Balck.[2]

Freeman Dyson

HERMANN THE OBSCURE

On 8 May 1945, the day World War II in Europe ended, General Hermann Balck presented himself to Major General Horace McBride, commander of the American 80th Infantry Division, in the Austrian town of Kirchdorf. Balck had come to arrange the surrender of the German 6th Army to American forces, desperate to ensure that his soldiers would not become prisoners of the Soviet Union. This act ended the career of an extraordinary panzer commander, although McBride and his victorious troops did not realize the importance of their new prisoner whose unfamiliar surname, Balck, meant nothing to them.

Balck had earlier established himself as one of the finest armoured warfare commanders in history during the Chir River battles, a series of desperate engagements fought on the frozen steppes of southern Russia during Germany's disastrous Stalingrad campaign. On 8 December 1942, when commanding the 11th Panzer Division, he annihilated the Soviet 1st Tank Corps at Sovchos 79, destroying fifty-three Red Army tanks. One week later, with only twenty-five operational panzers, Balck attacked the Soviet bridgehead at Nizhna Kalinovski and destroyed sixty-five Russian tanks while only losing three panzers.

Balck's extraordinary achievements at the Chir River earned him a well-deserved reputation within the *Wehrmacht* as a commander who led from the front and won battles despite fighting against overwhelming odds. The German High Command recognized his courageous leadership, awarding him the Knight's Cross with Oak Leaves, Swords and Diamonds, a prestigious medal given to only twenty-six other Germans during World War II. General Heinrich Gaedcke, who served under Balck on the Eastern Front, remembered him as a 'model field commander' and a 'man of unconventional, brilliant ideas and inspirations'.[3]

Despite Balck's exceptional military record, he received little recognition after the war. Unlike Erwin Rommel, Heinz Guderian and Erich von Manstein, who will forever be associated in the popular imagination as legendary German commanders, history has largely forgotten Hermann Balck. The historian Carlo D'Este accordingly observed that his name 'is conspicuously missing from the list of successful generals'.[4] David Zabecki similarly concluded that Balck is the 'greatest German general no one ever heard of'.[5]

Balck's obscurity in the English-speaking world partly resulted from the fact that he spent most of the war on the Eastern Front, distinguishing himself in battles unfamiliar to most westerners — the Kiev salient in 1943, Ternopil and Kovel in 1944, and the siege of Budapest in 1945. He only fought the Americans twice, at Salerno following the Allied invasion of Italy in 1943 and during the poorly remembered Lorraine campaign in 1944, when he opposed General George S. Patton.

Balck also contributed to his own obscurity by avoiding the spotlight after the war. While a prisoner in American custody, he refused to participate in historical work conducted by the United States Army's Historical Division, unlike many former German generals who used this opportunity to inflate their own reputations. After being released in 1947, Balck worked in a warehouse to support his family and made no effort to publicize his

Hermann Balck.
(Author's Collection)

past deeds. He remained silent when other *Wehrmacht* veterans wrote their memoirs, notably Guderian's *Panzer Leader* and Manstein's *Lost Victories*, which became bestsellers and ensured their post-war fame.

The few histories which did mention Balck immediately after the war often portrayed him in an unfavourable light. Hugh Cole, in *The Lorraine Campaign* (1950), unfairly described him as 'an ardent Nazi' with a 'reputation for arrogant and ruthless dealings with his subordinates' who was just 'the type of commander certain to win Hitler's confidence'.[6] Cole concluded that Balck was 'an optimist' who was 'prone to take too favorable a view of things when the situation failed to warrant optimism'.[7] Chester Wilmot in *The Struggle for Europe* (1952), clearly referencing Hugh Cole, similarly declared:

> The command [of Army Group G] was given to General Hermann
> Balck, an experienced tank commander and a notorious optimist with a
> reputation for ruthless aggression. This appointment was not welcomed
> by von Rundstedt, for Balck had no experience of operations against the
> Western Powers. With Hitler, however, this was no doubt a point in his
> favour.[8]

Actually, Balck had fought the western Allies in France in 1940, Greece in 1941 and Italy in 1943. Despite such slander, his legacy slowly emerged from obscurity and distortion, initially due to the efforts of Friedrich von Mellenthin. As a General Staff officer, Mellenthin had served as an operations and intelligence officer in Rommel's *Afrika Korps* before becoming Balck's chief-of-staff in the 48th Panzer Corps on the Eastern Front. After the war, Mellenthin wrote *Panzer Battles* (1956), which became a bestseller, and in this book he defended Balck's reputation and sought to correct the historical record. 'I regret that in that remarkable work, *The Struggle for Europe*,' Mellenthin explained, 'Chester Wilmot has followed the estimate of Balck's qualities given in the American official history, *The Lorraine Campaign*, where Balck is portrayed as a swashbuckling martinet.'[9] Mellenthin countered such impressions and concluded: 'If Manstein was Germany's greatest strategist during World War II, I think Balck has strong claims to be regarded as our finest field commander.'[10] Mellenthin also convinced Balck to end his long post-war silence.

After experiencing a devastating defeat in the jungles of Vietnam, the American Army sought to reform itself by refocusing on its traditional Cold War role of defending NATO against a feared Soviet invasion of Western Europe. However, in doing so it faced the dilemma of how to fight the Red Army and win despite being vastly outnumbered. The army's leadership sought the solution to this problem by studying the *Wehrmacht*'s Eastern Front operations and accordingly invited Mellenthin and Balck to America where they became military consultants, participating in symposiums, conferences and wargames during the late 1970s and early 1980s. The Americans found themselves in awe of Balck's first-hand accounts of his Eastern Front battles and General William E. DePuy, commander of Training and Doctrine Command, considered him to be 'the best division commander in the German Army'.[11] Balck's advice strongly shaped the American Army's AirLand Battle concept, which forms the basis of western military doctrine to this day.

Balck, through his engagement with the American military, gained a Sun Tzu-like reputation as officers frequently quoted his maxims as sage wisdom in their academic studies and military journals. In a typical example, Lieutenant Colonel Douglas Pryer declared in *Military Review*:

> Moltke cemented the support that military culture, education, and training gave to what had become decentralized command. Schools gave extensive tactical educations even to junior officers and non-commissioned officers. . . . Much later, the World War II German Gen. Hermann Balck would say: 'We lived off a century-long tradition, which is that in a critical situation the subordinate with an understanding of the overall situation can act or react responsibly. We always placed great emphasis on the independent action of the subordinates, even in peacetime training.'[12]

As Balck's cult status in the American military grew, the Army's Staff College taught its students that his command of the 11th Panzer Division during the Chir River battles constituted the epitome of military excellence.[13]

Balck recorded his thoughts in a journal between 1914 and 1945, which formed the basis of his long-overdue memoir *Order in Chaos*, first published in English in 2015.[14] The book reveals a thoroughly professional soldier and a deeply private man. Balck only hints at his domestic life and tells the reader nothing about his children until he encounters his son Friedrich-Wilhelm, a fellow soldier, in France in 1940. He then gives a purely military account on the burden of having offspring in one's chain of command. Balck, true to his reserved natured, only mentioned his wife once in his memoir when reminiscing about their time together in Slovakia when he was on leave from the front in 1943.

Balck's exploits have received the recognition they deserved within professional military circles and, over time, his battlefield success has also received significant attention in notable popular works such as Dennis Showalter's *Hitler's Panzers*, Peter McCarthy and Mike Syron's *Panzerkrieg* and James Holland's *The War in the West*. As historical memory of Balck has emerged from obscurity, the time is right for a wider audience to become acquainted with this remarkable leader of panzer troops.

HERMANN THE SOLDIER

Mathilde Balck gave birth to her son Hermann on 7 December 1893 in Danzig-Langfuhr in East Prussia. The Balck family came from Scandinavian roots, having migrated from Sweden to Finland in 1120, but after the Thirty Years' War, his branch of the family settled in Germany along the lower Elbe River. Balck's immediate ancestors had distinguished military careers; his great-grandfather migrated to England and served as an officer in the King's German Legion and on Wellington's staff during the Napoleonic Wars. Georg Balck, his grandfather, also moved to England and became an officer in the 93rd (Sutherland Highlanders) Regiment of Foot before losing his eyesight in the West Indies. The family practice of fighting for Britain ended during World War I when his father, Lieutenant General William Balck, commanded the German 51st Reserve Division, earning the *Pour le Mérite* (Blue Max), the Kaiser's highest award for valour.

After Germany's defeat, William Balck wrote *Development of Tactics — World War*, an authoritative account of Germany's recent military experience, and the English translation became an American Army textbook. Balck recalled that his father 'was the last great tactical theoretician of the Kaiser's army' who instilled in him 'extensive military and general mentorship'.[15] Balck's remarkable father, more importantly, taught him to understand ordinary people and instilled in him a progressive social conscience:

> I grew up and was educated as a soldier. But I also learned something else from my father, something even more significant — a deep sense and understanding for the lowest ranking troops and the mistakes of our social class.[16]

Balck, accordingly, developed a thorough understanding of his soldiers as people and led them with a strong sense of justice.

During World War I, the young Hermann Balck saw extensive action on the Western, Eastern, Italian and Balkan Fronts. In 1913, he became an officer candidate in the 10th *Jäger* (Light Infantry) Battalion based in Goslar, before attending the Hanoverian Military College in February 1914. Balck was promoted to second lieutenant as the guns of August raged. He first experienced combat while commanding a platoon from the 10th *Jäger* during the attack on the Liège fortress in Belgium on 8 August 1914:

> In the town we encountered the first dead bodies of Belgian farmers, small people with grimacing faces full of anger and deadly fear. Cattle were running around without their masters. A few women squatted with the remnants of their belongings, staring with empty eyes. This was our first glimpse of war.[17]

Balck later fought the French and the British on the Western Front. During an engagement at Fontaine-au-Pire, he learned a valuable lesson which he applied throughout his military career: 'A successful attack is less costly than a failed defense.'[18] At Ypres, Balck personally experienced the brutal violence:

> As shots rang out, the commander of 2nd Company, Captain Radtke, collapsed right next to me. He had been shot dead through the heart. I was hit in the left hip. I stumbled and fell right in front of the Englishman who had shot at me, and I was able to kill him with a pistol shot as he was rechambering his rifle.[19]

Before 1914 came to an end, Balck had become adjutant of the 10th *Jäger* and survived being shot in his right arm, left ear and back as well as suffering a grenade splinter in his hip. The army recognized his bravery, awarding him the Iron Crosses (1st Class and 2nd Class).

In 1915, Balck transferred to the 22nd Reserve *Jäger* Battalion and commanded its 4th Company in Poland, Serbia and Russia. During the brutal trench warfare near Pinsk, he learned another valuable lesson that would become the hallmark of his future command style:

> Although things were quiet during the day, a lively war between the trenches began at night. The Russians used every trick in the book, including confusing us with German speakers and conducting silent

ambushes from the rear. It was not always easy to keep our troops alert. They were innocently unsuspecting. I tried time and again to be in the right place when incidents happened, and often was able to prevent the worst.[20]

Balck, early in his military career, understood the need to be well forward with his men at the critical place to gain full situational awareness and exploit fleeting opportunities. He stayed with his company despite receiving shrapnel wounds in his right shoulder. After being given command of a *Jagdkommando* (special operations group) from the 5th Cavalry Division, Balck conducted raids behind Russian lines, including one patrol through the Rokitno swamps which lasted weeks.

In 1916, Balck returned to the 10th *Jäger* to command its machine gun company and, after leaving the Eastern Front, he fought in the mountains of Romania. As the war dragged on in 1917, he led his troops into battle in the Italian Alps as part of the division-sized *Alpenkorps*, where he survived bullet wounds to his chest, left arm and both hands. On another occasion, after an Italian machine gun propelled bullets into his chest and both arms, Balck returned to the front the next day with both arms in a sling.

In 1918, Balck successfully requested command of 4th Company of the 10th *Jäger* even though he knew the previous twelve company commanders had all been killed. He led the company in northern France, Macedonia, Serbia and Hungary. As the tide of war turned decisively against Germany and the spectre of revolution haunted the officers, Balck understood how to avoid the slide into the abyss:

Wherever the officers avoided the constant mass-produced mush, there was discontent; where the officers ate from the field kitchen, there was no sense of revolution. . . . No German soldier will turn against an officer who shares his joy and pain, death and danger.[21]

After shell splinters ripped into his hip and knee, Balck was awarded the Wound Badge in Gold and was recommended for the *Pour le Mérite*, but the war ended before he could be awarded the deserved medal.

After the armistice, as revolution in Germany ushered in the unstable

Weimar Republic, Balck and the survivors of the 10th *Jäger* returned to Goslar where the local workers' and soldiers' council mandated the battalion elect a soldiers' council. The troops unanimously elected Balck chairman of their council and, soon afterwards, the locals elected him head of the Goslar workers' and soldiers' committee.[22] During this chaotic time, a grateful veteran declared to Balck, 'I thank you, sir, in the name of all my comrades for everything you have done for our company.'[23] Hans Falkenstein, a private from the 10th *Jäger*, shared this sentiment in a letter to Balck, 'I participated with you as my company commander in the campaign in the West and in Serbia. I always like to remember you as a capable, courageous, and just leader.'[24]

As bloody frontier violence erupted between Germans and Poles, Balck and his unit, now renamed the Hanoverian Volunteer *Jäger* Battalion, fought in Poznań province during this savage ethnic conflict.

Although the Treaty of Versailles limited the *Reichswehr* to 4000 officers, Balck remained in the army, which is testimony to the faith the hierarchy placed in him as it only retained the very best officers. This small band of *Reichswehr* officers formed an elite cohort of exceptionally experienced leaders who saw themselves as heralds of a future army in a reborn Germany. The *Reichswehr* trained all its officers to accept higher levels of responsibility and to use their initiative to seize opportunities without the need to wait for orders. As these qualities were second nature to Balck, he thrived in the interwar army, becoming the adjutant of the 3rd *Jäger* Battalion.

In 1923, Balck transferred to the 18th Cavalry Regiment at Stuttgart to command its machine gun platoon. He swiftly rose through the ranks, being promoted to first lieutenant in 1924 and captain in 1929.

During the 1930s, Balck served in the 3rd Cavalry Division and commanded the 1st Bicycle Battalion. After serving as an exchange officer in the Swiss, Finnish and Hungarian armies, he twice turned down the opportunity to become a General Staff officer in preference to remaining a field officer:

> I loved the frontline life, the direct contact with the soldiers and the horses, working with living beings, and the hands-on training with the troops. Becoming a second stringer, as so often happened in the General

Staff, was not for me. Besides, as a member of the General Staff I could
not have pursued the many diverse intellectual interests I enjoyed so much.
Even my military interests, particularly military history, I was able to better
pursue on my personal time. As a General Staff officer one too often was
drowned in bureaucratic office work.[25]

Intellectual curiosity, self-motivated learning and a love of all things classical
were core traits of Balck's character. During World War I, he read from a
complete works of Shakespeare between battles on the Eastern Front and he
also immersed himself in Clausewitz's *On War*: 'Entertaining oneself during
quiet periods on the battlefield by reading the great philosopher of war
produced a strange sense of excitement.'[26]

When on leave from the front, Balck explored the great cities of Europe
to admire their historical treasures and cultural life. 'I drove to Warsaw,' he
recalled, 'where I enjoyed the Russian emperor's ballet dancers' and 'saw
Puccini's Tosca in Polish'.[27] He often visited Budapest and 'never missed the
chance to go sightseeing in this uniquely beautiful city'.[28] In Romania, Balck
explored the Teutonic Order castle at Focşani to admire its architecture. He
also possessed a deep love of antiquity and read his copy of Homer during
the Greek campaign in 1941. Later in Italy in 1943, Balck modified his
artillery plan to ensure that the Greek temples at Paestum remained outside
the bombardment zone.

Although Balck was a cultured man with a deep respect of antiquity,
he willingly fought for Hitler's tyrannical Third Reich and committed two
war crimes during the final stages of the conflict. In November 1944, Balck
ordered the summary execution of Lieutenant Colonel Johann Schottke,
who was found drunk in his bunker and unaware of where his artillery
batteries were located. The execution was conducted outside the framework
of German military justice. In the same month, Balck destroyed the French
town of Gérardmer, after the civilian population fled towards the Allied
lines, as part of a scorched earth policy.

After being promoted to major in 1935, Balck commanded the 1st Bicycle
Battalion in Tilsit before being promoted to lieutenant colonel in 1938. He
next worked in Guderian's Inspectorate of Mobile Troops in the Army High
Command, where he helped craft tactical and doctrinal concepts for cavalry,

motorized infantry and panzers. Balck remained in this position when the *Wehrmacht* invaded Poland on 1 September 1939, as Europe descended into another world war.

During the first month of World War II, Balck liaised with the panzer divisions to assist their reorganization and refitting following the Polish campaign while longing to again command troops at the front. The *Wehrmacht* obliged and gave him command of the 1st Motorized Rifle Regiment on 1 October 1939:

> My assignment as the commander of the 1st Rifle Regiment in Weimar came as quite a relief for me. I would not have chosen any other regiment. In addition to the good reputation the regiment and its officers had, I had just outfitted this unit with the most modern equipment. Everything was armored and mobile. It was the most modern regiment in the army.[29]

This book is about the making of Hermann Balck as a panzer commander and explains his transformation into a master of tactical warfare during the French, Greek and Stalingrad campaigns. However, it is also the story of a remarkable leader who, as Freeman Dyson explained, 'gaily jumped out of one tight squeeze into another, taking good care of his soldiers and never losing his sense of humor'.[30]

Balck commanded the 1st Motorized Rifle Regiment, within the 1st Panzer Division, during the French campaign in 1940. After crossing the Meuse River with his men, he created the decisive breakthrough at Sedan which allowed Guderian's panzers to race to the English Channel and surround the British Expeditionary Force at Dunkirk, instigating the fall of France. Despite this remarkable victory, Balck analysed German tactical shortcomings and theorized a new way in which infantry and tanks would co-operate in battlegroups — the *kampfgruppe* concept — which revolutionized the way panzer divisions fought, allowing them to later achieve stunning success on the Eastern Front.

During the Greek campaign in April 1941, Balck commanded the 3rd Panzer Regiment and put his *kampfgruppe* ideas into practice. Balck's innovative leadership enabled the panzers and infantry in his battlegroup to overcome seemingly impossible obstacles and secure victory against determined Australian and New Zealand soldiers, who defended the perilous roads and alpine passes near Mount Olympus. At Platamon Ridge on the Aegean coast, at the site of a medieval Frankish castle, *Kampfgruppe Balck* overran the New Zealand 21st Battalion in terrain the Allies considered unsuitable for tanks. The shattered New Zealanders regrouped in Tempe Gorge, the legendary home of Aristaeus, the son of Apollo and Cyrene, where they were reinforced by the Australian 2/2nd and 2/3rd Battalions. The Allied troops in the gorge hoped to stop Balck's soldiers in ideal defensive terrain; however, the panzers of *Kampfgruppe Balck* rolled through the Allied lines and continued on the road to Athens.

Balck's command of the 11th Panzer Division in southern Russia in 1942, during the summer offensive drive to the Don River and subsequent Stalingrad campaign, firmly established his place in history as a master of armoured warfare. At the Chir River, Balck fought a series of brutal engagements in the bleak Russian winter where he developed his 'fire brigade' tactics which were later used by the *Wehrmacht* to hold the Red Army at bay against impossible odds.

This book charts the critical period as Balck departed his infantry roots and first took command of an armoured unit, fully explaining his transformation into a uniquely gifted tactician — a journey which began in France.

CHAPTER ONE
BREAKTHROUGH AT SEDAN

THE SICKLE CUT

In 1914, the German Army invaded Belgium and Luxembourg in accordance with a plan devised by General Alfred von Schlieffen, which aimed to attack the French Army in the rear after conducting a massive single envelopment through the Low Countries. After achieving surprise and initial success, the Schlieffen Plan failed as the slow-moving German infantry could not maintain momentum and the French used their railways to redeploy troops, culminating in the Allied victory at the Battle of the Marne.

After the commencement of World War II, the German High Command planned to invade France with a mechanized rerun of the Schlieffen Plan, in which the *Wehrmacht* would outflank the Maginot Line and envelop the French Army by advancing in a circular route through Holland and northern Belgium. The Allies anticipated such a move, and without the element of surprise, the plan had no chance of success.

Lieutenant General Erich von Manstein, chief-of-staff of Army Group A, considered a revived Schlieffen Plan highly predictable and unable to secure victory, a sentiment Balck shared: 'The initial plan was a rerun of the Schlieffen Plan . . . we had to avoid it under all circumstances.'[1]

Manstein instead proposed his alternate 'sickle cut' plan in which Army Group B, under Colonel General Fedor von Bock, would invade Holland and northern Belgium with twenty-six infantry and three panzer divisions

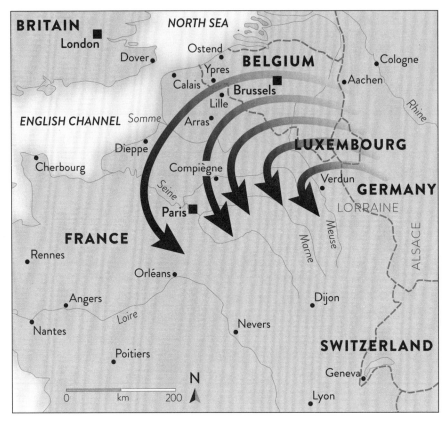

The Schlieffen Plan attempted in 1914.

as a feint to lure the best Allied units north by giving the impression that the Germans were attempting another Schlieffen Plan. With Allied attention focused in the north, Colonel General Gerd von Rundstedt's Army Group A, the main effort with forty-five infantry and seven panzer divisions, would quietly advance through the dense forests and rolling hills of the Ardennes in southern Belgium. Manstein assumed the Ardennes would be weakly defended as the Allies considered the area ill-suited to tanks. Therefore, he believed Rundstedt's panzers could take advantage of this weakness to swiftly advance through the Ardennes, cross the Meuse River and break through the French line at the town of Sedan before the Allies could effectively react. The panzers would then race to the English Channel and outflank the Allied armies marching north into Belgium and, once these forces were destroyed, the Germans would annihilate the rest of the French Army.

On 17 February 1940, Manstein briefed Hitler on his 'sickle cut' plan. The dictator, also dissatisfied with the General Staff's conventional thinking, sided with Manstein and approved the plan, a development Balck praised:

> Manstein gets all the credit for developing under difficult conditions a completely different scheme of maneuver . . . a blow at the pivotal joint of the enemy just as he was attempting to execute an encirclement.[2]

The panzers of Army Group A would be organized into two corps under General Ewald von Kleist, spearheaded by Lieutenant General Heinz Guderian's 19th Panzer Corps, consisting of the 1st, 2nd and 10th Panzer Divisions and the elite *Grossdeutschland* Regiment.

Balck's 1st Motorized Rifle Regiment, within the 1st Panzer Division, would be at the forefront of the 'sickle cut'. As Manstein's plan hinged on the need to swiftly cross the Meuse and overrun the French defenders at Sedan, Guderian avoided overly complex planning and instead gave his subordinates a great deal of initiative during exercises held at the Moselle River. Balck accordingly trained his men for the river crossing as he saw fit:

> . . . we rehearsed everything in detail in both map exercises and field exercises on similar terrain, under combat conditions, including live firing and air support. The Moselle River was the training stand-in for the Meuse. I was not satisfied until every man under my command was able to handle the rubber dinghies just like a combat engineer. I let the exercises run completely uninhibited to allow everybody to get used to independent thinking and acting. It was the best preparation for an offensive that I had ever seen.[3]

Meanwhile, the French Army, commanded by General Maurice Gamelin, assumed the Germans would repeat the Schlieffen Plan and accordingly planned to send thirty divisions, including his best mechanized units, into Belgium and Holland to defend the Dyle River.[4] After the German invasion, these units would race into the Low Countries to establish formidable

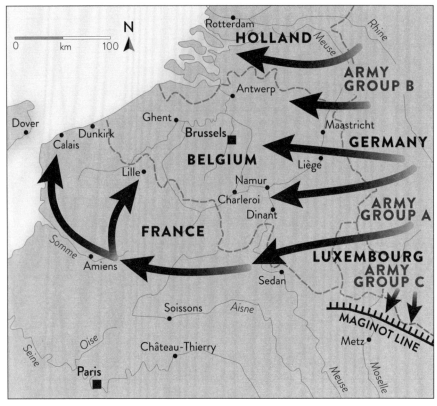

Manstein's 'Sickle Cut' plan to invade France in 1940.

defensive zones to stop the Germans before they reached French soil.[5] Although Sedan had traditionally been a gateway to France for invaders, notably for the Prussians in 1870, Gamelin considered the Ardennes 'Europe's best tank obstacle' due to the area's narrow roads which traversed thick woods and rolling hills.[6] However, the Ardennes, despite its terrain, offered the invaders a decent road network towards the Meuse.[7] As Gamelin considered a German attack at Sedan unlikely, he committed insufficient forces to its defence, allocating Brigadier General Pierre Lafontaine's 55th Infantry Division, a second-rate unit mostly manned by reserve soldiers, and the 147th Fortress Infantry Regiment to defend the west bank of the Meuse.[8]

Despite French weakness at Sedan, the German High Command only half-heartedly endorsed the 'sickle cut' plan. In early 1940, Rundstedt doubted the wisdom of placing his main effort at Sedan and Kleist considered a thrust to the English Channel too risky.[9] Bock advocated the complete abandonment of the 'sickle cut' as the *Wehrmacht* would be 'cramming the mass of the tank units together into the sparse roads of the Ardennes mountain country, as if there were no such thing as air power!'[10] On 17 March 1940, Army Group A's senior commanders conferred with Hitler at the Reich Chancellery. After Guderian explained his intention to cross the Meuse by the fifth day of the campaign, Lieutenant General Ernst Busch interjected, 'Well, I don't think you'll cross the river in the first place!'[11] Given the High Command's pessimism, the success of the 'sickle cut' would ultimately depend on the actions of field commanders like Guderian and Balck.

TOWARDS THE MEUSE

On 10 May 1940, Germany invaded the Low Countries. A small glider force captured the Belgian fortress of Eben Emael and German paratrooper landings in Holland convinced the Allies that Army Group B in the north constituted the main attack.[12] As Manstein predicted, the best Allied troops advanced into Belgium while the 134,000 soldiers and 1600 armoured vehicles of *Panzergruppe Kleist* — the largest mechanized force in history — quietly advanced through the Ardennes forest towards the Meuse River.[13]

Balck had been given temporary command of the 1st Panzer Division's advance guard consisting of the 1st Motorcycle Battalion, an armed reconnaissance troop and the 3rd Battalion of his own regiment. On the first day of the campaign, his troops invaded Luxembourg:

> The border gates did not slow us down much. Our infiltrated informants stood next to most of them, having prevented them from being closed. I drove forward to one of the motorcycle rifle companies that was advancing at a point ten kilometers ahead of the advance guard main body and caught up with them at the Belgian border.[14]

The 3rd Company (1st Motorcycle Battalion) and three armoured reconnaissance cars, after reaching the Belgian border around 0745 h, encountered the enemy at Martelange. The Belgian 1st Ardennes Light

Infantry Regiment defended a hill on the opposite side of the Sauer River, which dominated the town and blocked the road. The Belgians destroyed the bridge and opened fire from pillboxes and fortifications protected by minefields. A single T-13 tank fired its 47-mm gun, which kept the armoured cars at bay as their 20-mm cannons could not penetrate its armour, and the German advance came to a halt.

Balck arrived five minutes later and ordered the motorcycle troops to cross the Sauer and assault the hill, despite having no artillery support. This order contradicted conventional military logic because his soldiers would attack a similarly sized force occupying an excellent defensive position, but he nevertheless felt confident:

> Along the border lay the enemy bunkers that we were so familiar with from previous map exercises. They were silhouetted clearly in the terrain, but there was no movement. The Belgians seemed indecisive, almost as if they did not know there was a war going on. It was hard to believe. I immediately ordered the company to attack.[15]

The 3rd Company waded across the Sauer and attacked across 200 metres (218 yards) of open ground before storming the hill. Balck observed the bold assault that surprised the Belgians:

> The armored scout cars fired into the gun ports of the bunkers and the assault detachments moved forward. A Belgian tank or antitank gun tried to escape to the rear and the bunker crews started running. A few of the Belgians were cut down in our machine gun fire and we captured two machine guns, and five prisoners, including the Belgian platoon leader. It was all over in half an hour and we had broken through the Belgian border position with our surprise attack. Our losses were two killed and two wounded.[16]

After German engineers repaired the bridge, the 1st Panzer Division continued its advance through the Ardennes. Balck's first action of the war reflected his leadership style from the last war: forward command at the decisive point and immediately taking the initiative. Colonel Walter

Hermann Balck during the French Campaign.
(Author's Collection)

Krüger took command of the advance guard and Balck reverted to solely commanding his regiment.

The next morning, the 1st Panzer Division advanced towards the Semois River, the last major obstacle before the Meuse. The 1st Motorized Rifle Regiment shielded the southern flank of the advance and French mechanized cavalry harassed the invaders but imposed little delay. 'We moved forward quickly in the face of light enemy contact,' Balck recalled. 'Horses, equipment, the dead, the wounded, and shot-up supply convoys lay everywhere. The French fought extremely poorly.'[17] Army Group B advancing through northern Belgium and Holland remained the focus of French attention as the British Expeditionary Force occupied its defensive position along the Dyle River.

On 12 May, Balck's regiment exited the Ardennes and reached the Meuse River, south of Floing, in an exposed position: 'A French counterattack into one or both of my open flanks could have destroyed us, but everything remained quiet.'[18] Kleist ordered Guderian to commence the river-crossing operation in the afternoon of the next day. Although Kleist instructed Guderian to cross the Meuse 10 kilometres (6 miles) east of Sedan, the maverick panzer general instead decided to storm the river closer to the town.[19] After Guderian returned to his headquarters, he issued a brief two-page order to his subordinates which was almost identical to the exercises his subordinate commanders had conducted at the Moselle River.[20] The Germans were thoroughly prepared as they had spent months studying maps and photographs of the area and they knew the exact locations of the French bunkers.[21]

Guderian's 19th Panzer Corps would assault the river at four locations: Balck's regiment at Gaulier, the 10th Panzer Division further west near Wadelincourt, the *Grossdeutschland* north of Sedan and the 2nd Panzer Division near Donchery. Balck's men spent the night in their assembly area preparing for the crossing and Major General Friedrich Kirchner, commander of the 1st Panzer Division, signalled them: 'You are the spear point for the German attack. The eyes of all of Germany are focused upon you!'[22]

As the panzers emerged from the Ardennes, Lieutenant General Claude Grandsard, commander of the French 10th Corps, witnessed 'an almost uninterrupted descent of infantry, armored vehicles and motorized infantry'.[23] Artillery could have devastated the Germans on the east bank of the Meuse, but the French decided to conserve their ammunition for later use in a counter-attack. The French Air Force remained absent from the skies above the river as its leaders believed artillery would keep the Germans at bay. The French High Command continued to insist that the main German attack was advancing through Belgium further north.[24]

THE RIVER CROSSING

Dawn broke on 13 May to reveal a clear and sunny day. As Guderian's orders for the river crossing were almost identical to the Moselle exercises, Balck received a simple instruction: 'Act in accordance with War Game "Koblenz". Execute at 1600 hours today.'[25] The regiment's assault would be led by two battalions as the men had earlier rehearsed and they steeled themselves for the attack. 'For two hours we waited in tense anticipation,' Balck recalled. 'The orders were perfectly clear, and there was nothing more to be done.'[26] Once the men crossed the Meuse, they would have to capture the French bunkers on the opposite bank which protected the road to Sedan. One company of Panzer IV medium tanks, a battery of 75-mm guns and a company of 150-mm guns mounted on Panzer I chassis would support the men as they crossed the river.

Across the Meuse, the soldiers of the 55th French Infantry Division and the 147th Fortress Infantry Regiment waited to repulse the assault. 'The French artillery,' Balck noted, 'demonstrated its great effectiveness. Every movement we made was under fire and all traffic in the rear areas was affected.'[27] As the panzers had advanced beyond most of its artillery, the French had three times more guns than the Germans and Kleist lamented, 'my artillery only had 50 rounds per battery because the ammunition convoys were held up by the traffic jams on the roads in the Ardennes'.[28] Given French artillery superiority in the Meuse sector, the river crossing stood little chance of success unless the French guns were neutralized and for this task the *Luftwaffe* had been allocated a special mission.

The 1500 planes of the 8th Air Corps, including 300 Stuka dive-bombers, would support the river crossing with an unprecedented aerial bombardment, the largest of the French campaign. Guderian and *Luftwaffe* operations staff planned a continuous rolling air raid by small formations of planes continuing all day, aiming to deny the French any opportunity to recover.

The *Luftwaffe* operation at Sedan lasted five hours and involved 1215 bomber sorties over a sector of French lines around 4 kilometres (2.5 miles) wide. Although few guns were actually damaged, the aircraft silenced the French artillery as their crews fled in terror while the high-pitched sirens of Stukas accompanied their devastation of the area. The carnage also paralysed the 55th Infantry Division as the explosions cut its communication cables. A German soldier watching from the opposite bank witnessed a squadron of 'twelve aircraft pouncing simultaneously like predatory birds on their quarry, releasing their bomb load right over the target'. He continued, 'The enemy is hit here by an enormous annihilation strike and still, more squadrons keep coming on.'[29] Another German observer saw a 'sulfurous, yellowish-gray wall' rise on the other side of the river.[30] First Lieutenant Michard from the 55th Infantry Division survived the destruction:

> Explosions keep crashing all over the place. All you can feel is the nightmare noise of the bombs whose whistling becomes louder and louder the closer they get. . . . The noise from the siren of the diving aircraft drills into your ear and tears at your nerves. You feel as if you want to scream and roar.[31]

German soldiers crossing the Meuse River.
(Author's Collection)

'The attacking aircraft', Balck witnessed, 'went after the French artillery and put it out of action in the blink of an eye.'[32]

Under the cover of the air raids the Germans moved their 20-mm, 37-mm and 88-mm guns to the river's edge and they began shelling the French bunkers and gun emplacements at close range. Balck's men emerged from their trenches and prepared their collapsible boats in full view of the French bunkers across the river, but the engineers who were supposed to operate them failed to arrive. After the commander of the *Grossdeutschland*'s engineer battalion arrived, Balck declared, 'You are heaven sent. Here are the dinghies, put us across.' However, the officer replied, 'We are not trained to do that. We are assault engineers.'[33] Balck simply responded, 'Assaulting we can do by ourselves — for that we don't need you.'[34]

At 1600 h, the riflemen from the 2nd and 3rd Battalions began paddling across the Meuse at Gaulier while Panzer IV tanks and field guns pounded the opposite bank with direct fire as artillery suppressed the French defenders. The 1st Battalion followed the assault battalions as Stukas flew overhead.

French artillery shells landed ineffectively nearby, causing no harm, but the French soldiers defending the west bank opened fire with machine guns and threw grenades, damaging two boats. After the 2nd Battalion reached the opposite bank, bullets pinned the men down until the battalion commander rallied them to advance. Balck crossed the Meuse with the assaulting troops:

> I had thrust forward to the Meuse with one battalion after some brief fights with the French outposts, and I had set up my regimental command post up front there on the Meuse, along with the forward battalion. I went along with them to make sure that some ass wouldn't suddenly decide to stop on the way.[35]

Balck urged his men to move forward to capture the French bunkers defending the river and the assault battalions secured the west bank despite heavy machine gun fire: 'We attacked, just like on maneuvers. Prisoners flooded out of their bunkers, completely demoralized, and many of them senselessly drunk.'[36]

While Balck led from the front, his French opponent Lieutenant Colonel Pinaud, commander of the 147th Fortress Infantry Regiment, attempted to command his troops from his command post at Chaumont, 7 kilometres (4.5 miles) behind the lines. General Lafontaine similarly commanded the 55th Infantry Division from his bunker 8 kilometres (5 miles) south of Sedan. Balck, at the focal point with excellent situational awareness, reacted quickly to unexpected events, unlike his French adversaries who no longer had the ability to properly influence events.

After the regiment broke through the first line of French bunkers, Guderian, anxious to enlarge the bridgehead, crossed the river and found Balck who, in a humorous mood, declared, 'Joy riding in canoes on the Meuse is forbidden!'[37] Guderian had earlier lectured Balck and his men that crossing the river under enemy fire would not be a 'canoe trip'.[38] The troops needed to penetrate the French bunkers further up the hill which guarded the road to Sedan and Balck ordered his reserve battalion to advance: 'Let's go. Next orders briefing at that bunker up there on the hill.'[39] He moved forward first, believing that in 'such moments the leader has to expose himself' and 'show a disregard for danger'.[40]

The regiment advanced rapidly through the woods toward the Chateau de Bellevue, where Napoleon III had capitulated to Wilhelm I at the end of the Franco-Prussian War, as French machine gun fire from the high ground fell around them. As the men could not overcome the two lines of French bunkers defending the ground near Bellevue, they took cover in a river bank. Balck realized the need to keep his men moving forward to secure victory as the 'day was coming to an end and we still had to reach the dominating terrain'.[41]

At this critical time, Lieutenant Günther Korthals arrived with two combat engineer platoons from the 43rd Assault Engineer Battalion — specialists trained and equipped to destroy bunkers with explosive charges and flamethrowers. Korthals' platoons had become stuck in a traffic jam in the Ardennes, but after arriving at Gaulier, they crossed the river and moved forward. The engineers penetrated the first line of French bunkers and attacked the other fortifications from the rear, creating a gap which allowed Balck's riflemen to surge forward.

The regiment bypassed one bunker at Les Forges, before capturing two bunkers near the chateau, and the men reached the Bellevue–Torcy road around 1730 h. Another nearby bunker continued to resist, pouring machine gun fire around the assaulting infantry, until the men finally captured it 30 minutes later. After the riflemen passed Bellevue, the engineers attacked the bunkers on the western side of the road with flamethrowers.[42] 'I pushed and pushed', Balck noted, 'and by the time the sun was setting we owned the commanding hills and had destroyed the last enemy bunkers.'[43]

In the early evening, First Lieutenant Rossignol left the 55th Division's command post and almost immediately returned with news that retreating soldiers were passing through the area. French Brigadier General Edmond Ruby witnessed the spectacle:

> Suddenly, a wave of fleeing infantrymen and artillerymen came rushing at us on the road from Bulson. They hurried along, on vehicles or on foot, many of them without weapons but still carrying their packs, and shouted: 'The Panzers are in Bulson!' Some kept firing their rifles all around like crazy. . . . This was obviously a case of mass hysteria.[44]

There were actually no German soldiers near Bulson. General Lafontaine drew his pistol and waved it at his fleeing men, ordering them to stop, but the soldiers ignored him as the 55th Infantry Division disintegrated.[45]

After overcoming the French bunkers, Balck's regiment advanced south towards the dominant heights of La Boulette, which overlooked Sedan. The men made rapid progress until high ground slowed their movement and the exhaustion caused by three days of continuous operations became manifest. Balck, however, refused to contemplate a pause as he wanted to capture Hill 301 at La Boulette that night. At this critical moment, his thoughts turned to the battle of Mount Kemmel in Flanders, a pivotal moment in his life.

As a *Jäger* company commander in 1918, Balck received orders to attack Mount Kemmel, which dominated the area. On 25 April, his *Jägers* seized the heights, but orders prevented them from advancing further, allowing the French 3rd Cavalry Division to restore the line. 'If we had taken advantage of the great tactical success we had gained', Balck reasoned, 'and had used it for a push northward toward Poperinge, we would have gotten into the rear of the Allied forces there. Pushed against the sea, they would have been totally destroyed.'[46] Haunted by this wasted opportunity, he was determined to act boldly and not to repeat this mistake at Sedan:

> We had accomplished a huge success. My totally exhausted troops fell into a leaden sleep. The enemy was gone and there was a huge gap in his lines. I thought back to Mount Kemmel, where we had achieved a similar great success, but no senior leadership had been at the point to follow through to a victory. It was my great good luck that I was allowed to lead at a point where I had seen others in the First World War fail so critically.[47]

Balck ordered his regiment to advance another 10 kilometres (6 miles) but his adjutant, Lieutenant Andreas Braune-Krickau, protested. 'Sir, that would lead to the destruction of the regiment.' 'No,' Balck replied. 'It will lead to the destruction of the French.'[48] The battalion commanders insisted that the men were too exhausted to move, but Balck declared that the regiment would advance after one hour of rest.

The tired men of the 2nd Battalion advanced towards La Boulette and engaged the French 2/331st Battalion, convincing Lieutenant Langrenay of

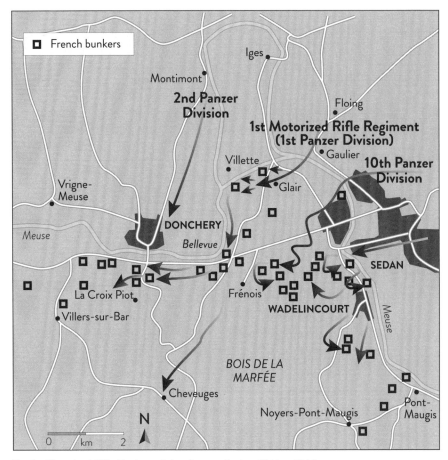

The 1st Motorized Rifle Regiment's breakout at Sedan, 13 May 1940.

the 7th Company to withdraw.[49] The 3rd Company of the 1/331st Battalion defended the key high ground of La Boulette and Captain Litalien could see that enemy fire 'progressively increased in intensity' as his men struggled to contain the German advance.[50] By 2130 h, Balck's men had overrun the left flank of the French defence and were pressuring the right flank. Litalien ordered a withdrawal as the German riflemen stormed La Boulette, capturing Hill 301 and forty French soldiers. The regiment next captured Cheveuges village, which opened a critical gap in the French line, and Balck signalled the 1st Panzer Division headquarters: '1st Rifle Regiment took commanding heights just north of Cheveuges at 2240. Last enemy bunker in our hands.

Complete breakthrough. Elements, 1st Motorized Rifle Regiment, sent toward Chéhéry and heights to the east thereof.'[51] Reconnaissance teams advanced south and reached the northern edge of Chéhéry around midnight and the day ended with the regiment having advanced 8 kilometres (5 miles) beyond the French forts.

Guderian's panzer corps attempted six major river crossings that day, but only three succeeded. The *Grossdeutschland* crossed the Meuse north of Sedan, suffering heavy casualties, and the regiment advanced slower than Balck's men further to the west. The 10th Panzer Division's river assault stalled under heavy artillery fire and only a small force reached the opposite bank and secured a limited beachhead. The 2nd Panzer Division attempted a crossing near Donchery but faced strong machine gun fire and artillery, and only a small element established a bridgehead. By dusk, the Germans had linked their three bridgeheads into a single position.

In the evening, a ferry began transporting anti-tank guns and light guns across the Meuse and by sunset five infantry battalions and one motorcycle battalion had crossed the river. During the night, engineers constructed a pontoon bridge at Gaulier where Balck's men had crossed and the first vehicle reached the west bank at ten minutes past midnight. The first panzers did not cross until 0720 h.[52]

On the morning of 14 May, the 1st Motorized Rifle Regiment, having advanced far beyond the Meuse, was exposed in a narrow corridor and vulnerable to counter-attacks. Balck joined his forward elements at Chéhéry where he expected the French to attack, but he needed reinforcements to resist a determined assault: 'We had one antitank gun with us, which I had towed forward with my command car. The division's Panzer brigade was also still on the other side of the Meuse, and the troops were completely spent.'[53] Guderian arrived and instructed Balck to 'hold out for another one to two hours and the Panzer brigade will be here'.[54]

The French High Command, now aware of the German threat at Sedan, ordered the Allied air forces to destroy the solitary bridge over the Meuse at Gaulier, committing 152 bombers and 250 fighters to the mission. Guderian, however, realized the importance of the bridge and concentrated 303 anti-aircraft flak guns around Sedan and *Luftwaffe* fighters patrolled overhead.[55] The Allied air attacks continued all day as brave British and French pilots flew straight into dense flak and German fighters. The Allies lost fifty-two bombers and fifty fighters, but the bridge remained intact.

General Grandsard, commander of the French 10th Corps, had ordered Lafontaine to counter-attack at Bulson the previous night, allocating him the 213th and 205th Infantry Regiments and the 7th and 4th Tank Battalions. After the men halted halfway to Bulson near Chémery to wait for dawn, Lafontaine, unlike Balck, did nothing to urge them forward. At 0220 h, General Grandsard authorized Colonel Chaligne, the senior command post officer, to commence the counter-attack as Lafontaine had not yet arrived. After Lafontaine appeared ten minutes later, he refused to commence the operation without written orders from Grandsard, which did not arrive until 0445 h.[56] When Lafontaine finally issued his orders fifteen minutes later, his astonished officers could not believe that his plan was identical to an earlier exercise which had been rehearsed several times three weeks previously. Lafontaine could have issued the same orders nine hours earlier but felt compelled to follow the procedures of the French command system. In contrast, Guderian and Balck wasted no time and simply issued brief verbal orders, referencing earlier exercises.

The French counter-attack finally commenced at 0730 h and the 213th Infantry Regiment and the 7th Tank Battalion advanced towards the German bridgehead as low-flying planes supported their assault. Balck soon received a report of the French advance: 'Strong French tank elements moving toward Chéhéry . . . our antitank guns cannot penetrate the French armor . . . we have to withdraw.' Balck refused to contemplate retreat and responded, 'The order is to stay in place. The regimental staff will stay also.'[57]

Balck ordered an engineer company, which had just arrived, to reinforce the defence, but he feared the French tanks would overrun his position. 'We needed our Panzers,' he recalled. 'Then a motorcycle messenger arrived, reporting that the Panzer brigade had crossed the Meuse and would close with us within half an hour.'[58] An officer from *Grossdeutschland* informed Balck that 50-mm anti-tank guns would soon arrive. After engine noises were heard coming from the river, two field kitchens arrived, infuriating Balck: 'The devil himself must have sent them to taunt us.'[59] After the anti-tank guns finally arrived, Balck deployed them as the French tanks approached:

The first gun went into position but was knocked out by the French tanks. The second gun went into battery and opened fire, setting one tank ablaze, then a second and a third. The French attack faltered, and the courageous antitank crews from the Grossdeutschland kept firing.[60]

The panzers arrived around 0900 h and secured the high ground a few minutes before the first French tanks appeared.[61] As Balck's men had been adequately reinforced, the Germans routed the counter-attack, destroying fifty French tanks, and he proudly noted: 'We had overcome the crisis and not a single man of my regiment had left his position during the hellish episode. Consequently, our losses were minimal.'[62]

The French counter-attack had suffered from poor co-ordination due to an insufficient number of radios, and the delay caused by Lafontaine's hesitation cost the French the opportunity to overrun the German bridgehead before reinforcements arrived. An earlier assault would have smashed into weak defences before the panzers crossed the Meuse and destroyed the bridgehead. Lafontaine's needless nine-hour delay would ultimately spell the doom of France.

As the regiment waited for its trucks to continue the advance, the men finally had a chance to sleep until a French air raid interrupted their rest. The men defended themselves with machine guns and a nearby 20-mm anti-aircraft gun supplemented their fire as Balck witnessed low-flying French planes being struck by fire and exploding as they hit the ground: 'In just a few minutes that crisis was over and hardly any of the courageous French pilots could have survived.'[63] The regiment captured the village of Singly later that day and the men continued advancing west at dusk, capturing numerous French soldiers along the way.

CHAPTER TWO
THE FALL OF FRANCE

THE ROAD TO DUNKIRK

On 14 May 1940, Lieutenant General Heinz Guderian's 19th Panzer Corps had punched an 80-kilometre (50-mile) gap in the French lines and, by the afternoon, his three panzer divisions had crossed the Meuse. After the 1st Panzer Division captured the Malmy Bridge near Chémery, he had to decide whether to secure the bridgehead or exploit the Sedan gap by ordering the panzers west towards the English Channel. Guderian, sensing an operational breakthrough, ordered the 1st and 2nd Panzer Divisions 30 kilometres (18.5 miles) west towards Rethel while leaving the 10th Panzer Division and the *Grossdeutschland* Regiment behind to protect the bridgehead. General Ewald von Kleist, commander of Army Group A, instead wanted to first consolidate the bridgehead and restricted the panzers' advance to 8 kilometres (5 miles).[1]

On 15 May, the German High Command forbade any further advance by Guderian's panzer corps until the infantry divisions of the 12th Army had secured its southern flank. Guderian, however, disregarded the order and his panzers continued advancing towards the English Channel, despite the threat to their flanks. As the other panzer commanders followed Guderian's example, the High Command lost control of the 'sickle cut'.[2]

The 1st Motorized Rifle Regiment advanced along the road to Bouvellemont until it encountered French resistance at the village of La Horgne, defended by North African soldiers from the 3rd Spahi Brigade.

The lead battalion attacked, but its assault stalled at the edge of the village as another battalion attempted to envelop the village through a forest. Balck observed the violent fighting as the Spahi brigade 'fought like devils' and 'had to be dug out of their entrenched positions'.[3] He rallied his men as his adjutant Lieutenant Andreas Braune-Krickau witnessed:

> Lieutenant Colonel Balck, accustomed to satisfying himself personally about any situation, hurried forward. Suddenly he appeared right at the entrance to the village and in the middle of the front line. Inspired by the presence of their commanding officer, the companies renewed the attack and, in tough fighting, forced their way into the first houses of the village. But again they had to go to earth. There were casualties, and the wounded came back with chilling reports — a crisis had arisen, but everybody kept his head, for the regimental commander was there with the men.[4]

The Germans captured the village despite fierce resistance and Balck was impressed by the bravery of the French troops: 'The 3rd Spahi Brigade had ceased to exist, sacrificing themselves for France. I issued special orders to treat the few surviving prisoners well.'[5]

The regiment continued its advance towards Bouvellemont across open country and, as the men approached the village, French machine guns opened fire. A battalion from the French 15th Armoured Rifle Regiment defended the village and Balck realized his soldiers were close to breaking point: 'The troops were completely exhausted. The rations were gone and there was nothing to drink in the extreme heat. Ammunition was low.'[6] Balck gathered his officers, who declared that after a good night's rest the men would attack the next day, but he replied, 'Gentlemen, we will attack, or we will lose the victory. If you're not going, then I'll just take the village myself.'[7] Balck began walking alone through a field towards the village as Braune-Krickau observed:

> The men in the ranks watched wide-eyed. 'D'you see the "old man"? Are you going to let him go on alone?' They shouted to one another. Then still dead-tired, half-sleeping men sprang electrified from their slit trenches, and all of a sudden they had caught up with the regimental commander.[8]

As Balck continued towards the village, his men rushed forward:

> Troops and officers, who just a few seconds ago could not move anymore, started to pass me. Nobody rushed from cover to cover, they all just stormed ahead. Their bayonets reflecting in the setting sun. There was no stopping them. . . . I had not miscalculated. No German soldier will abandon an officer who moves forward.[9]

The regiment stormed Bouvellemont and destroyed the French battalion, capturing eight tanks in brutal street fighting. One German rifleman saw Balck standing 'like a tower in the battle, equipped with only a field walking cane, gasmask and pistol'.[10] Braune-Krickau learned from a radio announcement that the regiment's exploits had been recognized at the highest level: 'the Fuhrer had awarded Lieutenant Colonel Balck the Knight's Cross of the Iron Cross, every man in the regiment was rightly proud of it. Every one of them regarded it as his own Knight's Cross.'[11]

With Bouvellemont in German hands, nearby French units retreated, and the panzers resumed their advance and repulsed a poorly co-ordinated counter-attack by the French 3rd Armoured Division. No significant opposition now remained between Guderian's panzer corps and the English Channel.

On the morning of 16 May, Guderian visited Bouvellemont and saw Balck's 'dirty face and his red-rimmed eyes' which 'showed that he had spent a hard day and a sleepless night'.[12] The regiment advanced towards the Oise River as Balck witnessed the disintegration of the French Army:

> We advanced through the withdrawing French troops. Some units were still in their garrisons. None of them seemed to be thinking about fighting. Occasionally enemy tanks tried to attack our columns and were quickly destroyed. Nobody bothered with the prisoners; somebody else would collect them up.[13]

After Balck captured the Oise River crossing on 18 May, he took temporary command of the 1st Panzer Brigade, relieving Colonel Johannes Nedtwig who had suffered a breakdown caused by physical exhaustion. Balck now

German soldiers advance past French prisoners of war.
(Bundesarchiv, Bild 101I-126-0322-03)

commanded the 1st Motorcycle Battalion containing his son, Officer Cadet Friedrich-Wilhelm, which made him uncomfortable:

> It is always an awkward situation to have your own son under your command. For the father it is an additional heavy burden, and for the son it can easily be that he sees things in a slightly distorted light.[14]

Balck, proud of Friedrich-Wilhelm's exploits, boasted:

> Friedrich-Wilhelm had developed brilliantly. He was the first German soldier to reach the enemy side of the Meuse. I saw him again for the first time during the war in the same place where in 1914 I had met my father for the first time during that war.[15]

On 20 May, Guderian's panzers reached the English Channel near Abbeville, surrounding some 1.7 million Allied troops.[16] After the 1st Panzer Brigade advanced from the Péronne bridgehead without being relieved by the 10th

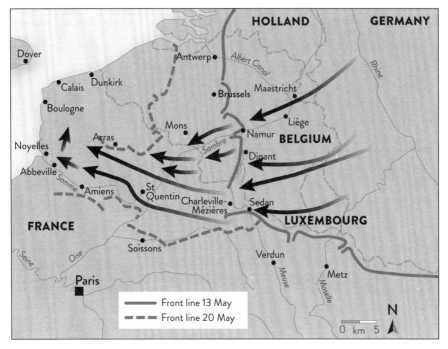

The German advance from Sedan to the English Channel, May 1940.

Panzer Division, an enraged Colonel Landgraf challenged this decision as it weakened the German position. Balck, however, calmly replied, 'If we lost it, you can always take it again.'[17]

Balck's brigade captured Amiens after a brief battle and, after repulsing a counter-attack from a British battalion from the Royal Sussex Regiment, the men crossed the Somme. The brigade advanced north two days later, approaching Calais and Dunkirk. After Balck received orders to capture the bridge across the canal at Bourbourg, he resisted the temptation to micromanage the attack:

> Eckinger's battalion forced its way across and established a bridgehead. They captured six guns and completely destroyed the enemy. Observing the attack from the roof of a house, I had the distinct impression that nothing was going right. Finally, I got down from the roof, sat down in my easy chair, and read Le Figaro. Sometimes you have to force yourself to

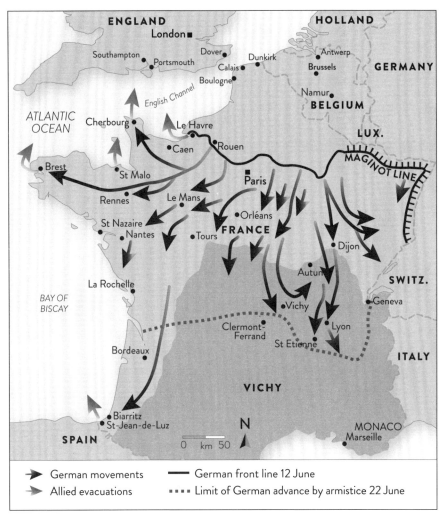

The Fall of France, June 1940.

trust reliable people who are leading at the front. In the end, everything worked out down to the second.[18]

Although the Royal Navy rescued 370,000 men from Dunkirk, the Germans took 1.2 million prisoners and began preparing for the next phase of the campaign. Balck's men got some rest and he took the time to see Rodin's famous *Burghers of Calais* sculpture.

TRIUMPH IN THE WEST

After Dunkirk, the French campaign continued and Balck explained that 'our follow-on mission was the destruction of the remaining French army'.[19] The 1st Panzer Brigade protected the left flank of the 1st Panzer Division as German forces attacked the French positions along the Aisne River.

General Maxime Weygand, who had replaced General Maurice Gamelin as commander of the French Army, organized his forces in depth by fortifying nearby villages. Balck's men first encountered such a village at Juniville where he ordered the 1st Motorcycle Battalion to attack. After their assault failed despite strong artillery support, Balck ordered his 2nd Battalion to launch an enveloping attack to approach the village from the rear, but just before this attack commenced, the French conducted an armoured counter-attack. Balck's troops repulsed the assault with artillery and 35-mm anti-tank guns, though one French tank even reached his command post:

> One tank circled us and chased us around the woods. My antitank
> guns fired thirty-six rounds and only missed twice. But the hits did not
> penetrate. Finally, when we managed to knock off one of the tracks we
> were able to fire into the less thickly armored areas. Even then only four or
> five rounds actually penetrated the tank. The crew finally bolted; every one
> of them was wounded.[20]

After the French counter-attack faltered, Balck's men fought their way into Juniville as brave French defenders from the 127th Infantry Regiment resisted with machine gun and mortars from well-fortified positions. After an assault gun battalion reinforced the troops, the German attack gained momentum and the men secured the village before sunset. Balck's brigade continued south, passing through retreating French convoys, but the French Army was not yet defeated:

> Whenever we encountered any resistance one battery would stop
> and engage, while everything else kept moving forward. On occasion
> individual tanks put up resistance. One time I had stopped and had
> stepped away from my command vehicle when my entire staff was killed
> by a prematurely exploding round from one of our own Panzers.[21]

A German Panzer II light tank during the French campaign.
(Bundesarchiv, Bild 101I-382-0248-33A)

On 18 June, the brigade approached Belfort and the men overran a road block, captured Fort Les Basses Perches and occupied the town, but French soldiers opened fire from nearby buildings, forts and the citadel. Balck ordered his panzers to advance and return fire. After the 2nd Battalion arrived, he planned a co-ordinated attack with panzers, artillery and engineer support:

> The attack started at 1400 hours. I established my command post at Fort Les Basses Perches, at the place where my Uncle Schmidt had earned his Iron Cross in 1870. A beaming Guderian stood in my command post. Fort after fort fell after only short heavy howitzer shelling. Finally, the citadel fell.[22]

The brigade continued south and advanced through the Vosges Mountains and eventually reached the Swiss border. The campaign ended after France and Germany signed an armistice on 22 June, ushering in Marshal Pétain's Vichy regime.

After the fall of France, Balck and his men travelled through the country they had helped conquer:

We spent almost half a year of peaceful quiet in God's most marvelous country — first near Paris . . . and then along the Loire River amid the French royal castles. I had always been fascinated by France, with its culture, its gothic style, and its castles. I took advantage of the opportunity to indulge my interests in architecture and history. I led my officers on numerous staff rides through all of France, all the way down to the northern border of Spain. These trips also served the purpose of getting them out of Paris. A rest and relaxation site had been established near Saint-Malo, where Brittany and Normandy meet and Mont Saint Michel rises from the sea. I was pleased to see that many more of my officers than I had expected were receptive to those great cultural experiences.[23]

Balck's actions during the French campaign earned him clasps to the Iron Cross (1st Class), the Iron Cross (2nd Class), the Knight's Cross and the Panzer Combat Badge. The army also promoted him to colonel on 1 August 1940. The remarkable exploits of the 1st Motorized Rifle Regiment had resulted from Balck's command presence, as the historian Robert Doughty explained:

. . . the ability of Lieutenant Colonel Balck to maintain the will to fight of his regiment stands as the best example of the German style of leadership on the battlefield. . . . Not one to lead from the rear, Balck's personal example maintained the momentum of the attack when some of the German soldiers faltered.[24]

Alistair Horne concurred with this assessment:

Balck was a most forceful personality . . . and there were certainly not many Second World War commanders who could exact more from their troops . . . his qualities as a leader undoubtedly contributed most significantly to Guderian's success.[25]

The regiment's adjutant, Lieutenant Braune-Krickau, simply declared, 'it was the CO who worked miracles in the front line by his own example'.[26]

Although Balck's assault across the Meuse triggered the breakthrough at

Sedan — the decisive moment of the French campaign — his contribution is largely forgotten, as John Mosier concluded:

> In the popular mythology, Rommel led the crossing of the Meuse at Sedan, attacked the Maginot Line, and routed the slow-moving French. . . . In reality, not much of this had actually happened. The man responsible for the crossing of the Meuse at Sedan was Balck.[27]

Balck, despite his success at Sedan, knew the battle had been a closely contested struggle as the French had almost destroyed his bridgehead. The lessons he drew from this revelation would soon reshape the entire way the *Wehrmacht* conducted combat operations.

KAMPFGRUPPEN

The *Wehrmacht* was not a mechanized army and had invaded Poland with only six panzer, four light and four motorized infantry divisions, while forty infantry divisions comprised the bulk of the force.[28] The panzers were technologically and numerically inferior to Allied tanks on the Western Front, where 3500 superior French and British tanks outclassed 2500 German tanks — mostly light Panzer I, Panzer II and captured Czech models.[29] The *Wehrmacht* in France also lacked motorized transport and relied on horses to move its artillery.[30] The Germans did, however, organize their armoured forces differently to the Allies. The French mostly distributed their superior armour to support infantry units while the Germans concentrated their inferior tanks in panzer divisions, giving them local superiority at the decisive point in the Ardennes.

The *Wehrmacht* outfought the Allies during the French campaign and owed its success in a large measure to sound command principles. During World War I, high-ranking commanders had used telegraphs and telephones to control their units. As a result, they lost touch with reality on the ground as Balck explained:

> With the mass armies it was thought to be no longer possible for a commander to lead from the front or from the point of action. Telephony

had to be used to control the mass army, and therefore the commander had to attempt to influence the battle from a desk at the rear connected with his troops by telephone.[31]

Guderian knew that these devices no longer provided commanders with effective control because static cables could not be used by fast-moving mechanized units. As the higher command often only had vague knowledge of where their units were located, the provision of up-to-date orders became impossible.[32]

Guderian, who served as a signals officer during World War I, appreciated the potential of field radios in panzers and advocated equipping all armoured vehicles with wirelesses to allow unprecedented co-ordination. He also envisaged field commanders possessing special command vehicles equipped with long-range radios, enabling them to race between focal points and issue orders on the move.

Guderian's marriage of the tank and radio was a critical German innovation which, as Balck explained, freed the leadership 'from the telephone line, and the German general was once again leading personally from the front'.[33] Balck also realized that equipping all panzers with radios 'allowed both small and large tank units to be commanded and maneuvered with a swiftness and flexibility that no other army was able to match. As a result, our tanks were able to defeat tanks that were quite superior in firepower and armor.'[34] The *Wehrmacht*'s use of radios liberated forward commanders like Balck from command posts, unlike their French opponents who continued the World War I tradition of commanding from bunkers with field telephones.

The freedom enjoyed by German commanders was enhanced by its culture, which celebrated initiative and delegated responsibility. The *Wehrmacht* was built upon the Prussian concept of *auftragstaktik* (mission tactics), in which junior leaders enjoyed unparalleled levels of initiative, giving them much freedom in determining how to undertake their missions.[35] This mindset allowed commanders like Balck at the front to immediately exploit opportunities by giving brief verbal orders to subordinates over the radio.

Another aspect of German tactical excellence displayed in France was combined arms co-operation. After World War I, the army's commander-in-

German infantry co-operating with a Panzer III medium tank.
(Bundesarchiv, Bild 1011-259-1392-21A)

chief, Hans von Seeckt, oversaw a study of the conflict, resulting in the manual *Leadership and Battle with Combined Arms*, which envisaged infantry, artillery, armour, cavalry and aircraft working together in mutually supporting roles.[36]

In 1933, Generals Ludwig Beck, Werner von Fritsch and Otto von Stulpnagel wrote the manual *Truppenführung* (Unit Command), which built upon Seeckt's legacy, further emphasizing combined arms co-operation by advocating mobile operations with tanks, infantry, artillery, engineers and aircraft all working closely together as combined arms teams.[37] The *Truppenführung* stressed that no single arm, including panzers, could achieve tactical success on its own as only the harmonious co-operation of all arms achieves victory.[38]

After the fall of France, the *Wehrmacht* further enhanced its combined arms methods due to Balck realizing the shortcomings of the panzers. The Germans had organized panzers in rigid groups which lacked flexibility and diminished combined arms co-operation. After Balck and his men crossed the Meuse, Guderian held the panzer regiments back to preserve them for the operational breakthrough, effectively keeping his infantry and panzer units separate. As a result, the first panzer did not cross the Meuse until 0720 h on 14 May, the day after the river assault, leaving Balck without armoured support. Consequently, his men endured savage combat, assaulting French bunkers at close quarters with pistols, grenades and hand-to-hand fighting. The German victory at Sedan had been won by the infantry, as the historian Dennis Showalter explained:

> May 13 was the Day of the Rifleman — the lieutenants and sergeants and rear-rank privates of Hermann Balck's 1st Regiment, of Grossdeutschland and their counterparts. . . . Never again would panzer commanders — successful ones at least — treat the truck-riders and motorcyclists as a supporting cast.[39]

Balck realized that the French counter-attack at Chémery on 14 May was almost successful. Despite the courage of his men, they would not have been able to stop the French tanks on their own and only the arrival of the *Grossdeutschland*'s anti-tank guns and the 1st Panzer Brigade in the nick of time saved his regiment. Balck concluded that Guderian's separation of infantry and panzers in separate echelons was a mistake: 'The idea of separate assignments for tanks and infantry was a sin against the essence of tactics.'[40] The assault across the Meuse exposed the weakness of German armoured doctrine as Friedrich von Mellenthin, Balck's future chief-of-staff, explained:

> At that time it was customary to draw a sharp distinction between rifle units and armored units. This theory proved unsound. Had Colonel Balck had tanks under his command during the Meuse crossing, things would have been much easier. It would have been possible to ferry single tanks across the river, and there would have been no need to send the troops forward without any tank support on the night 13/14 May.[41]

Balck accordingly advocated that infantry and tanks needed to work closer together and proposed mixing infantry, armour and other supporting arms into more flexible *kampfgruppen* — battlegroups. As the Meuse crossing demonstrated the need for greater infantry and tank co-operation, the 1st Panzer Division reorganized its panzer and motorized infantry brigades into two 'battlegroups', each comprising two panzer battalions and two infantry battalions as well as artillery, engineers and anti-tank elements. After Balck took temporary command of the 1st Panzer Brigade, he began experimenting with his *kampfgruppe* concept:

> That was the success of the battlegroup, that you needed only one armored regiment if you employed all the other necessary arms together in the battlegroup. Thus, when I took over my brigade after Sedan, the second armored regiment had already been given to another battlegroup. My old infantry regiment was similarly split: My new brigade had one of its battalions; the remaining two infantry battalions were with the other battlegroup.[42]

After the fall of France, the *Wehrmacht* accepted Balck's idea of merging infantry and panzer forces into more flexible combined arms *kampfgruppen*. 'The Battle of Sedan in May 1940 is of considerable significance in the development of armoured warfare,' Mellenthin explained, because 'at Balck's suggestion, after Sedan tanks and infantry were combined in mixed battle groups.'[43] Mellenthin also stressed that the '*Kampfgruppen* embodied a principle as old as war itself — the concentration of all arms at the same time in the same area.'[44]

The *kampfgruppe* envisaged ad hoc organizations tailored to meet particular circumstances and were self-contained and able to fight independently.[45] This new thinking fed into Hitler's decision to expand Germany's ten panzer divisions to twenty-one divisions for the invasion of the Soviet Union, reducing the number of tanks in each division from around 300 in two regiments to around 150 in one regiment.[46] The new panzer divisions contained a better balance of armour and other arms, allowing greater flexibility and the increased numbers of heavier Panzer III and IV medium tanks, which progressively replaced the lighter Panzer II tanks, compensated for the reduction in overall tank numbers.[47] Most of the new divisions had enough armoured personnel carriers to carry a rifle company which could support the panzers in forests and villages by assaulting enemy infantry and anti-tank guns.[48] The new divisions on the Eastern Front were better able to eliminate pockets of resistance and protect their flanks due to the increased levels of infantry support.

By 1942, the *Wehrmacht* finally overcame the distinction between tank and infantry elements within the panzer divisions with the near universal replacement of armoured and infantry regiments and brigades with combined arms *kampfgruppen*.[49] Although Balck would eventually command his own armoured *kampfgruppe* in the titanic battles of the Eastern Front, he would first do so in Greece.

CHAPTER THREE
INTERVENTION IN THE BALKANS

3RD PANZER REGIMENT

On 12 December 1940, Balck received orders to take command of the 3rd Panzer Regiment: 'I was not at all happy to leave my great 1st Rifle Regiment to which I had grown so attached over the last few years.'[1] Before the war, the 12th Cavalry Regiment had been reorganized into a motorized infantry regiment and, after the unit acquired tanks in 1936, it became the 3rd Panzer Regiment, attached to the 2nd Panzer Division. The regiment participated in the *Anschluss* (annexation) of Austria in 1938 and, after the unit relocated to Vienna, most of the men were Austrians.[2]

After the outbreak of war, the 3rd Panzer Regiment, as part of the 2nd Panzer Division commanded by Major General Rudolf Veiel, had sustained heavy casualties in Poland during its advance to Kraków. In the French campaign, the regiment raced through the Ardennes at the tip of the spear, crossing the Meuse River on 14 May before advancing to St Quentin. The regiment followed the rest of the 2nd Panzer Division towards the English Channel and saw action near Dunkirk. After the fall of France, the regiment deployed to Poland and later returned to Austria.

Balck arrived in the garrison town of Mödling in Austria on 17 December and formally took command of the 3rd Panzer Regiment:

I immediately liked what I saw. The unit's first commander, Colonel . . .
Josef Harpe, had similar ideas about training as I had; so I did not have
to change anything . . . the officers and the NCOs were still mostly from
Saxony. The enlisted were mostly from Vienna, but they had served
the regiment quite well. The Viennese were technically competent and
they obeyed their officers. Since the latter were far above average, my
command functions during combat operations could be limited to keeping
the troops communicating and coordinating everything.[3]

Balck also found that his new regimental adjutant, First Lieutenant Rämsch,
understood the technical capabilities of the panzers, but more importantly
he knew the men through 'a rare understanding of human behavior that was
deeply rooted in his love for even the lowest ranking soldier'.[4]

The troops had established good relations with the townsfolk of Mödling.
Balck noticed that the local Austrian National Socialists possessed a higher
level of culture compared with Germany, which he attributed to the fact
that the Austrian Nazis originated from the traditional German People's
Party of Austria.

The 3rd Panzer Regiment contained a regimental headquarters company
and two panzer battalions. The regiment possessed forty-five Panzer II light
tanks, fifty-one Panzer III medium tanks, twenty Panzer IV medium tanks
and three command tanks. Balck's first assignment with his new command
would be the German invasion of Greece, an enterprise ordered by Hitler
to rescue his Italian ally Benito Mussolini.

THE GRECO–ITALIAN WAR

Hitler never intended to intervene in the Balkans because he feared that
any military actions in the region would disrupt the importation of critical
raw materials to Germany. As the Balkans supplied Germany with food,
bauxite, copper, lead, zinc and Romanian oil, Hitler intended to secure the
Third Reich's interests through diplomacy by enticing Hungary, Romania,
Bulgaria and Yugoslavia to join the Axis Pact. If Hitler could peacefully
bring the Balkans into Germany's orbit, he would be free to concentrate
on his greatest gamble — Operation Barbarossa, the invasion of the Soviet

Union — but events in the region would spiral beyond his control.

After the outbreak of war in 1939, a series of border alterations in the Balkans threatened the traditional status quo. Under the terms of the Hitler–Stalin Pact, the Soviet Union annexed Bessarabia and northern Bukovina from Romania in June 1940. Romania subsequently lost additional territory after the Second Vienna Arbitration, mediated by Germany, ceded southern Dobrudja to Bulgaria and one-third of Transylvania to Hungary in August 1940. This loss of territory and prestige created a political crisis in Romania which General Ion Antonescu resolved by overthrowing the government of King Carol II. The pragmatic Antonescu, believing that closer ties to Germany would reverse Romania's recent losses over time, courted Hitler and Romania drifted into the German sphere of influence. This development became apparent to the world when a German military mission arrived in the country on 7 October 1940 with orders to protect the oilfields, train the Romanian military and prepare for Operation Barbarossa.[5]

Hitler's Balkan strategy seemed to be working when Hungary joined the Axis on 20 November 1940 and Romania followed three days later. However, the German dictator failed to appreciate that his success had come at the expense of his closest ally. Mussolini had declared war on Britain and France on 10 June 1940, believing that Italy should fight a 'parallel war' with Germany by capitalizing on Hitler's victories in order to allow Italy to secure her own strategic interests. The two Axis allies consequently failed to develop a co-ordinated strategy and Italian forces fought their own war against the British in the Mediterranean and North Africa. This lack of co-ordination became even more apparent as German diplomacy transformed the Balkans.

Mussolini rightfully felt humiliated by the arrival of German soldiers in Romania as Hitler had previously agreed that the Balkans were an Italian sphere of interest. Mussolini had met Hitler on 4 October 1940, and the *Führer* had made no mention of his impending move into Romania.[6] Mussolini, wounded by this lack of respect, decided to reassert Italian influence in the Balkans by invading Greece.[7] On 12 October, he informed his foreign minister, Galeazzo Ciano, that Italy would invade Greece in sixteen days, declaring, 'Hitler always faces me with a fait accompli. This time I am going to pay him back in his own coin. He will find out in the papers that I have occupied Greece.'[8] Ciano shared Mussolini's optimism, believing that with 'one hard blow' Greece would 'utterly collapse in a few hours'.[9] Ciano insisted that 'Two hundred airplanes over Athens would suffice to make the Greek government capitulate'.[10]

As Mussolini's best troops were fighting the British in North Africa, the Italian Army largely committed lesser tier units to the upcoming Greek campaign.[11] Marshal Pietro Badoglio, the Army chief-of-staff, pleaded with Mussolini that he needed three months to make adequate preparations for the invasion of Greece, including the recall of 600,000 demobilized troops who had been sent home on agriculture leave. Mussolini ignored this advice, believing the conquest of Greece would involve little bloodshed and resemble the German annexation of Czechoslovakia. After Badoglio insisted that Hitler be informed of their plans, Mussolini thundered, 'Did they ask us anything about attacking Norway? Did they ask our opinion when they wanted to start the offensive in die [the] West? They have acted precisely as if we did not exist.'[12]

On 27 October 1940, hours before an Italian ultimatum would be presented to Greece, Ciano informed the German government of the impending invasion. Hitler attempted to stop the attack, as Field Marshal Wilhelm Keitel explained: 'The Fuhrer described this "encore" by our Ally as downright madness, and at once decided to go down through Munich for a meeting with Mussolini.'[13] Hitler arrived in Florence too late to stop the invasion and, as he approached Mussolini, the Italian dictator announced, '*Führer*, we are on the march.'[14]

The Italian ambassador, Emanuele Grazzi, issued an ultimatum to the Greek premier General Ioannis Metaxas, who ruled an unpopular authoritarian regime. Grazzi accused Greece of permitting the Royal Navy to use her ports and demanded that Italy occupy the islands of Corfu and Crete, Epirus (on the north-west coast) and Piraeus (a port near Athens).[15] After Grazzi threatened that Italian troops would invade in seven hours, Metaxas replied, 'I could not make a decision to sell my house on a few hours' notice. How do you expect me to sell my country? No!'[16] Metaxas, defiant in the face of aggression, ordered a military mobilization.

Italian aggression unified Greece behind Metaxas and his popular rejection of the ultimatum. The Greek Army, commanded by General

Italian soldiers during the invasion of Greece.
(Author's Collection)

Alexandros Papagos, mobilized 230,000 soldiers. Despite obsolete weapons and equipment, Greek soldiers enjoyed the advantages of shorter supply lines, local knowledge of the mountainous terrain and superior morale conjured from a burning desire to defend their country. Papagos planned to allow the Italians to advance into Greece before defeating them on favourable terrain.

On 28 October, Italy invaded Greece from Albania with 162,000 soldiers, mostly conscripts and older reservists. The Italians advanced in three columns: a thrust along the coast towards Igoumenitsa, the elite 3rd Julia Alpine Division towards the Pindus Mountains and another thrust towards Kalpaki. Despite Italian predictions of an almost bloodless war, the invaders encountered fierce Greek resistance in the Epirus Mountains where torrents of rain transformed dirt roads into impassable rivers of mud. The Italians advanced 60 kilometres (37 miles) along the coast but made less progress elsewhere. After the Julia Division engaged determined Greek soldiers defending the Metsovo Pass, the Italian unit retreated with 2500 casualties. The completely inadequate Italian supply system soon collapsed, leaving the troops overextended and vulnerable in hostile territory.[17]

The Italian Invasion of Greece, 28 October 1940.

As the Italian offensive stalled, Greek troops launched local counter-attacks and Papagos conducted a co-ordinated counter-offensive along the entire front on 14 November. The brave Greeks pushed the demoralized Italian invaders back 80 kilometres (50 miles) to the border and entered Albania, capturing Koritza and 2000 prisoners. The Greeks subsequently advanced 50 kilometres (31 miles) into Albania, threatening the strategic port of Valona.

Mussolini, realizing the extent of the disaster, recalled the 600,000 demobilized soldiers and began rushing reinforcements to Albania.[18] On 23 December, the Greek offensive eventually ran out of steam due to harsh

The Greek counter-offensive into Albania, November 1940.

terrain and appalling winter weather, and a stalemate took hold along the entire front. Mussolini's fait accompli had failed and, after he requested German assistance, fifty *Luftwaffe* Junkers 52 transport aircraft arrived to help move reinforcements and supplies between Italy and Albania.[19] Hitler, despite his anger at Mussolini, could not afford to abandon his ally because the Italian invasion had created an opportunity for British forces to return to continental Europe, threatening his interests in the Balkans and grand ambition to conquer Russia.

Greek soldiers on the Albanian Front.
(Author's Collection)

OPERATION MARITA

The Italian invasion of Albania on 7 April 1939 created fears in Britain of Axis designs on Greece, resulting in a British guarantee of Greek independence. However, after Italy invaded Greece, the Greek Government did not seek assistance from Britain in order to avoid giving Hitler a pretext for German intervention. Churchill nevertheless hoped that Greek victories against the Italians might keep Turkey neutral and prevent the Axis powers from dominating the Balkans.[20] He also believed that providing the Greeks with arms might cause the Balkans to rally against Hitler. Churchill accordingly informed Metaxas, 'We will give you all the help in our power' and ordered the planning of military assistance to Greece.[21]

In November 1940, the Greek Government accepted Churchill's offer to defend Crete and a British battalion landed on the island and soon afterwards a Royal Air Force (RAF) Squadron and anti-aircraft batteries arrived in the country. By 16 November, the British presence in Greece, known as Barbarity Force, grew to five RAF squadrons under the command of Air Vice-Marshal John D'Albiac. Barbarity Force supported Greek forces in Albania and, by the end of March 1941, the RAF had shot down over ninety enemy aircraft while suffering only eight losses.

Hitler, alarmed at the possibility of British air raids against the Ploesti oilfields in Romania, decided to invade Greece and issued Directive No. 18 on 12 November 1940. He ordered the *Wehrmacht* to 'be prepared, if necessary, to occupy — from Bulgaria — the Greek mainland north of the Aegean Sea'. One month later, Hitler issued Directive No. 20 which increased the scope of the invasion as the dictator now sought to seize 'the north coast of the Aegean and, should this be necessary, the entire mainland of Greece'. The invasion — Operation Marita — would commence in the spring of 1941, and planned to secure the Balkans before Operation Barbarossa. The invasion force would consist of twenty-four divisions under the command of the 12th Army which would assemble in Romania and Bulgaria.

The first elements of the 12th Army, commanded by Field Marshal Wilhelm List, arrived in Romania in December and the *Luftwaffe* began developing airfields in the country. List had served as a staff officer during World War I, commanding the 14th Army during the Polish campaign in 1939 and the 12th Army in France in 1940. Although the German High Command ordered List to be prepared to enter Bulgaria by 25 January 1941, the country had not yet signed the Axis Pact. The 12th Army's deployment to Romania slowed due to the harsh winter and, by the end of January, only two panzer and two infantry divisions had arrived.[22]

As the German build-up in Romania continued, Italian soldiers on the Albanian front endured appalling weather during the winter of 1940–41, made worse by their inadequate cold-weather clothing and unreliable supply lines. They suffered 30,000 casualties from frostbite and every day the surgeons in the military hospital in Tirana performed seemingly endless amputations.[23] Greek soldiers clothed in ragged uniforms likewise endured intense suffering, living on meagre rations of bread and olives, and 11,000 of them fell victim to frostbite.[24]

As fear of German intervention grew in Greece in early 1941, the Greek government sought greater British support. On 13 January 1941, Metaxas met a British delegation in Athens and requested nine British divisions be deployed to eastern Macedonia and western Thrace before the Germans could invade from Bulgaria; however, the British did not have such a force available.[25] General Archibald Wavell, Commander-in-Chief Middle East, could instead only offer the Greeks two or three divisions. Metaxas rightly feared that the arrival of insufficient British forces in Greece would provoke German intervention without being strong enough to resist the invasion. Therefore, he agreed to only accept a British force of this size if the Germans entered Bulgaria.[26] After Metaxas died of tonsillitis on 29 January 1941, Alexandros Koryzis replaced him as premier.

As Germany prepared to invade Greece, British forces in North Africa captured Tobruk on 22 January 1941 and the rout of the Italian Army in Cyrenaica increased the prospect of sending more Allied troops to Greece. On 6 February, the British captured Benghazi, which seemingly secured their gains in North Africa, and the British War Cabinet suspended operations beyond Cyrenaica in order to send the largest possible force to Greece.[27]

Wavell ordered the 2nd New Zealand Division, the 6th and 7th Australian Divisions, the 1st Armoured Brigade and the Polish Brigade to defend Greece. He assigned Lieutenant General Henry 'Jumbo' Wilson to command these 100,000 soldiers, now known as W Force.[28] Wilson had fought in the Boer War and served on the Western Front in World War I. After being given command of British Troops in Egypt in June 1939, he commanded the Western Desert Force which expelled the Italians from Egypt during Operation Compass in December 1940.

The 6th Australian Division had fought the Italians in Libya; however, the 7th Australian Division and the 2nd New Zealand Division had not yet seen combat and the men were still undergoing training in Egypt. On 17 February, Wavell told Major General Bernard Freyberg that his New Zealand Division would be sent to Greece as the advance guard to defend Macedonia until the Australians arrived. Wavell meanwhile faced the difficult task of organizing how W Force would be transported to Greece and concentrate its combat strength before the Germans invaded.

On 22 February, Wavell and Papagos met in Athens where the Allies again faced the vexing problem of not wishing to deploy a British force into northern Greece before the Germans entered Bulgaria.[29] Papagos realized that the Metaxas Line along the Greek–Bulgarian border, which defended Salonika, could only be held with Yugoslav support. He also added that, if Yugoslavia joined the Allies, Salonika would have to be held as the railway from the port was the only means of suppling the country. However, given the uncertain attitude of the Yugoslavs, he proposed withdrawing from the Metaxas Line to the more southerly Aliakmon Line, where the Anglo-Greek troops could concentrate their defence. Wavell agreed with this logic and later reflected: 'The proposals of General Papagos appeared to offer a reasonable prospect of establishing an effective defence against German aggression in the north-east of Greece.'[30] Papagos, however, had no intention of commencing the withdrawal from the Metaxas Line until Yugoslav intentions became clear.

Papagos also worried that a German invasion of Yugoslavia could allow its forces to outflank the Metaxas Line and enter northern Greece through the Monastir Gap in southern Serbia, a valley extending from Prilep in Yugoslavia to Servia in Greece. Despite this fear, he recalled the fierce Serbian resistance to the Austro-Hungarian invasion in 1914 and, in any event, he reasoned that there would be time to strengthen the Yugoslav border if the Germans did invade.[31] Papagos also drew confidence from the mountainous terrain of Greece, which was ideal for conducting defensive warfare and would naturally slow the German advance.

On 1 March, Bulgaria joined the Axis Pact and the next day German soldiers entered the country from Romania while the *Luftwaffe* arrived at airfields near Sofia and Plovdiv.[32] As the *Wehrmacht* reached the Greek–Bulgarian border, Field Marshal List rallied his soldiers:

> The Fuhrer calls us to new deeds. This advance means the protection of Bulgaria; our struggle is with England, if she dares threaten our German soil from the fringes of the Balkans. I place my faith in the spirit of determination of the veteran formations of the 12th Army and am sure that neither the rigours of weather nor the difficulties of terrain will halt our victorious advance.[33]

The 3rd Panzer Regiment, as part of the 2nd Panzer Division, received orders to head to the Balkans as part of Operation Marita. Balck knew the upcoming Greek campaign aimed to eliminate British influence in the region:

Mussolini had foolishly attacked Greece, but was clearly rebuffed in Albania. We could not abandon him now, especially considering Churchill's long-standing concept of conquering Europe through its soft underbelly, the Balkans.[34]

The 'Aliakmon Line'.

On 5 March, the regiment departed Austria and commenced its journey to Bulgaria. Balck remembered that 'All of Mödling was at the train station, seeing us off with enthusiasm'.[35] The men travelled by train through Hungary and, at Budapest, Balck witnessed crowds 'yelling "Heil Hitler!" and giving the Hitler salute'.[36] The train stopped frequently in Hungary to allow oncoming traffic to pass. During these breaks, Balck conversed with members of the minority Romanian population, who wore traditional leather shoes and hand-woven fabrics.

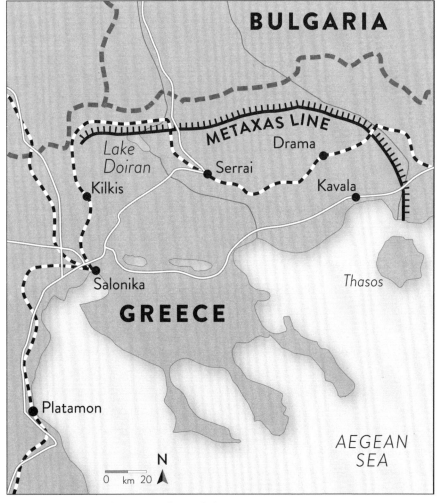

The 'Metaxas Line' defending the Greco-Bulgarian border.

On 11 March, the regiment reached Romania as the train crossed the plains near the Moldova River. Balck found the landscape near the Bulgarian border intoxicating:

> The Danube Valley with its majestic plains and the far hills of the Dobruja Region were relaxing to the eye after the Bărăgan Plain. For a long time we stopped, waiting for a locomotive near the old Trajan's Wall.[37]

After the men reached Bulgaria, enthusiastic crowds greeted them. Balck recovered from his two-week journey with a bath in Sofia before attending Easter mass in the St Alexander Nevsky Cathedral. He also explored the area:

> On one Sunday I managed to get away to the famous Rila Monastery. From village to village I saw the young men hiking to the dances. The sound of the recorder could be heard everywhere, and the men and women moved in quintuple time, dressed in magical old costumes that were different from town to town. It was an unforgettable image.[38]

In the meantime, the men of the 3rd Panzer Regiment quartered near Kyustendil as the countdown to Operation Marita continued.

THE ARRIVAL OF W FORCE

The German entry into Bulgaria convinced Papagos to change his strategy. Instead of withdrawing from the Bulgarian border to the Aliakmon Line, he proposed holding the Metaxas Line since the Germans might invade during the withdrawal and catch his troops off guard. Papagos informed Wilson that three Greek divisions from the Central Macedonian Army would defend the Aliakmon Line. W Force moved north towards the line, which Wilson planned to hold with the Greek forces in the western sector and his troops in the eastern sector. The 6th Australian Division would hold the Veria Pass, the 2nd New Zealand Division would guard the Aegean coast and the 1st Armoured Brigade would move further north to the Axios River on the Macedonian plain to delay the German advance.[39]

The first troops of the 1st British Armoured Brigade, the 6th Australian

Soldiers from the 2/2nd Australian Battalion conversing with Greek soldiers.
(AWM)

Division and the 2nd New Zealand Division left for Greece on 5 March. The next day, Freyberg addressed his men embarking in Alexandria:

> In the course of the next few days we may be fighting in defence of Greece, the birthplace of culture and of learning. We shall be meeting our real enemy, the Germans, who have set out with the avowed object of smashing the British Empire. It is clear, therefore, that wherever we fight we shall be fighting not only for Greece but also in defence of our own homes.[40]

On 7 March, elements of the 1st Armoured Brigade, commanded by Brigadier Harold Charrington, arrived in Greece and headed north to the Axios River. The first soldiers from the 2nd New Zealand Division also disembarked and moved north towards the Aliakmon Line.

As the British build-up in Greece continued, the Italian Army recovered from its near disaster in Albania as reinforcements stabilized the front. On 9 March 1941, the Italians launched a spring offensive with 50,000 troops across a 30-kilometre (18.5-mile) front in the Trebeshine Mountains, while Mussolini personally watched the onslaught from an observation post.[41] The Greeks once again held their ground and Mussolini returned to Italy twelve days later after his army sustained 12,000 casualties.[42] The victorious Greek soldiers nevertheless suffered heavy attrition and Papagos redeployed additional forces from Macedonia and Thrace to reinforce the Albanian front, despite the risk of a German invasion through Bulgaria. The Eastern Macedonian Army now defended the Metaxas Line with only four divisions while the Central Macedonian Army guarded a weak line from the Aegean coast near Mount Olympus to the Yugoslav border with two understrength divisions.[43]

After the New Zealanders arrived at the Aliakmon Line, the 19th Greek Motorized Division moved north to the Lake Doiran sector near the Greek–Yugoslav border. By 18 March, the 1st Armoured Brigade and half of the New Zealand Division had arrived in Greece, and three days later the 6th Australian Division began arriving in the country and the 16th Australian Brigade soon moved north towards Servia Pass.

By the end of March, the New Zealand Division was firmly in place in the Katerini-Olympus area on the Aliakmon Line and had constructed an anti-tank ditch. Freyberg's divisional cavalry regiment deployed further north on the Katerini plain near the Aliakmon River, planning to delay any German attempt to cross the river. Freyberg complained that his two forward brigades could not hold the line and advocated a withdrawal back to Olympus Pass because 'the enemy will have no difficulty in penetrating at any place where he chooses to concentrate'.[44] General Wilson, however, refused as the Katerini position had not yet been threatened.

Meanwhile, List finalized his plans to invade Greece from Bulgaria. The 18th Mountain Corps, the main effort, would break through the Metaxas Line on both sides of the Rupel Pass to allow the 1st Armoured Group to capture Salonika. However, breaching the Metaxas Line would be no easy task. The Greeks had constructed a system of strong fortifications, consisting of concrete pillboxes extending 200 kilometres (124 miles) from the mouth of the Nestos River to the Yugoslav border. Balck later explained the formidable nature of the Greek defences:

German Panzer IV medium tanks in the Balkans.
(Bundesarchiv, Bild 101I-175-1266-05A)

> The fortifications were very modern and offered complete protection
> against Stukas and heavy sustained fire. The weapons were protected by
> concrete or armor. The design more or less mirrored the Maginot Line.
> River sections, impassable mountain terrain, and artificial obstacles made
> the line even more complex. The whole layout was cleverly adapted to the
> surrounding terrain. They also used numerous false bunkers. The fires of
> all weapons interlocked.[45]

Once the invaders breached the Metaxas Line, they would still have to fight
through the narrow mountain passes of Greece, ideal defensive terrain
which would negate the effectiveness of armoured vehicles.

As Hitler planned the conquest of Greece, he also pressured Yugoslavia
to join the Axis. The Yugoslav Government, wishing to preserve peace,
signed the Axis Pact on 25 March in a ceremony in Vienna, guaranteeing
Yugoslav sovereignty.[46] The entry of Yugoslavia into the Axis was a disaster

for the Allies. Wilson consequently urged Papagos to withdraw his forces south from the Metaxas Line to the Aliakmon Line because northern Greece and Salonika could no longer be held. Papagos reluctantly agreed and announced that he would move his forces south from the Bulgarian border; however, once again the strategic situation rapidly changed.

Yugoslavia's membership of the Axis sent divisive shockwaves through the multi-ethnic country. While most Croatians supported Germany, angry demonstrations erupted across Serbia where public opinion condemned the new alliance.[47] Two days after Yugoslavia joined the pact, Brigadier Bora Mirković launched an anti-German coup in Belgrade which dissolved the regency and installed General Dusan Simović as premier in a Serbian-dominated regime. Anti-German demonstrations continued throughout Serbia as the Yugoslav Army mobilized.

The Yugoslav coup restored Allied optimism in the Balkans and Churchill cherished 'renewed hope at forming a Balkan front with Turkey comprising 70 Allied divisions'.[48] Papagos proposed a new strategy with a continuous defensive front from the Adriatic to the Black Sea. He envisaged Yugoslav troops helping Greek forces to expel the Italians from Albania, before transferring east to concentrate on the German threat from Bulgaria. Therefore, he asked Wilson to move his forces north to the Metaxas Line as Salonika now had to be held to supply Yugoslavia.[49] Papagos' plan, however, was contingent upon the Yugoslav Army conducting a strong defence of southern Serbia, which guarded the Monastir and Doiran gaps leading into Greece, before operations in Albania concluded. Lacking faith in the Yugoslav Army, Wilson informed Papagos that there would be no British move north until the situation in Yugoslavia had been clarified.[50]

In Germany, an enraged Hitler summoned senior military leaders to the Reichstag and announced his desire to 'destroy Yugoslavia as a military power and sovereign state'.[51] He ordered an invasion of Yugoslavia to be conducted in parallel with Operation Marita, codenamed Operation 25, after Hitler's directive of the same number. The *Wehrmacht* committed twenty-eight divisions, including seven panzer and three motorized divisions, to both invasions, which would simultaneously commence on 6 April. The *Luftwaffe* allocated 1000 aircraft, one quarter of its strength, under the 4th Air Fleet to support operations in both Yugoslavia and Greece.

The German 2nd Army, based in Austria and Hungary under Field Marshal Maximilian von Weichs, would crush Yugoslav resistance and advance towards Zagreb, Sarajevo and Belgrade with the assistance of the 2nd Italian Army and the 3rd Hungarian Army. The 12th Army's 41st Motorized Corps and 1st Panzer Group would invade southern Yugoslavia from Bulgaria and advance towards Belgrade via Nis.

The invasion of Yugoslavia would greatly assist operations in Greece as the Germans could now outflank the Metaxas Line through southern Yugoslavia and seize Salonika via the Doiran Gap. List, therefore, altered his plan and ordered the 12th Army to invade Greece and southern Yugoslavia in a double envelopment with 680,000 men, 1200 panzers and 1100 artillery pieces.[52] The 30th Infantry Corps commanded by Major General Otto Hartmann would concentrate on the coast and attack the eastern sector of the Metaxas Line behind Nestos and seize all Greek ports in the northern Aegean. The 40th Panzer Corps, commanded by General Georg Stumme, would invade southern Yugoslavia and capture Skopje, cutting the strategic railway line connecting Yugoslavia and Greece, before turning south towards Greece via the Monastir Gap to isolate the Greek Army in Albania and link up with Italians near Lake Ohrid.

General Franz Boehme's 18th Mountain Corps — consisting of the 2nd Panzer Division, the 5th and 6th *Gebirgsjäger* (Mountain) Divisions, the 72nd Infantry Division and the 125th Infantry Regiment — assembled in southern Bulgaria near the Greek border. The two mountain divisions would attack the western sector of the Metaxas Line and seize the Rupel Gorge while the two infantry divisions attacked the line further east. The 2nd Panzer Division, which included the 3rd Panzer Regiment, would invade southeast Yugoslavia through the Strumica Valley and move south towards Lake Doiran and the Axios Valley. Balck realized that such a move would unhinge the Metaxas Line:

> That gave us the opportunity to push one Panzer division through Yugoslavia toward Salonika, even though the roads were poor. The thrust through the poorly fortified terrain west of Lake Dojran would achieve an envelopment and completely dislodge the entire Metaxas Line.[53]

After capturing Salonika, the 18th Mountain Corps would attack W Force on the Aliakmon Line before advancing further south towards Athens and the Peloponnese.

In early April, the Greek Army fielded 540,000 men, but its soldiers were still poorly equipped with World War I equipment and artillery with few tanks and anti-aircraft guns.[54] The 70,000 soldiers of the Eastern Macedonian Army, mostly older reservists and inexperienced troops, commanded by Lieutenant General Konstantinos Bakopoulos, guarded the Metaxas Line from forts designed to garrison over 200,000 troops. By this time, the Yugoslav Army had only mobilized two-thirds of 800,000 soldiers and its men also suffered from a lack modern equipment as well as deep political, religious and ethnic divisions.

After Rommel's *Afrika Korps* landed at Tripoli in February 1941, altering the balance of forces in North Africa, he captured Benghazi on 4 April. Wavell decided not to send the 7th Australian Division and the Polish Brigade to Greece because these forces were now needed to defend Libya. The reduced British commitment to Greece meant that by April, W Force consisted of only one and a half infantry divisions and an armoured brigade, totalling 58,000 men, 176 tanks and 427 field guns. The RAF had around eighty aircraft in Greece with two Hurricane squadrons and two Blenheim squadrons based near Larissa in central Greece to support Anglo-Greek soldiers facing the German invasion, while two other squadrons defended the Albanian front and three squadrons remained in Athens.

As Salonika could be bombed by the *Luftwaffe* from Bulgaria, W Force on the Aliakmon Line had to be supplied from the port of Piraeus near Athens along a road and railway line which ran north through Larissa and continued north through the Tempe Gorge and across a narrow coastal strip via the Platamon Tunnel to Salonika. The main roads through the mountain were narrow and heavy rain made them ill-suited for motor vehicles. Once off the roads, only infantry and pack animals could pass through the rough terrain.

By the evening of 5 April, the day before the invasion, German soldiers made their final preparations and Balck contemplated his role in the operation:

[The 2nd Panzer Division] prepared to launch the thrust west onto Strumica. After reaching that town we were supposed to turn south and move west of Lake Dojran, directly toward Kilkis-Salonica. My mission was to push forward on the southern bank of the Strumica River with one Panzer battalion, one infantry battalion, and one artillery battalion.[55]

As the men of the 3rd Panzer Regiment moved into their assembly areas, Balck observed the majestic mountains in the distance: 'It was a mild, beautiful night. In the bright moonlight we could see the mountains of Greece and Yugoslavia.'[56] The tranquillity would not survive the dawn.

CHAPTER FOUR
THE SHADOW OF OLYMPUS

THE ROAD TO SALONIKA

On 6 April 1941, Germany invaded Yugoslavia and the *Luftwaffe* conducted a massive terror-bombing raid on Belgrade, killing 17,000 inhabitants and destroying half the city. The 2nd Army attacked Croatia from Austria and Hungary while the 41st Motorized Corps and the 1st Panzer Group invaded Serbia from Bulgaria. The Italian 2nd Army crossed the Julian Alps into Yugoslavia and advanced along the Adriatic coast towards Ljubljana.

Meanwhile, Field Marshal Wilhelm List's 12th Army invaded southern Yugoslavia and Greece from Bulgaria. The 40th Panzer Corps, commanded by General Georg Stumme, rolled into Serbia and advanced towards Skopje and the Monastir Gap, the gateway to central Greece. Stumme's panzers overwhelmed the 7th Yugoslav Division as the *Luftwaffe* relentlessly bombed the retreating Yugoslav columns. By evening, his men had reached the Axios River.[1] General Otto Hartmann's 30th Infantry Corps attacked the eastern sector of the Metaxas Line along the Aegean coast. The 164th Division attacked Fort Echinos, but fierce Greek resistance halted their advance while the 50th Division advanced towards Komotini and encircled Fort Nymphaea.[2]

General Franz Boehme's 18th Mountain Corps assaulted the Metaxas Line near the Rupel Gorge. The 5th *Gebirgsjäger* Division, mountain infantry

German mountain soldiers in Greece.
(Bundesarchiv, Bild 101I-163-0319-03A)

armed with light artillery and howitzers, assaulted the forts at Rupel, Istibei and Kelkayia, but despite heavy artillery bombardment and airstrikes from Stuka dive-bombers, the Greeks defenders repulsed the invaders.[3] The 6th *Gebirgsjäger* attacked the line at Demir Kapou and Kale Bair while the 72nd Division attacked three forts, but by the end of the day, the Germans had only captured one fort in the Struma Valley. The *Wehrmacht* had underestimated the Greek defences as Balck freely acknowledged:

> On the German side our knowledge of the layout of the Metaxas Line was nebulous at best. German and Bulgarian intelligence had failed completely to identify the improvements that had been made to the positions. Had we known all that in advance, we most likely would have developed a different scheme of maneuver.[4]

As the mountaineers assaulted the Metexas Line, the 2nd Panzer Division, also part of the 18th Mountain Corps, invaded southern Yugoslavia from

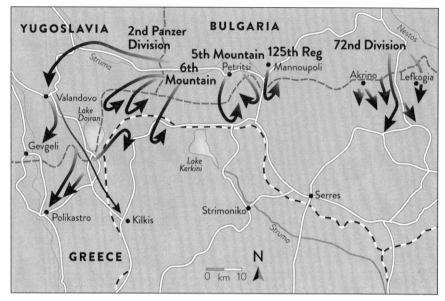

The 2nd Panzer Division flanks the Metaxas Line, 6–8 April 1941.

Bulgaria. List had ordered Major General Rudolf Veiel to race through the Doiran Gap into the Axios Valley and capture Salonika.

The 3rd Panzer Regiment, at the forefront of the invasion, crossed the Serbian frontier. 'On 6 April at 0520 hours we were at the ready,' Balck recalled. 'The Yugoslavian border guards had fled and the Bulgarian border guards were happily shooting into the air, waving us through.'[5] Balck's panzers advanced west through the Strimoll Valley, encountering little resistance:

> Once we got across the border the roads usable for tanks ended. I had to get in behind our right column, which had been advancing faster on improved roadways and already had destroyed the Yugoslav 49th Infantry Regiment, capturing two hundred prisoners and sixteen guns. There was hardly any resistance.[6]

The harsh terrain and weather caused further delay as rain had transformed dirt roads into pools of mud. Balck's men took two hours to pull their vehicles through:

I had driven ahead and was sitting in the middle of a field waiting for everything to close up. Slowly the first vehicle, then the first Panzer emerged from the mud, as the regiment followed piecemeal. Fortunately, there was no enemy. Salonika was close, but the damned mud near the border had slowed us down.[7]

Despite delays caused by demolitions, minefields and mud, the regiment reached the town of Strumica, its objective for the first day of the campaign, where resistance stiffened. The men encountered a deep anti-tank ditch and concrete obstacles defended by determined Yugoslav soldiers from the 3rd Army armed with machine guns and anti-tank guns. Balck noted the strong resistance his men faced in his after-action report:

The lead platoon of Leutnant Brunenbusch opens fire on the enemy, who has taken positions on the opposing slope in a dense thicket. The remaining platoons sheltering in the trench are trying to find a crossing, but cannot proceed. One tank after another hits a mine and is disabled. Due to the dense thicket, use of these weapons is impossible.[8]

German engineers, covered by fire from supporting panzers, flak and machine guns, created a path through the minefield and used explosives to demolish the anti-tank obstacles, allowing the motorized infantry to overwhelm the Yugoslav defenders and the panzers to resume their advance. The regiment encountered further Yugoslav resistance outside Strumica after a reconnaissance team and two Panzer IV medium tanks crossed a bridge. Balck observed the assault: 'One tank "conquers" a gun emplacement. Single enemy positions in houses, from which the battalion commander is fired at, are silenced by some HE rounds.'[9] By evening, the 2nd Panzer Division had reached the Axios Valley near the Greek border, south of Lake Doiran.

General Alexandros Papagos received reports of the German attacks on the Metaxas Line and southern Serbia. He requested a Yugoslav counter-attack against the 2nd Panzer Division's flank as it advanced towards the Strumica Valley.[10] Although the Yugoslavs attacked, their forces lacked strength and the Germans repulsed their assault without difficulty.

Papagos also ordered the Greek 19th Motorized Division, commanded

German artillery in Greece.
(Bundesarchiv, Bild 101I-163-0319-07A)

by General Nikolaos Liubas, to stop the panzers east of Lake Doiran. The division, which guarded the eastern shore of the lake and the Greek–Yugoslav frontier near the Axios River, had earlier fought on the Albanian front and possessed an odd assortment of captured Italian Fiat tanks, ten British Vickers light tanks and several dozen Bren gun carriers.[11] The poorly equipped division, which in reality was only brigade strength, defended 30 kilometres (18.5 miles) of front and was the only Allied unit between the 2nd Panzer Division and Salonika.

The *Luftwaffe* bombed the port of Piraeus near Athens that night, damaging the ammunition ship SS *Clan Fraser* which later exploded. The blast also destroyed six merchant vessels, twenty smaller ships, harbour infrastructure and nearby trains. The damage to the port would create supply problems for the Allies for the rest of the campaign because they now had to rely upon smaller ports such as Khalkis, Stilis and Volos.[12]

On 7 April, Balck advanced unopposed through the Axios Valley 'over the winding mountain pass, crossing countless bridges', but roads cratered by explosives caused delays. 'Our pioneers work continuously,' he noted. 'Later this day, 12 Serbian tanks are surprised and all are destroyed.'[13] After sunset, Balck slept in his Volkswagen *Kübelwagen* command car until bright headlights from two vehicles broke his slumber:

> I thought that they must be out of their minds, driving around like that in the middle of a war. I woke up the regimental clerk and told him, 'Go straighten them out, will you?' As he stood right in front of the lead truck I could hear shouting and confused voices. I was out of my vehicle in a flash and immediately realized that I was standing in the middle of a Greek company.[14]

Balck and five soldiers from his headquarters staff realized they were surrounded by sixty enemy soldiers. He boldly walked towards the Greek soldiers: 'I pulled my pistol, instinctively grabbed the rifle from the first Greek soldier, and started yelling at them. That did it. The Greeks immediately formed up, standing at attention.'[15] Balck's staff took the Greek troops prisoner.

Further east, the German divisions continued their assault on the Metaxas Line. The 5th *Gebirgsjäger* captured three forts while the 6th *Gebirgsjäger* breached the line and reached the railway to Salonika in the evening.[16] The 72nd Division advanced through the Yiannen Valley and penetrated the line south of Nevrokop, threatening to envelop the Rupel Pass.[17] The 30th Infantry Corps bypassed the Greek forts at Echinos and Nymphaea as soldiers from the 50th Division marched towards Salonika and the 164th Division advanced east towards Alexandroupolis.[18]

On 8 April, the 30th Infantry Corps reached the Aegean coast after overcoming strong Greek resistance. The 164th Division captured Fort Echinos and occupied Xanthi while the 50th Division advanced towards the Nestos River. The 5th *Gebirgsjäger* attacked Fort Rupel, but the defenders repulsed their assaults, inflicting heavy casualties on the mountain troops.

Meanwhile, the 2nd Panzer Division advanced south towards Lake Doiran, crossing the Greek border before advancing towards Akritas. The German advance guard, supported by the *Luftwaffe*, overwhelmed the Greek 19th Motorized Division, which had no means of conducting an adequate defence. By midday, the Germans had captured Akritas and forced the

Greeks to retreat from the high ground at Obeliskos.[19] The advance guard continued towards Kilkis while the survivors of the 19th Motorized Division retreated southwards after General Lioumbas ordered his men to withdraw. The panzers resumed their advance through open country towards Salonika.

The 3rd Panzer Regiment, which did not participate in fighting near Akritas, followed the vanguard through the Doiran Gap and the Axios Valley. Balck once again struggled against the elements:

> I had managed to get the tanks, one rifle company, and one battery out of the mud. By that point the ground in the mud patch had been torn up so completely that nothing else could move. With the small force I had available I pushed on via Kilkis toward Salonika.[20]

As Balck's regiment slowly advanced towards Kilkis on the road to Salonika, General Konstantinos Bakopoulos, commander of the Eastern Macedonian Army, received reports of panzers advancing through the Doiran Gap, which threatened Salonika and the Metaxas Line. He consequently ordered a general withdrawal towards the Aegean ports.[21] At night, Bakopoulos sent an envoy to the 2nd Panzer Division to propose a regional ceasefire with a caveat that Greek soldiers could retain their weapons. However, he stressed to his commanders that they were honour bound to continue resisting until a ceasefire had been signed. General Veil, after signalling the terms of the proposal to List, agreed to the ceasefire, which would begin in the morning, although the question of the Greeks retaining their arms would be settled later during negotiations.[22] Balck believed that Bakopoulos had lost his nerve because the Eastern Macedonian Army could have held out longer:

> . . . the situation for the Greeks at that point was not that unfavorable. They still held considerable sectors of the Metaxas Line and especially the important Roupel Pass. The Greek commander did not really know what was moving against Salonika. In fact, it was only elements of a division whose main body was still far behind at the border, stuck in the mud. Our Panzers positioned near Salonika only had gas for a few more kilometers, not enough for a real fight. No supplies would make it forward for forty-eight hours. Would the Greeks still have surrendered if they had known all

that? The old adage is never to give up in war; the enemy is at least as bad off as you are.[23]

The 2nd Panzer Division entered Kilkis just before midnight and Balck noted, 'After a speedy ride we reach the gates of Thessaloniki [Salonika].'[24] The panzers had advanced through harsh terrain which, as List explained, was a remarkable achievement:

> With infinite pains and after a number of tanks had been eliminated for technical reasons, the formation overcame mountains, boggy paths and inundated country and reached open country south of the mountains with still enough tanks to be capable of the decisive breakthrough towards Salonika.[25]

On the morning of 9 April, the 2nd Panzer Division rolled unopposed into Salonika, encircling the Metaxas Line. As panzers paraded through the streets, Balck witnessed a strangely festive populace:

> The world had gone totally crazy. The city was packed with people shouting, 'Heil Hitler, Heil Hitler, Bravo, Bravo!' Flowers were thrown into our vehicles. All hands were raised in the Hitler salute. Were we occupying an enemy town, or were we returning back home to a victory parade?[26]

In the early afternoon, the Eastern Macedonian Army formally capitulated after Bakopoulos signed a surrender document in Veiel's presence at the German Consulate. As the ceasefire came into effect, the remaining Greek forts on the Metaxas Line surrendered and the Germans took 60,000 prisoners and, as Balck explained, 'we had to deal with the traditional ethnic and national hostilities of the Balkans. During the surrender the Greeks specifically requested not to be handed over to the Italians or the Bulgarians.'[27] The commander of the 72nd Division congratulated the Greeks on their courageous defence of their forts, declaring that he had not witnessed such stubborn resistance in Poland and France.[28] Balck shared his high opinion of the valiant Greeks:

The 2nd Panzer Division captures Salonika, 9 April 1941.

Overall the Greek troops had fought brilliantly and quite tenaciously. They had been the toughest of all of our adversaries so far. They even fired on diving Stukas with their rifles. Their fortifications were cleverly designed. The fighting was more difficult than for the Maginot Line.[29]

The battle for the Metaxas Line resulted in 1200 Greek casualties while 720 Germans had been killed and 2200 wounded.[30]

In Yugoslavia, resistance in southern Serbia disintegrated as the 40th Panzer Corps destroyed the 3rd Yugoslav Army and captured Skopje in Macedonia. The SS *Leibstandarte* Adolf Hitler Regiment, the *Führer*'s personal bodyguard unit commanded by Josef 'Sepp' Dietrich, advanced into the Monastir Valley and captured Prilep, cutting the vital railway between Belgrade and Salonika, threatening the Monastir Gap. The next day, the Germans captured Nis and continued towards Belgrade while the

The Fall of Yugoslavia, April 1941.

Leibstandarte seized the Monastir Gap, opening another gateway into Greece.

Weichs's 2nd Army continued its advance across Yugoslavia, meeting only sporadic resistance as pro-German Croatian units mutinied, seizing Zagreb on 10 April where Croatian nationalists declared independence. Two days later, the 46th Panzer Corps captured Belgrade and, as the collapse of the

Lieutenant General Thomas Blamey (left), Lieutenant General Henry Wilson (centre) and Major General Bernard Freyberg (right).
(AWM)

country could no longer be prevented, the Yugoslav High Command asked for an armistice, which was signed on 17 April.

ABANDONING THE ALIAKMON LINE

As Germany invaded Greece on 6 April, Anglo-Greek soldiers defended the Aliakmon Line from the Aegean Sea to the Yugoslav frontier. The 2nd New Zealand Division, commanded by Major General Bernard Freyberg, defended the line from the Aegean to the northern foothills of Mount Olympus with the 6th Brigade in the coastal sector, the 4th Brigade in the west and the 5th Brigade in reserve at Olympus Pass. Freyberg, with insufficient troops, defended zones normally allocated to battalions with companies.[31]

Lieutenant General Thomas Blamey, commander of the 1st Australian Corps, realizing the weakness of the defence, advocated the immediate withdrawal of the 2nd Division from the Aliakmon Line to Olympus Pass. Lieutenant General Henry Wilson disagreed because a retreat would abandon the railhead at Katerini, the main supply route of the Greek Army in eastern Albania, and force the Allies to rely on the low-grade mountain road from Larissa.[32] Freyberg agreed with Blamey and made preparations for a withdrawal to Mount Olympus, believing that Wilson would soon change his mind. Freyberg's instincts proved correct when Wilson's staff began drafting plans for a withdrawal to an 'intermediate line' from Olympus Pass to the Vermio Mountains.[33] As the defeat of Yugoslavia seemed certain, Wilson decided to withdraw. The New Zealand troops on the Aliakmon Line would retreat from the Macedonian plain, abandoning much of their wire and mines by the anti-tank ditch they had spent almost a month preparing.

On 8 April, Papagos, realizing that the Germans could enter the heartland of Greece through the Doiran and Monastir gaps, decided to withdraw Greek forces from Albania in order to form a new line across the Greek peninsula. W Force would hold its 'intermediate line' while Greek forces defended the line further west from Lake Vegoritida to the Florina Valley at Vevi. Wilson planned to defend the 'intermediate line' long enough to allow Greek forces to withdraw from Albania and allow W Force to establish the 'Olympus–Aliakmon Line', further south from Mount Olympus to the Aliakmon River and south-west to Servia.[34]

Wilson meanwhile established a force at Vevi under Major General Iven Mackay based on the 19th Australian Brigade, which included the 1st Armoured Brigade, to defend Vevi and the Kleidi Pass. After Brigadier Harold Charrington ordered the 1st Armoured Brigade to withdraw back across the Aliakmon River towards the 'intermediate line', he reminded his men that as British soldiers would soon fight the Germans in Europe for the first time since Dunkirk, the world will be watching with 'heartfelt interest'.[35]

As the 2nd Panzer Division advanced towards Salonika from the Doiran Gap, Papagos requested reinforcements from the 1st Armoured Brigade, but Wilson refused, having already decided to withdraw. Balck strongly disagreed with Wilson's decision because W Force could have attacked the German flank while it was stuck in the spring mud on the road to Salonika. 'Considering the condition of the division's lead elements,' he argued, 'there was no doubt who would have been successful. But instead, the English corps just stood by without intervening as the East Macedonia Army Detachment was destroyed.'[36] The lack of co-operation between Greek and British forces

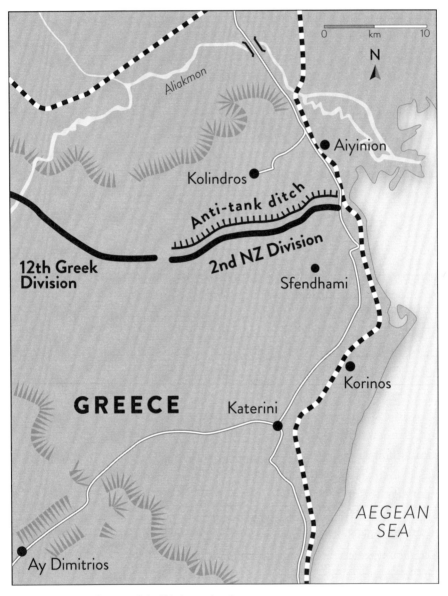

The New Zealand Sector of the 'Aliakmon Line'.

would plague the Allies for the remainder of the Greek campaign.

As the 2nd New Zealand Division deployed to the 'intermediate line', the 4th Brigade moved towards Servia Pass while the 6th Brigade retreated

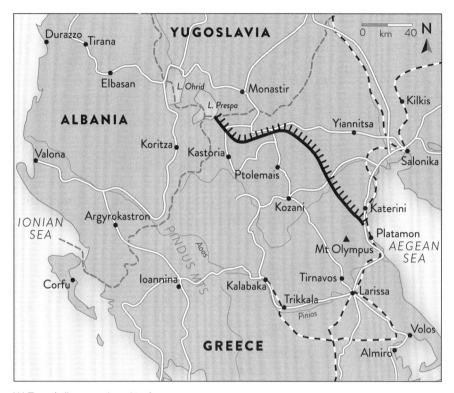

W Force's 'Intermediate Line'.

south towards Olympus Pass. Freyberg also ordered the 21st New Zealand Battalion, from the 5th Brigade, to move north by train from Athens to defend the Platamon Tunnel on the Aegean coast, on the extreme eastern flank of the new line.[37] The Allied plan to defend Mount Olympus seemed feasible, as Balck explained, given 'the incredible defensive advantage of the mountainous terrain and the traditional toughness and courage of the British soldiers'.[38]

On 9 April, Wilson confirmed that the 'intermediate line' would consist of Mackay Force at Vevi, the 20th and 12th Greek Divisions in the Vermio Mountains, the 16th Australian Brigade at Veria, the 4th New Zealand Brigade at Servia and the rest of the 2nd Division at Olympus Pass.[39] Mackay Force had to defend Vevi for as long as possible to allow the Greeks to retreat from Macedonia and Albania before eventually withdrawing south to the 4th Brigade position at Servia.

THE BATTLE OF VEVI

General Mackay placed Brigadier George Vasey in charge of defending Vevi where the Monastir Valley narrows into the Kleidi Pass with the 2/4th and 2/8th Australian Battalions, the 1st Rangers from the 1st Armoured Brigade, the 2/1st Australian Anti-tank Regiment, New Zealand machine gun detachments and two artillery regiments. Vasey planned to hold the northern entrance to the pass, south of Vevi village. The 2/4th Battalion moved into the hills on the left flank to defend Mala Reka ridge and the 2/8th Battalion guarded a ridge on the right flank. Vasey positioned the Rangers in the centre, south of Vevi, to defend the line behind a minefield, supported by the 2/1st Australian Anti-tank Regiment and the New Zealand machine gunners.

After the fall of Salonika, List believed that his 12th Army could swiftly advance into central Greece and destroy W Force before outflanking the Greek forces retreating from Albania. He ordered Boehme's 18th Mountain Corps in the Aegean sector to advance towards Mount Olympus and Stumme's 40th Panzer Corps to advance through the Monastir Gap and attack the Allied position at Vevi in order to drive a wedge between Anglo forces and the Greek Army in Albania. List intended both German thrusts to form a pincer towards the vital Allied supply base at Larissa in central Greece, which List judged would 'be fatal to the Greek and British forces'.[40] Stumme accordingly ordered his spearheads to advance to Vevi.

On 10 April, the *Leibstandarte*'s 2nd Reconnaissance Battalion linked up with the Italians advancing from Albania near Lake Ohrid while the bulk of the regiment advanced through the Monastir Gap. Its lead motorcycle column, followed by trucks and armoured cars, encountered a troop of three Marmon-Herrington armoured cars from the New Zealand Divisional Cavalry, which had entered Yugoslavia to delay the German advance by destroying bridges. After a brief firefight, the New Zealanders withdrew south towards the Kleidi Pass.

Stumme's advance guard — *Kampfgruppe Witt* — a battlegroup drawn from the *Leibstandarte*'s 1st Battalion commanded by Major Fritz Witt, approached Vevi and probed the defences of the Kleidi Pass. The SS troops attacked the 2/8th Battalion's position near Hill 997 while a reconnaissance platoon attempted to flank Mackay Force north-east of the village.[41] As Allied artillery

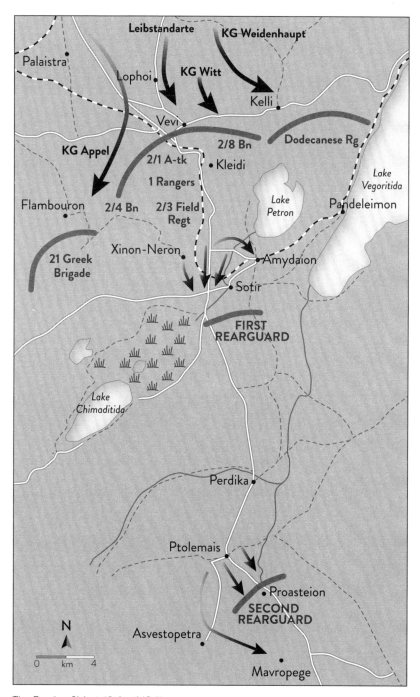

The Battle of Vevi, 12 April 1941.

shelled German troops arriving on trucks, Witt decided to halt his attack and wait for more troops and heavy weapons to arrive. *Kampfgruppe Witt* halted as Australian soldiers watched enemy vehicle convoys and armour arriving from the north. The bulk of the *Leibstandarte* had arrived by dusk and, during the night, German patrols probed the Allied defences.

The next day, Stumme planned to seize the Kleidi Pass, which would allow his panzer corps to cut the Allied retreat by linking up with units from the 18th Mountain Corps advancing through the Edessa Pass. The *Leibstandarte*, reinforced by tanks from the 9th Panzer Division and artillery, seized Vevi. In the early evening, Witt ordered his 7th Company, supported by two StuG III assault guns, to attack the high ground on the right flank of the 2/8th Australian Battalion. However, the attack stalled after defending artillery fire disrupted the German advance and the assault guns withdrew. Despite this setback, the infantry pressed forward and captured several forward posts before machine gun fire forced them to retreat to Vevi. After nightfall, Stumme planned a methodical attack to commence the next day. The 9th Panzer Division would attack the Allied line between Mackay Force and the 21st Greek Brigade, while *Kampfgruppe Witt* attacked the Kleidi Pass.

On the morning of 12 April, Witt's 1st Company advanced towards the boundary between the 2/8th Australian Battalion and the 1st Rangers, supported by mortar and machine gun fire. Despite accurate Allied artillery fire and vicious hand-to-hand fighting, the German assault forced the Australian companies on the left flank to retreat up the ridge, but the battalion's right flank stopped the German advance.[42] The 1st Rangers witnessed the withdrawal of the two Australian companies and, believing that the entire battalion had been overrun, retreated. In the early afternoon, *Kampfgruppe Witt* launched an assault, supported by assault guns, which forced the Australian battalions to withdraw south and the *Leibstandarte* seized the Kleidi Pass.

Stumme now needed to capture Servia Pass before he could advance towards Larissa. The 9th Panzer Division advanced towards the pass while the bulk of the *Leibstandarte* headed west to Kastoria to destroy the 3rd Greek Corps and cut off the withdrawal of Greek soldiers from Albania.

Mackay Force withdrew towards Servia where the 4th New Zealand Brigade defended the pass, a naturally strong defensive position where the

Byzantine Emperor Justinian I had built a castle in the sixth century AD. As the men retreated south, the rearguard delayed the German advance and Brigadier Charrington took personal command of the blocking force at Sotir along a stream, which consisted of two squadrons from the 3rd Royal Tank Regiment and one from the 4th Hussars. At dusk, a company from *Kampfgruppe Witt* contacted the rearguard, but the Germans stopped for the night on the opposite side of the stream. During the night, Stumme formed a battlegroup from the 9th Panzer Division and the 59th Motorcycle Battalion, commanded by Lieutenant Colonel Willibald Borowietz, to advance through Witt's troops towards Kozani in the morning, followed by the 33rd Panzer Regiment.[43]

On the morning of 13 April, *Kampfgruppe Borowietz* launched a series of unco-ordinated attacks against Sotir Ridge. Despite Allied artillery and machine gun fire, a small German detachment crossed the stream, but a squadron of Charrington's tanks and the Rangers' Bren gun carriers repulsed the German assault. After the rearguard checked the German advance, it withdrew to the second defensive position south of Ptolemais where a stream created a natural anti-tank ditch. The Rangers defended a ridge, the bulk of the 4th Hussars and a squadron of tanks guarded the right flank and a squadron from the 4th Hussars supported by anti-tank guns covered the left flank.

At midday, *Kampfgruppe Borowietz* and elements of the 33rd Panzer Regiment reached Ptolemais. In the early afternoon, German artillery shelled Ptolemais Ridge as panzers advanced towards the village.[44] Allied artillery fire convinced the Germans to avoid a frontal attack. Just before nightfall, thirty-two panzers attempted to flank the rearguard and encountered Allied armour, initiating the only significant tank battle of the Greek campaign.[45] After the rearguard destroyed six panzers, Charrington, realizing his force might be cut off, ordered a withdrawal to Servia Pass. The 1st Armoured Brigade had suffered heavy losses as the Germans knocked out at least six tanks and twenty-one others, after mechanical breakdowns, were destroyed by their crews, effectively wiping out the Allied armoured force in Greece.

As Mackay Force retreated south, Wilson decided to withdraw W Force to Thermopylae where 'British Imperial troops could hold without reliance

An RAF Blenheim in Greece.
(© IWM)

on Allied [Greek] support'.[46] Although this would abandon all of Greece except the Peloponnese and Athens, Wilson did not consult with Papagos beforehand and the Greek general continued to plan the defence of the Olympus–Aliakmon Line.[47] As Balck observed, 'the English divisions were like rocks in the surf, refusing any kind of coordination with the Greeks'.[48] Wilson's main problem now was the need to hold the vital crossroads at Larissa, which his men would have to retreat through on the road to Thermopylae. Meanwhile in Cairo, Admiral Andrew Cunningham, the Royal Navy's Commander-in-Chief of the Mediterranean, considered evacuating W Force from Greece. The Royal Navy consequently began preparations under the codename Operation Demon.

The RAF had attempted to disrupt the German advance but the *Luftwaffe*, possessing forward airfields, maintained air superiority over the battlefield and British bombers suffered heavy casualties. Air Vice-Marshal D'Albiac ordered his remaining planes to redeploy to Athens and by mid-

The 'Olympus–Aliakmon Line'.

April RAF strength in Greece was reduced to just twenty-six Blenheims, eighteen Hurricanes and twelve Gladiators.[49] However, Balck argued that Allied air power could have been decisive in Greece:

> I am convinced that the English could have completely stopped the German conquest of Greece if they had properly employed their air [force]. The roads were narrow mountain roads filled to overflowing with our columns. By hitting us at the right points they could have caused us boundless losses.[50]

On 14 April, a battlegroup created from the German 9th Panzer Division commanded by Colonel Hans Graf von Sponeck advanced towards Servia Pass. *Kampfgruppe Sponeck* occupied Kozani just before midday and continued towards the Aliakmon River, hoping to capture the pass before the Allies established a proper defence.[51] In the afternoon, observation posts of the

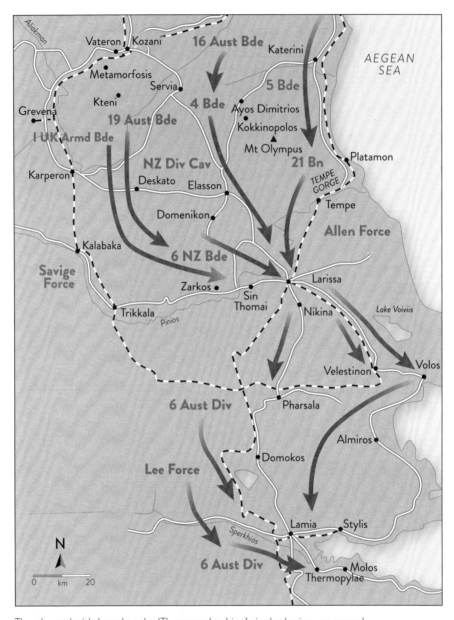

The planned withdrawal to the 'Thermopylae Line' via the Larissa crossroads.

4th New Zealand Brigade spotted German vehicles, including over thirty panzers, advancing south towards the river. In the early evening, elements of *Kampfgruppe Sponeck* crossed the river near a demolished bridge, but Allied artillery checked their further advance.

THE ADVANCE FROM SALONIKA

After the fall of Salonika, the 3rd Panzer Regiment quartered in Nicopolis. As the men rested, Balck became transfixed by the majesty of Mount Olympus, home of the Greek gods:

> When I opened my window in the morning I could see snow-covered Mount Olympus against the blue sky, hovering over the dense fog of the Warda Plains. It was overwhelming. I had seen a lot of the world. Nothing compared to Mount Olympus. So there I sat, pensively in awe, holding a copy of Homer that I had brought along. I never put him away while I was in Greece.[52]

Balck contemplated the next phase of the campaign after List ordered the 18th Mountain Corps to advance south towards Katerini and Mount Olympus. The 6th *Gebirgsjäger* would march from Veroia and climb the mountain's northern slopes while the 2nd Panzer Division would cross the Aliakmon River and force the passes closer to the Aegean coast before converging on Larissa. Balck explained how German planning concentrated on capturing the town:

> The Twelfth Army initiated the pincer movement against the British Expeditionary Corps. On the German left wing the 2nd Panzer Division was supposed to attack on both sides of Mount Olympus, with the 6th Mountain Division attacking across Mount Olympus, thrusting toward Thessaly. Larissa was the objective for all forces.[53]

After Boehme ordered the 18th Mountain Corps to advance south on 11 April, its forward reconnaissance elements moved through the Axios plain. The 6th *Gebirgsjäger* crossed the Vardar and Aliakmon rivers before

British soldiers in Greece.
(© IWM)

commencing its ascent up the foothills of Mount Olympus.[54] The 2nd Panzer Division waited for petrol resupplies and, the next day, Boehme ordered Veiel to advance south along the Aegean coast to Platamon and through Olympus Pass.

By 13 April, the 5th and 6th New Zealand Brigades planned to hold Olympus Pass to allow the remainder of W Force to withdraw through Larissa — the critical junction where all key roads from northern Greece converged. The retreat to the Thermopylae Line also depended upon the 21st New Zealand Battalion defending the narrow pass at Platamon between Mount Olympus and the Aegean Sea. If the Germans captured Larissa before the retreating Allied troops passed through, W Force would be doomed.

In the afternoon, the advance guard of the 2nd Panzer Division crossed the Aliakmon River near Nicelion.[55] The next day, List reported that 'the English have abandoned, apparently in panic, the positions in the Aliakmon bend east and SE of Verria prepared weeks ago'. He also noted that the 18th Mountain Corps 'will advance on Larissa from its bridgeheads south and east of Verria with its main weight (2 Pz Div) going through Katerini'.[56] Balck knew that his objective 'was the destruction of the English forces, which would result in the conquest of all of Greece'.[57]

CHAPTER FIVE
THE BATTLE OF PLATAMON RIDGE

THE CASTLE BY THE SEA

On 9 April 1941, the 21st New Zealand Battalion, commanded by Lieutenant Colonel Neil 'Polly' Macky, arrived at Platamon station following a train journey from Athens. The men had travelled through the green fields, forests and clearings of Greece, during the Balkan spring with its hyacinths, irises and violets. They could now see the snow-covered peak of Mount Olympus in the distance. Macky had orders to defend Platamon Ridge on the Aegean coast, east of Mount Olympus, which guarded the northern approach to Tempe Gorge and Larissa on the extreme right of Lieutenant General Henry Wilson's 'intermediate line'.

After being raised in Auckland on 12 January 1940, the 21st Battalion trained in Britain before arriving in Egypt on 8 March 1941. The battalion departed for Greece on 29 March and, after arriving, the unit remained in Athens until 8 April, when Macky received orders to move north. The New Zealand soldiers, unlike the experienced German veterans they would soon face, had only received limited training and had no combat experience.

The eastern slopes of Mount Olympus almost reach the Aegean Sea near Platamon station on the Larissa–Katerini railway. The line enters a tunnel further north at Platamon Ridge, which rises sharply to 60 metres (200 feet) and extends 1600 metres (1 mile) from the coast to Panteleimon

Lieutenant Colonel
Neil 'Polly' Macky,
commander of the 21st
New Zealand Battalion.
(Author's Collection)

Platamon Castle.
(Author's Collection)

village, located in the foothills of Olympus, where several mountain tracks converge. The nearby ground is hard, rocky and covered with scrub. A track east of the tunnel near the coast could not be used by vehicles, but a saddle track further west bypassed the tunnel and rejoined the railway line to Tempe Gorge.

A ruined castle located by the Aegean beside great cliffs above the sea dominated Platamon Ridge. In 1204, the Frankish crusader Marquis of Montferrat invaded the Byzantine Empire and occupied Larissa, Thermopylae and Tempe Gorge. The Franks established the fiefdom of Boudonitza and built Platamon Castle on the site of an ancient Greek fort from the Hellenic era. The Ottoman Turks invaded the area in the fourteenth century and rebuilt the castle with a stone tower in the middle surrounded by a stone wall and gate tower. In 1941, the castle's outer walls remained sound although its central tower had begun to crumble.[1]

Platamon Ridge, also known as Castle Hill, was a natural obstacle and chokepoint, making it an ideal location to frustrate the German advance to Larissa. Any enemy soldiers advancing south from Katerini had to move

Soldiers from the 21st New Zealand Battalion on their train journey to Platamon.
(Author's Collection)

through a narrow gap between the sea cliffs to the east and the inaccessible ridges of Mount Olympus to the west, across ground which offered little cover except for some rocks, olive and mulberry trees.[2] The view from Platamon Ridge gave the defenders excellent observation on the approaches from the north, although scrub on the lower ridges could conceal advancing enemy soldiers.

Brigadier James Hargest, commander of the 5th New Zealand Brigade, ordered Macky to defend Platamon 'from which there will be NO retirement'.[3] Macky established his headquarters behind the castle and placed his mortar platoon, commanded by Second-Lieutenant Wilson, nearby and the crews assembled their two 3-inch mortars. He later moved his headquarters into a sandbagged dugout near the mortar platoon and located the regimental aid post in a house further south. Macky positioned his companies in a line extending up the ridge to defend the area from the seaside cliffs to the slopes of Mount Olympus.

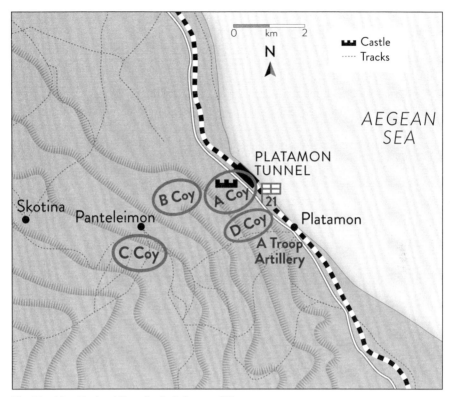

The 21st New Zealand Battalion's defence of Platamon.

A Company (Captain McClymont) defended the coastal sector and dug into the crest of the ridge among the bay trees, oleanders and Aleppo pines along the northern face. 8 Platoon defended the right flank above the entrance to the tunnel, 7 Platoon guarded the centre and 9 Platoon defended the left flank and saddle track.[4]

B Company (Captain Le Lievre) occupied the central sector higher up the ridge in front of Hill 266, which emerged out of the ridge west of the saddle track, near mule tracks, shrubs and ravines. 10 Platoon defended the right flank while 11 Platoon and 12 Platoon defended opposite sides of a ravine which ran between the saddle track to the east and 10 Platoon to the west.[5]

C Company (Captain Tongue) defended the western flank near Panteleimon village at the junction of three tracks surrounded by oaks and chestnut trees. The company guarded the tracks from the village through

The view from Platamon Castle facing north.
(Author's Collection)

thick woods which the Germans could infiltrate through to Platamon station further south to outflank Platamon Ridge.[6] 14 Platoon and 15 Platoon defended the mule trails while Captain Tongue kept 13 Platoon in reserve on the path to the saddle track near his headquarters.

D Company (Captain Trousdale) remained in reserve south of the ridge with 17 Platoon on the right flank, 18 Platoon on the left flank and 16 Platoon at the rear near the southern entrance of the tunnel.[7]

Macky ordered his Bren gun carrier platoon, which possessed ten carriers, light tracked armoured vehicles, commanded by Lieutenant Dee, to deploy south of Platamon station and patrol the coast from Platamon Tunnel to the Pinios River. A Troop from the 5th Field Regiment supported the battalion with four 25-pounder field guns commanded by Lieutenant Lawrence Williams. Macky placed the guns near the coast south of Platamon station under the shade of willow trees and their fire would be directed from

The view from Platamon Castle facing west.
(Author's Collection)

observation posts in the high ground. New Zealand engineers from the 19th Army Troops Company, commanded by Lieutenant Jones, arrived with a naval depth charge, mines and gelignite to collapse the roof of the tunnel and to crater the saddle track, rendering it impassable to vehicles.[8]

The New Zealanders defending Platamon totalled just over 700 soldiers. The majority of the men had been civilians in Auckland before the war, but some of the older soldiers had served in World War I, including all the company commanders. Macky had won the Military Cross on the Western Front in 1916 and between the wars he had been a solicitor in Auckland, although he continued to serve in the part-time Territorials.[9]

On the morning of 10 April, Macky received a letter from Major General Bernard Freyberg ordering him to hold Platamon 'at all costs'.[10] Freyberg advised Macky to 'expect infantry only, as the country was impassable to tanks', even though an earlier intelligence report concluded that vehicles could traverse the coastal route and trucks had recently towed guns across the ridge.[11] As Freyberg believed panzers could not operate in the area, he did not allocate any anti-tank guns to the 21st Battalion.

The New Zealand soldiers expected German patrols to probe their position within twenty-four hours, but the only sign of the enemy were reconnaissance aircraft circling overhead. The next day, the men witnessed an Allied fighter shoot down a German plane over the Aegean Sea. As the New Zealanders waited for the German attack, the men dug trenches and weapons pits and the engineers assisted by using explosives to break the hard ground.

On the morning of 14 April, a train from Katerini passed through Platamon and a Greek general on board told them that this train was the last to leave the town, which the Germans now occupied. In the afternoon, a train from Larissa arrived with Freyberg on board who informed Macky that the Olympus–Aliakmon Line could not be held. Therefore, Wilson had ordered a retreat to the Thermopylae Line, which made the 21st Battalion's defence even more critical as Platamon Ridge, and Tempe Gorge to the south, had to be held long enough to allow W Force to withdraw through Larissa. Freyberg accordingly ordered Macky 'to hold at Platamon until instructed to the contrary'.[12]

As the New Zealanders prepared the defence of Platamon, the 3rd Panzer Regiment advanced south from Salonika behind the 2nd Panzer Division's vanguard until Balck received orders to lead the push: 'When the advance guard reached Katerini the order came through: "Tanks to the front!" "Aha!" we thought. "Now things are happening." And so it was. The whole regiment moved up, along the narrow track, past endless motorized columns.'[13] Major General Rudolf Veiel ordered a reconnaissance force based on the 2nd Motorcycle Battalion, commanded by Lieutenant Colonel Carl Stollbrock, to move south from Katerini and investigate the coastal road to Platamon.[14] All panzer divisions had a motorcycle battalion, primarily used for reconnaissance as Balck explained:

The motorcycle infantry was particularly important in order to get very, very quickly to the decisive point. The motorcycles were very valuable as a pure means of rapid movement and, as a result, motorcycle units were often far out in front of the tanks.[15]

In the evening, Stollbrock's battalion approached Platamon followed by engineer, artillery and machine gun detachments.

Macky meanwhile held a conference with his senior officers, but proceedings were interrupted after an observation post reported seeing the flickering light of the sun reflecting off vehicle windscreens in the north, heralding the approach of the Germans. Macky ordered Lieutenant Jones to immediately detonate the tunnel and, after 350 pounds of gelignite and the depth charge exploded, smoke poured from both entrances, but the roof remained intact. The engineers subsequently detonated 50 pounds (22 kg) of gelignite placed in a breach in the roof which caused the tunnel to collapse. After the engineers had cratered the saddle track and laid a small anti-tank minefield in the forward slopes of the ridge, they headed south to prepare demolitions in Tempe Gorge.[16]

Lieutenant Williams left the conference and rushed to his observation post and, on arrival, spotted a German reconnaissance patrol observing Platamon Ridge 4 kilometres (2.5 miles) away near Panteleimon.[17] Williams ordered his field artillery to open fire. The 21st Battalion's baptism of fire began as New Zealand field guns opened fire at 4050 metres (4430 yards). The German patrol took cover in an olive grove as light armoured vehicles approached from the north. Although the artillery targeted the vehicles, dust and the sun reflecting off windshields obscured observation and reduced accuracy; however, the bombardment halted the vehicles and motorcycle troops.

The German patrol, before the artillery opened fire, had observed New Zealand soldiers defending pits on the forward slopes of Platamon Ridge.[18] Stollbrock concluded that the Allied defence was focused around the castle but not the surrounding area. He accordingly ordered a dawn attack, confident it would be sufficient to overwhelm the seemingly weak Allied defence. As most New Zealand soldiers manning the pits had not yet opened fire and remained concealed in good camouflage, Stollbrock did not realize

German motorcycle soldiers advancing through Greece.
(Bundesarchiv, Bild 146-1979-123-28)

the true strength of the Allied position.[19]

As engineers, artillery and machine gun detachments from the 2nd Panzer Division reinforced the 2nd Motorcycle Battalion that night, the New Zealanders witnessed headlights from a heavy stream of vehicle traffic assembling in the plain below the ridge. The four field guns and two mortars fired at German troop concentrations, and the New Zealand troops witnessed the fire from burning trucks and heard the screams of wounded German soldiers.[20]

Captain Tongue from C Company reported to Macky that German artillery and vehicles had parked across the plain and that over 100 tanks could be seen. Macky, sceptical of this number, signalled Anzac Corps headquarters that 50 tanks and 150 other vehicles had halted in front of Platamon.[21] As no panzers had yet arrived, the 'tanks' were actually armoured personnel carriers.

The New Zealand soldiers anxiously waited in their pits as the sound of heavy vehicles and artillery echoed across the plain. Some men cleaned their rifles while others wrote letters home, knowing the Germans would attack at dawn. Shortly before midnight, the 2nd Panzer Division's operational log noted that the unit will 'advance south and destroy the English wherever they are found'.[22]

THE FIRST ATTACK

On 15 April, General Veiel reorganized the 2nd Panzer Division into two *kampfgruppen*. The first battlegroup consisted of the 2nd Infantry Regiment, the 2nd Battalion (3rd Panzer Regiment), a detachment of the 38th Anti-tank Unit, engineer detachments and two artillery regiments. Veiel ordered this force to attack Olympus Pass and advance to Larissa via Elassona. The second battlegroup included the 2nd Motorcycle Battalion, the 1st Battalion (3rd Panzer Regiment), the 2nd Battalion (304th Infantry Regiment), the remainder of the 38th Anti-tank Unit and two artillery batteries. Veiel placed Balck in command of the second *kampfgruppe* and ordered him to advance along the coastal route towards the 21st New Zealand Battalion at Platamon before advancing towards Larissa via Tempe Gorge. Veiel reminded both battlegroup commanders that they must 'push on with no halts, reach Larissa as soon as possible and re-establish contact with the enemy'.[23] If Balck reached Larissa before the bulk of W Force passed through the town, he could cut off and destroy Wilson's troops.

In the morning, Stollbrock learned that the New Zealand position defending Platamon Ridge was stronger than he earlier believed, but he did not alter the attack plan. The 2nd Motorcycle Battalion formed up in an assault position in front of the castle — their objective — which could clearly be seen on the summit of the ridge. German artillery bombarded Castle Hill near A Company for one hour with little effect because the well-camouflaged New Zealand pits had not been located. The dismounted motorcycle troops from Stollbrock's lead company advanced through the dense undergrowth until they reached the forward slopes of Platamon Ridge. As the attackers climbed the hill, New Zealand soldiers from A Company unleashed heavy frontal fire on them from their pits in the high ground, inflicting heavy casualties and wounding the company commander. Although the attack stalled, a few motorcycle soldiers reached the clearing

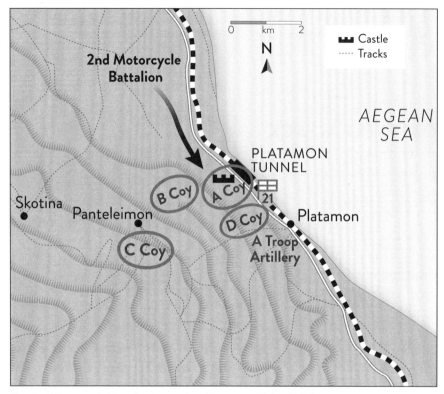

The 2nd Motorcycle Battalion's attack at Platamon, 15 April 1941.

in front of 7 Platoon before New Zealand fire and hand grenades thrown by Lieutenant Southworth convinced them to retreat.[24]

The soldiers of B Company rained heavy flanking fire on the lead German company from the high ground to the west as the forward observers called in artillery fire from A Troop. Private Perry Wouldes recalled that the Germans 'didn't know what hit them as we opened fire for they just crumbled at the knees and didn't move. . . . As soon as we happened to see a bunch moving, we let them have it again.'[25] The German company, pinned down with heavy casualties, withdrew through the scrub as patrols probed the 21st Battalion's front. The four artillery pieces of A Troop bombarded the motorcycle troops with such intensity the Germans believed the Allies had eight to twelve guns. Stollbrock lamented that New Zealand artillery 'plagued us, front and rear, right and left . . . things were damned sour with

Platamon Castle under bombardment from German artillery.
(Author's Collection)

us for a while'.[26] German artillery fire continued to shell the ground around the castle, mostly missing the soldiers of A Company, although the signallers had to repair the telephone wire eleven times between the observation post and Battalion Headquarters.

Stollbrock, frustrated by the heavy losses his men had sustained, sent another motorcycle company to attack B Company's position in order to allow his lead company to resume the attack on A Company. Although the New Zealand defenders successfully pinned down these troops, a German patrol crept forward and located exactly where the New Zealand left flank ended. The patrol returned with the disheartening news that the enemy held the ridge all the way to Panteleimon village.[27] Stollbrock's attack had failed because of poor reconnaissance, insufficient artillery and the lack of direct fire support from heavy weapons.[28] Despite the failure of the first attack, the Germans now possessed a good picture of the New Zealand positions, but Stollbrock would not lead the next assault.[29]

THE SECOND ATTACK

In the afternoon, Balck arrived at the front and took command of all German forces near Platamon. After assessing the situation, he realized the strength of the Allied position:

At midday on 15 Apr the head of the division was halted by stubborn English resistance at Pandeleimon on Mount Olympus. There the English had taken up position on a ridge running right down to the sea and greeted us with accurate shellfire. From their lofty position in an old castle they had splendid observation.[30]

Although the first attack had been poorly co-ordinated, Balck's forward presence gave the Germans a powerful edge.[31] The lead company of motorcycle troops in front of the castle could not withdraw and remained pinned down by New Zealand fire until after dark. The rest of the 2nd Motorcycle Battalion had gone to ground, protected by the dense undergrowth and boulders on the forward slopes of Castle Hill. Balck consequently ordered the battalion to withdraw further back to reorganize and called forward his panzers.

The 1st Battalion (3rd Panzer Regiment), commanded by Lieutenant Colonel Karl von Decker, approached Platamon along the coast road from Katerini. Decker had served as a junior officer during World War I in East Prussia, Poland, Russia, Latvia, Belgium and France, earning both the Iron Cross (1st Class) and Iron Cross (2nd Class). He remained in the army between the wars, serving with the 29th Reserve *Jäger* Regiment, the 5th *Jäger* Regiment and the 6th Cavalry Regiment. After the outbreak of war, Decker fought in the Polish campaign, commanding the 38th Armoured Detachment within the 2nd Panzer Division. He was promoted to lieutenant colonel on 1 April 1940 and commanded the 1st Battalion (3rd Panzer Regiment) in France.

After arriving in Katerini, Decker learned that his battalion 'was attached to the Kampfgruppe Oberst Balck' and that he 'had the assignment of taking Pandelejmon, the rail line road to Platamonos, and break through to Tempital'.[32] The panzer battalion reached Platamon shortly before 1800 h.

After personally conducting a reconnaissance of the area, Balck decided to send his infantry on a wide outflanking movement through the difficult forward slopes of Mount Olympus, which he reasoned would be lightly defended because the New Zealanders would not expect an attack through this harsh terrain.[33] He accordingly ordered Decker's panzers to launch an attack along the coast directly in front of Castle Hill while the 2nd Motorcycle Battalion outflanked the New Zealand defence near Panteleimon village.

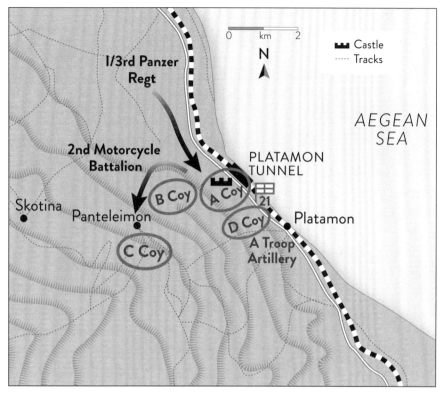

Kampfgruppe Balck's attack at Platamon, 15 April 1941.

At 1900 h, the 2nd Motorcycle Battalion commenced its enveloping attack against the left flank of the New Zealand defence. Two companies conducted a frontal attack against C Company while the other company ascended the higher ground further west to outflank the position, marching through difficult mountainous terrain with slopes 700 metres (765 yards) high.[34]

Captain Tongue informed Macky that infantry were attacking his position. The men of C Company had witnessed the German build-up around Panteleimon during the day and suspected the enemy had reached the village. Private Bosworth from 15 Platoon crept forward to investigate and a Greek civilian confirmed that the Germans had indeed occupied the village.[35] By dusk, the dismounted motorcycle troops had forced 14 Platoon from its position, but the harsh terrain and fading light stalled further progress.

Decker's panzers meanwhile advanced along the track between A and B Companies and halted 1200 metres (1312 yards) from the castle. The Panzer III and Panzer IV medium tanks opened fire on the New Zealand positions while a troop of five Panzer II light tanks advanced towards the castle along the saddle track, which offered the only approach to the ridge. Decker noted in his after-action report: 'About 1800 hours, the Panzers carried the attack farther forward against the castle.'[36]

The soldiers of A and B Companies engaged the light panzers with rifles, machine guns and Boys anti-tank rifles while forward observers directed artillery and mortar fire on the tanks. The small-arms fire from the higher ground struck the panzers, causing sparks as bullets ricocheted off their armour. As the light panzers advanced, the New Zealand artillery could no longer target them due to the angle of the ridge. Macky signalled Anzac Corps Headquarters, 'enemy infantry and tanks massing opposite my centre' and soon added 'centre penetrated, position serious'.[37] The hail of fire unleashed by the infantry failed to halt the German armour, but the rough terrain and demolished track closer to the castle forced the panzers to stop. Decker noted that the rough ground caused all five of his Panzer II tanks to throw 'their tracks directly in front of the enemy defence lines'.[38] Seven Panzer III medium tanks attempted to advance through the ravine in front of 11 and 12 Platoons, but artillery and mortar fire disrupted their movement and the impassable ground forced them to retreat.[39] Balck realized that his armoured attack had failed:

It was clear that our frontal attack was bogging down. We could not observe the enemy in the jagged, bushy terrain; the Panzers could not mount a reasonable attack; and our artillery fire was relegated to complete ineffectiveness. I halted the attack temporarily, reconnoitered, and determined that our present course of action could not succeed.[40]

A relieved Macky signalled Anzac Corps Headquarters: 'tanks have withdrawn in face of our harassing fire. Present position quiet except for infiltration left flank. Casualties slight but finding it difficult to prevent entry of tanks.'[41]

At sunset, German counter-battery fire struck the artillery of A Troop and one shell landed near a field gun, killing the sergeant and wounding four crewmen. The panzers withdrew, but all five Panzer II light tanks with broken tracks were abandoned. 'After dark,' as Decker reported, 'the platoon leader abandoned the Panzers and returned to the Abteilung [battalion] with all the crews, weapons, and equipment. These five Pz.Kpfw.IIs stood together in front of the enemy barricade and were not accessible by either party.'[42] Balck signalled the bad news to General Veiel: 'The fight for the castle began at nightfall. End not yet in sight. Very fierce resistance, and terrible country.'[43]

During the night, New Zealand artillery harassed the panzer laager as German reinforcements arrived. The 4th Company (2nd Motorcycle Battalion) reached the front and deployed near C Company's position under the cover of darkness. The 2nd Battalion (304th Infantry Regiment) and additional engineer and artillery detachments also arrived at night. *Kampfgruppe Balck* now possessed 100 panzers and over 2000 soldiers from the 304th Infantry Regiment and 2nd Motorcycle Battalion as well as twelve 105-mm and four 150-mm artillery pieces.[44] The Germans now had superiority over the 700 men of the 21st Battalion who were only supported by one troop of 25-pounders and one section of engineers.

Balck planned a dawn attack to be launched the next day. Decker's panzers supported by an infantry company would conduct a frontal attack against Castle Hill at the gap between A and B Companies while the 2nd Motorcycle Battalion would seize the high ground near C Company and envelop the New Zealander defenders. The 2nd Battalion (304th Infantry Regiment) would circle around further west and attack C Company from the rear as Balck explained:

> The battalion itself was to move beyond the ridge, and without letting the enemy push them back, penetrate deep into their rearward lines. 'Do not end up in front of the enemy, under any circumstances,' I ordered, 'even if your adjacent unit is crying for support.' We spent the night moving forward through horrible terrain.[45]

The attack would commence after a preliminary artillery bombardment and both assaults would commence simultaneously to overwhelm the 21st Battalion.

The 2nd Motorcycle Battalion would outflank C Company from the slopes above Panteleimon village after enduring a far wider flanking march through far rougher mountainous terrain than had earlier been attempted. Balck had effectively ordered his dismounted motorcycle troops to become mountain soldiers, a task he was familiar with given his mountain warfare experience in the Romanian and Italian Alps with the 10th *Jäger* Battalion during World War I. As Balck understood what men can endure in alpine conditions, he had no pity when the motorcycle troops complained about their mission:

> As soon as they arrived, I took away their motorcycles and used them as mountain troops against the New Zealanders' positions in the hills. After all, I'm an old mountain infantry man myself. I told them, 'Don't cross this line. You can cry as much as you like but take the long way around and come from the rear.'[46]

After flares lit up the night sky, New Zealand soldiers searched for targets and fired towards the sound of soldiers walking in the darkness, often inviting return fire, while the field guns of A Troop knocked several panzers and armoured cars out of action.[47] The New Zealand artillery continued firing during the night, especially at the German infiltration on the left flank. As the guns crews only had eighty rounds left per gun, they kept their harassing fire to a minimum. German patrols moved through the scrub in the lower slopes and artillery bombarded A Company as the men of *Kampfgruppe Balck* moved into their assembly areas.

The German infiltration in front of B Company convinced Major Le Lievre to move 11 Platoon from its forward pits into a reserve position behind 12 Platoon. C Company also yielded ground as infiltration continued on the left flank and a German patrol advanced across the ridge between 13 and 14 Platoons, firing tracer bullets and flares.[48] The close proximity of German troops to B and C Companies prevented German artillery from harassing the New Zealand positions because of the risk of friendly fire.[49]

THE THIRD ATTACK

At dawn, *Kampfgruppe Balck* prepared to assault Platamon Ridge. 'At 0900 hours on 16 April we were to be ready,' Balck recalled. 'Shortly prior to that I had formed up the Panzer battalion, one rifle company, and one engineer company to fix the enemy frontally, while the artillery brought the ridge under fire.'[50] At 0900 h, German artillery, mortars and direct fire from around fifty panzers bombarded Castle Hill and the surrounding area, blanketing A Company's position above the tunnel with high explosive and smoke shells. The four 25-pounder field guns of A Troop could not match the intensity of the German bombardment and the observation post on Platamon Castle could not direct their fire because of the smoke. As ammunition for the field guns ran low, the artillerymen of A Troop had to ignore several German targets to preserve their rounds.[51]

As the bombardment suppressed the New Zealand defenders, the 2nd Company (2nd Motorcycle Battalion) advanced through the smoke screen towards the enemy positions between Hill 266 and Platamon Castle. As the dismounted motorcycle troops approached the forward posts, the New Zealanders opened fire, slowing their progress. After German infiltration threatened to surround 12 Platoon, Captain Le Lievre ordered his men to withdraw to the south side of Hill 266 held by 11 Platoon.

At the same time two panzer companies advanced along the saddle track towards the crest of the ridge with engineer support. Balck watched the tanks attempt to force their way up the ridge:

In the morning the attack was continued after a heavy preliminary bombardment, this time with the engineers in support. The right hand company of tanks forced its way forward through the scrub and over rocks and in spite of the steepness of the hillside got on to the top of the ridge. The country was a mass of wire obstacles and swarming with the enemy. In the thick scrub visibility was scarcely a yard from the tanks and hardly a trace was to be seen of the enemy except an occasional infantryman running back. The tanks pressed forward along a narrow mule path. Many of them shed their tracks on the boulders or split their assemblies and finally the leading troop ran on to mines. Every tank became a casualty and completely blocked the path.[52]

Lieutenant Yeoman from 11 Platoon witnessed the armoured assault:

> The section posts of A Company had excellent fields of fire. But enemy tanks forcing their way through the foothills to the N[orth] and crashing through the scrub were able to keep hull down and come within 2-300 yards of A Coy.[53]

B Company, under pressure from the panzers and infantry, withdrew behind Hill 266, except for 10 Platoon which remained forward. A Company held its ground as fire from the high ground above Panteleimon village rained down on D Company. German artillery kept cutting the telephone cable between A Troop and the observation post on Platamon Castle, making effective artillery fire difficult. As the panzers seemed likely to break through, Lieutenant Paterson, A Troop's gun position officer, reconnoitred anti-tank positions for the field guns, but the gunners did not have enough ammunition to be used in a direct-fire role.

After the craters and terrain of the saddle track completely blocked the panzers' advance, Decker sent some tanks along a detour path, but the rocks along the route began breaking their tracks and a minefield finally halted their advance. Balck witnessed one tank in front of him hit a mine and explode:

> As a piece of paper came flying back from the smoke cloud, Rämsch caught it. It was a picture of a woman. Then from the smoke an uninjured lieutenant emerged who had commanded the destroyed tank. We handed him the picture of his wife. In total surprise he said, 'But I have it here in my breast pocket . . .' It was not there anymore. Who knows how such things happen.[54]

Two panzers tried to find another way over the ridge through a swamp only to become stuck in the soft ground.

After marching through the mountains, the 2nd Battalion (304th Infantry Regiment) and the rest of the 2nd Motorcycle Battalion flanked the New Zealand position and threatened to encircle C Company.[55] One motorcycle company had advanced in a wide flanking move behind

A destroyed German Panzer IV
medium tank at Platamon.
(Author's Collection)

Panteleimon while the other companies attacked the front and flank of
C Company, concentrating on 15 Platoon on the extreme left of the New
Zealand line. The men of 7 Section, commanded by Corporal Bert Howe,
defending the track from Panteleimon, witnessed a group of Germans
casually walking in four columns from the village towards their position.
Howe's men opened fire, causing the Germans to scatter. However, they
quickly reorganized and attacked with supporting mortar and machine
gun fire. After reaching the position, the Germans engaged the New
Zealanders in brutal hand-to-hand fighting.

The 2nd Motorcycle Battalion's attack stalled until the 2nd Battalion
(304th Infantry Regiment) arrived.[56] The Germans surrounded 7 and 8
Sections from 15 Platoon and, after forcing the defenders to surrender, they
demanded food from their new prisoners as they had not eaten for twenty-

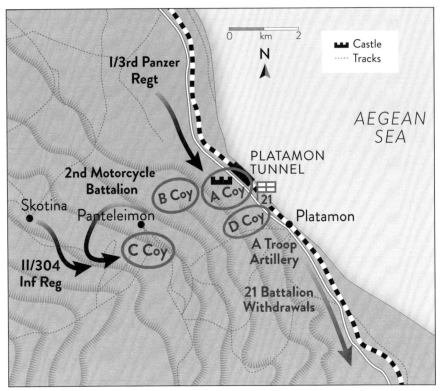

Kampfgruppe Balck's attack at Platamon, 16 April 1941.

four hours.[57] Friedrich von Mellenthin, Balck's future chief-of-staff, noted that the attack through the unforgiving mountainous terrain 'showed that the thorough training and splendid physical condition of our riflemen had produced results'.[58]

After the rout of 15 Platoon, Captain Tongue ordered Lieutenant O'Neill to lead a fighting patrol from 13 Platoon up the south side of the ridge to stop the German advance, but enemy small-arms fire pinned down the force. Sergeant Kibblewhite, despite being wounded three times, crawled forward alone to draw enemy fire away from the rest of the patrol. As a result, the patrol slowly advanced to 15 Platoon's area, only to discover that its survivors had already withdrawn.

As the German attack forced 14 Platoon to fall back closer to C Company Headquarters, Captain Tongue feared encirclement. Therefore, he ordered

14 Platoon and the survivors of 15 Platoon to withdraw down the ridge while 13 Platoon provided covering fire. After O'Neill's patrol returned, his men joined the orderly withdrawal.[59] Balck later reflected on the collapse of the 21st Battalion's left flank: 'I brought the motorcycle infantry down into the rear of the New Zealanders and their resistance fell apart.'[60]

As the Germans now controlled Panteleimon village and C Company's position, they could advance down the ridge and outflank the rest of the 21st Battalion. Macky, faced with the prospect of being surrounded, ordered his men to withdraw from Platamon Ridge.[61] The New Zealanders destroyed equipment that could not be transported, but hot food which had already been cooked was left behind to feed stragglers.[62] Macky intended to fall back to a new defensive line near the Platamon railway station, but as the ground nearby was ill-suited for defence he decided to cross the Pinios River and establish a new defensive position in Tempe Gorge.[63]

The 21st Battalion withdrew in haste as the men left behind their blankets, coats, field telephone cable and digging tools. The signallers broadcast a final message before destroying their wireless: 'WT station 21 Bn closing down. Getting out.'[64] As German artillery continued to bombard A Troop, the gunners towed their field guns away under fire and Lieutenant Paterson recalled that 'every man behaved with great coolness and there were no casualties'.[65] A Troop and the Bren gun carriers left Platamon and withdrew towards Tempe Gorge.

Balck, realizing that the New Zealanders were withdrawing, ordered the few remaining operational panzers of the 1st Company to advance 'regardless of the terrain' and they resumed their advance along the saddle track towards the crest of the ridge.[66] The tanks attempted to take the castle but, as Balck explained, the 'steep and narrow mountain roads with their numerous turns proved almost impossible to be negotiated by the heavy vehicles. German pioneers had to widen them by blasting away the rocks.'[67] Five panzers eventually reached the saddle, and Decker's after-action report praised his troops:

The attack succeeded. The 1.Kompanie lost one Panzer and the 3.Kompanie lost two Panzers to mines that were scattered about the terrain. The reinforced 2.Kompanie reached the rail line road without suffering any losses. From here, further advance was blocked because the enemy had blown up the rail line tunnel.[68]

A Company descended the ridge in good order followed by D Company and later B Company. 18 Platoon kept steady fire on the forward German troops who took cover in the scrub as B Company retreated. The exhausted survivors of C Company were the last New Zealanders to leave Platamon Ridge along with the men of 18 Platoon. The soldiers of 21st Battalion retreated towards Tempe Gorge.

As the New Zealanders abandoned their positions, small groups of German infantry moved up the ridge and hoisted their flag on the castle. The Germans captured Platamon Ridge around 1100 h and Balck noted that his men found 'large stores of canned food and tents . . . signs of a hasty panic-stricken flight. . . . That was fine for the tank crews, for in this type of country the field kitchens could not possibly get forward.'[69]

The battle of Platamon Ridge vindicated Balck's *kampfgruppe* concept. General Veiel had assigned Balck a tailor-made battlegroup with the right balance of infantry, panzer, engineer and artillery elements, giving him a highly flexible combined arms force. Balck had also used his troops in an unconventional manner as Mellenthin correctly concluded: 'Balck's success is to be ascribed to his boldness in separating his infantry from their transport and sending them off on wide-flanking moves, which should really have been entrusted to trained mountain troops.'[70]

Kampfgruppe Balck suffered around 262 casualties and Balck noted there were '149 wounded in hospital at Katerini and a large number still with forward troops'.[71] One Panzer II light tank and two Panzer III medium tanks had been destroyed and most surviving panzers needed to have their tracks repaired before they could continue the advance.

During the battle, eight New Zealanders had been killed, ten wounded and eighteen taken prisoner. Although they had delayed *Kampfgruppe Balck* for thirty-six hours, Macky failed to achieve his mission as the Germans could now access the coast road and railway to Larissa via Tempe Gorge.[72] Macky had fought the battle like a World War I commander and the French at Sedan — from a command post with a field telephone. In contrast, Balck led from the front, giving verbal orders, and his forward presence was a critical factor as the historian David Greentree explained: 'At Platamon, for example, Oberst Hermann Balck, the Kampfgruppe commander, was at the forefront and could issue orders that were relevant to the events as they happened on the battlefield.'[73] The historian Peter Willian Wood similarly concluded:

> German tactics were poor until Balck assumed control. With his organisational skills, drive and intuition based on previous combat experience, Balck literally drove his exhausted men, in spite of the terrain difficulties for infantryman and panzer alike, at the New Zealanders.[74]

Macky had little control over events during the battle and did not send out patrols, order counter-attacks or use his reserve (D Company). However, Freyberg had failed to provide the 21st Battalion with anti-tank guns, incorrectly believing that panzers could not operate in the rugged terrain. He also provided Macky with insufficient artillery and ammunition.

Balck could not immediately pursue the retreating New Zealanders because his panzers had to stop at the crest of the ridge and wait for his engineers to clear the mines and rocks. 'The mule path that we had been moving forward on had to be reinforced to handle tanks and wheeled vehicles', he explained. 'That took time, a lot of time.'[75]

General Veiel noted that *Kampfgruppe Balck* had engaged in 'bitter fighting against troops of 2 NZ Div'.[76] The Germans could now threaten Tempe Gorge, the last major obstacle before Larissa, with *Kampfgruppe Balck* advancing from the coast and the mountain troops from the 6th *Gebirgsjäger* Division descending Mount Olympus. General Veiel ordered his men to 'force the Tempe sector and push straight through to Larissa'.[77] The fate of W Force in Greece would soon be decided at Tempe Gorge.

CHAPTER SIX
THE RACE TO LARISSA

THE RETREAT TO THERMOPYLAE

On 15 April 1941, *Kampfgruppe Sponeck* prepared to attack the 4th New Zealand Brigade at Servia Pass and before dawn two companies from the 11th Infantry Regiment crossed the Aliakmon River. As they approached the pass, soldiers from the 19th New Zealand Battalion ambushed them with small-arms fire, mortars and grenades as they were silhouetted in the moonlight. At dawn, the German survivors, almost out of ammunition and under artillery bombardment, found themselves trapped. Colonel Hans Graf von Sponeck ordered the 1st Battalion (11th Infantry Regiment) to cross the river and rescue their comrades, but the troops made slow progress and New Zealand fire harassed the Germans for the rest of the day.[1] *Kampfgruppe Sponeck* suffered 290 casualties while only two New Zealanders were killed and six wounded.[2]

The stiff resistance convinced Major General Alfred Ritter von Hubicki, commander of the 9th Panzer Division, to wait for more artillery to arrive before resuming the attack at Servia Pass. He convinced General Georg Stumme to attempt an encirclement of the pass from Kalabaka.[3] The 5th Panzer Division would advance towards Kalabaka while the SS *Leibstandarte* Adolf Hitler Regiment advanced south to Elassona, which would also threaten the pass. The *Leibstandarte* soon reached the Kastoria–Grevena road, further isolating the Greek Army in Albania.

Meanwhile, the 2nd Panzer Division's western battlegroup engaged the 5th New Zealand Brigade position at Olympus Pass. After a brief bombardment, a small detachment of German motorcycle troops attacked the 22nd Battalion's position, but machine gun fire stopped their advance and the 28th (Maori) Battalion repulsed an assault by five panzers. In the afternoon, the Maori observed German infantry in the Mavroneri ravine and opened fire at close range, but the Germans captured their forward posts. A Maori counter-attack soon afterwards forced the Germans back into the ravine.[4] Although the 23rd Battalion repulsed a number of attacks during the day, the Germans broke through its forward positions in the evening. The 22nd Battalion held the exit from Olympus Pass and, after nightfall, the 5th Brigade withdrew from the pass through dense mist and headed towards Larissa.

As the Allies resisted the German onslaught, Lieutenant General Henry Wilson formally ordered W Force to withdraw to the Thermopylae Line. In order to support the retreat, the 1st Armoured Brigade, the 17th Australian Brigade, the 6th New Zealand Brigade and the 19th Australian Brigade would form rearguards to protect the major road and rail lines to Larissa. The 5th Brigade at Olympus, the 4th Brigade at Servia and 17th Brigade at Kalabaka would withdraw through the rearguards on the night of 17 April on their way to the Thermopylae Line. The next night, the 6th Brigade at Elassona, the 16th Brigade at Zarkos and the 21st Battalion at Platamon would withdraw, followed by the 1st Armoured Brigade early the next day.[5]

After Field Marshal Wilhelm List realized the British intended to evacuate Greece, the campaign became a pursuit as his 12th Army raced to capture W Force before the men could embark on ships at the coast. List withdrew his infantry divisions, which lacked mobility, and his panzer divisions, the *Leibstandarte* and the *Gebirgsjäger* mountain troops continued the campaign. As the Germans raced forward, their advance guards often lost contact with higher headquarters and their logistics system struggled to supply the front line, although captured food and fuel enabled them to sustain the pursuit.[6]

The Achilles heel of Wilson's plan to withdraw to the Thermopylae Line remained the crossroads at Larissa, through which all retreating brigades had to transit. If the Germans captured Larissa before the Allies could withdraw through the town, W Force would be cut off and forced to surrender. Despite List's ambition, the German thrusts stalled as the 2nd

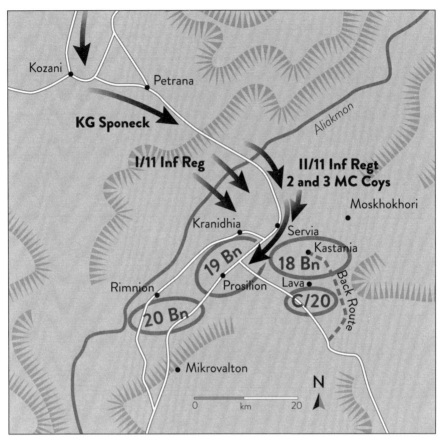

The Battle of Servia, 15 April 1941.

Panzer Division's western battlegroup failed to capture Olympus Pass and the 40th Panzer Corps had been repulsed at Servia Pass. *Kampfgruppe Balck*, advancing from Platamon to Tempe Gorge, represented the greatest threat to Larissa. General Franz Boehme, commander of the 18th Mountain Corps, accordingly signalled the 2nd Panzer Division: 'Please push on with all possible speed to Elason and Larissa. Very important to reach Larissa.'[7] If Balck captured the crossroads before the bulk of W Force could withdraw through the town, the British expeditionary force would be doomed.

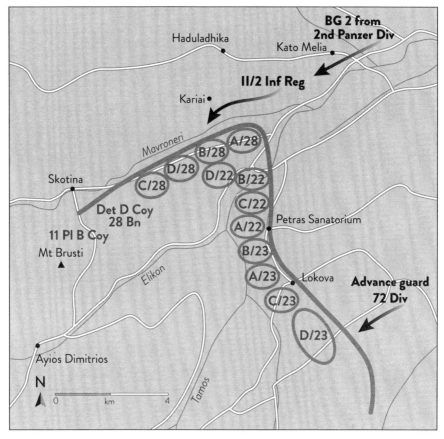

The 5th New Zealand Brigade's defence of Olympus Pass, 14–17 April 1941.

THE VALE OF TEMPE

An earthquake in prehistoric times had created a long gorge along the Pinios River, known to ancient poets as the Vale of Tempe. The narrow valley is flanked with steep walls of rock, 20 to 30 metres (65–100 feet) high, and it extends for 10 kilometres (6 miles) through the mountains south-east of Mount Olympus. Its lower ground is covered in hyacinths, cyclamens and crocuses while, higher up, Judas trees and chestnuts line the gorge. In the valley between the second and third ridges, vineyards and olive groves cover the landscape. Mount Ossa dominates the southern side of the gorge, surrounded in all directions by highland gullies. The railway from Katerini passes through the gorge on the northern bank of the river. At the western

The Vale of Tempe.
(Contributor: X3A Collection/Alamy Stock Photo)

entrance of the gorge, the railway crosses the river near the railway station at Tempe village — a small settlement with white houses, peach trees and a Greek Orthodox church — before turning south towards Larissa, 24 kilometres (15 miles) away. A road follows the southern bank of the river beside the ridges of Mount Ossa. The village of Itia lies on the north side of the river, west of Tempe village. Five kilometres (3 miles) further west, the larger village of Gonnos is located in the foothills where the mountain trails lead to Mount Olympus.

In antiquity, the Greeks believed Aristaeus, the son of Apollo and Cyrene, inhabited the Vale of Tempe where he chased Eurydice, wife of Orpheus. Goethe set the Walpurgis Night scene in his play *Faust* in the Tempe Valley where Mephistopheles asks the question, 'Are any Britons here? They are always travelling, to track down sites of battles.'

The Tempe Gorge is a naturally strong defensive position with its narrow pass and fast-flowing river. Since antiquity, the gorge has also been an invasion route into the plains of Thessaly and the heart of Greece. According to Herodotus and Pliny, 10,000 Greek hoplites, citizen-soldiers armed with

Soldiers from the 21st New Zealand Battalion during the withdrawal from Platamon to
Tempe Gorge.
(Author's Collection)

spears and shields, occupied the gorge hoping to stop the Persian invasion led
by Xerxes in 480 BC; however, they abandoned their position, fearing the
enemy would outflank them through two nearby passes from the southern
slopes of Mount Olympus.[8] The Greeks instead made their famous stand at
Thermopylae further south where 3500 warriors, led by King Leonidas and
his 300 Spartans, inflicted 20,000 casualties on the Persians.[9]

On 16 April, Lieutenant General Thomas Blamey, commander of the
Anzac Corps, received a message from Major General Bernard Freyberg
indicating the 21st New Zealand Battalion had withdrawn from Platamon

and radio contact with Lieutenant Colonel Macky had ceased.[10] Blamey accordingly decided to abandon the Zarkos rearguard and ordered the 16th Australian Brigade, commanded by Brigadier Arthur Allen, to reinforce the 21st Battalion and defend the western entrance of Tempe Gorge.[11] Allen now commanded a brigade group centred on the 2/2nd and 2/3rd Australian Battalions and the 21st New Zealand Battalion, supported by the 26th Battery (4th New Zealand Field Regiment), L Troop (7th New Zealand Anti-Tank Regiment), A Troop (2/1st Australian Anti-Tank Regiment) and eleven Bren gun carriers from the 2/5th and 2/11th Australian Battalions.

Allen departed for the gorge that night and ordered Lieutenant Colonel Donald James Lamb, commander of the 2/3rd Battalion, to follow him.[12] Lamb, born on 21 August 1903, had been a sales manager before the war. He later became an officer, following in the footsteps of his father, Malcolm St John Lamb, who had served in the Boer War and commanded the 34th Battalion during World War I. Lieutenant Colonel Lamb now prepared to redeploy his battalion to Tempe Gorge.

In the morning, Lieutenant Colonel Frederick Chilton, commander of the 2/2nd Battalion, reported to Anzac Corps Headquarters where Brigadier Sydney Rowell ordered him to defend Tempe Gorge alongside the 21st Battalion for 'possibly three or four days'.[13] Chilton, born in 1905, had studied law at the University of Sydney and had become a militia officer after joining the Sydney University Regiment. After commanding the battalion's D Company, he took command of the unit and fought the Italians in North Africa before arriving in Greece.

After withdrawing from Platamon, the 21st Battalion marched through olive groves and sandy flats before reaching the Pinios River near the eastern entrance to Tempe Gorge. The men rested under trees and in wheat fields while *Luftwaffe* bombers returning from missions passed overhead. Blamey had sent Brigadier Cyril Clowes to contact the battalion and take any action necessary to secure the defence of the gorge.[14] Clowes found Macky at the ferry crossing on the Pinios near the eastern entrance. After discussing their options, both men agreed that the eastern entrance could not be held as German mountain troops could march over Mount Olympus and capture the western entrance, trapping them in the gorge. Clowes accordingly ordered Macky to defend the western entrance from the south bank of the river as it was 'essential to deny the Gorge to the enemy till 19th April even if it meant extinction'.[15] Clowes promised Macky reinforcements within twenty-four hours and cautioned him to keep a close eye on the north bank as the Germans would likely attempt to infiltrate along the railway line.

New Zealand engineers ferried trucks and field guns across the river while gun tractors, ammunition limbers and Bren gun carriers travelled along the north bank of the river to cross the railway bridge at Tempe village. After all men had crossed the river, the engineers sank the ferry and the 21st Battalion reached the western entrance of Tempe Gorge as dusk approached.

An engineer section from the 19th Army Troops Company used a Bren gun carrier to tow a railway car inside the tunnel on the north bank which blocked the route. Another section of engineers demolished the railway bridge further downstream after the last vehicle had crossed. On the south bank, the engineers used explosives to create a roadblock in the gorge 5 kilometres (3 miles) east of Tempe village and, with their work completed, they departed for Larissa. 10 Platoon commanded by Second-Lieutenant Rose guarded the roadblock as Major Le Lievre deployed the rest of B Company along a stream 1600 metres (1750 yards) inside the gorge near the village of Ampelakia.[16]

Macky established his battalion headquarters in a house in Tempe village shortly before dusk. After sunset, Chilton arrived with a carrier platoon and met with Macky, informing him that his 2/2nd Battalion would arrive later that night. Macky explained that, although his battalion had almost been surrounded at Platamon, the men had managed to fight their way out but were fatigued by the strain of recent fighting. 'As it was now dark', Chilton recalled, 'it was agreed that I should meet him early next morning and mutually arrange for the defence of the position.'[17] Chilton established his headquarters further south in a shepherd's hut near Evangelismos village.

The 2/2nd Battalion arrived at night and Chilton deployed his companies near the gorge entrance. Further west along the south bank of the river opposite Gonnos village, artillery batteries also began to arrive. During the night, a Greek man, arrested as a suspected fifth columnist, was brought to Chilton's headquarters for questioning but refused to enter the hut. When Major Paul Cullen, commander of Headquarters Company, attempted to strike the man with a revolver, he accidentally hit Chilton's arm, breaking his wrist.[18]

On the morning of 17 April, Chilton, with his arm in a sling, and Macky conducted a reconnaissance of Tempe Gorge with Lieutenant Colonel Graham Parkinson (4th New Zealand Field Regiment), Major Stewart (4th Field Regiment), Lieutenant Williams (5th Field Regiment) and Lieutenant Longmore (7th Anti-Tank Regiment). Chilton and Macky planned the defence with urgency because they sensed the Germans might appear at any moment. The 21st Battalion would defend the western entrance of the gorge against *Kampfgruppe Balck* from the high ground and ridges on the south bank from the road block to Tempe village. Meanwhile, the Australians would defend the river west of the village against German mountain soldiers approaching from Mount Olympus. As further insurance against panzers, Chilton also ordered a new crater to be blown inside the gorge near a spur 500 metres (546 yards) from the roadblock. Macky suggested taking command of the entire defence until Brigadier Allen arrived but Chilton refused so the Allied defence remained split. Chilton also sent a patrol into the gorge to discover whether the crossing at the eastern entrance had been seized.

In the 21st Battalion sector, Macky deployed D Company (Captain Trousdale) on the right flank in the high ground to defend the village of Ampelakia. To prevent infiltration through the goat tracks, he detached 11 Platoon from B Company to patrol the gorge about 3 kilometres (1.8 miles) forward of Ampelakia. C Company (Captain Tongue) defended the left flank of D Company, south of the gorge road and east of Tempe village. 13 Platoon guarded the flat across the road while 14 and 15 Platoons held the high ground further up the ridge towards Ampelakia.

Macky ordered B Company (Major Le Lievre) to guard the entrance of the gorge from the south bank on a spur opposite the demolished railway tunnel on the northern bank. 10 Platoon continued to defend the roadblock directly south of the tunnel entrance while 12 Platoon dug in on a spur. In the evening, engineers from the 2/1st Australian Field Company used naval depth-charges to crater the road below the spur in accordance with Chilton's orders. A Company (Captain McClymont) formed a reserve south of Tempe village on a ridge in all-round defence, ready to meet an attack across the river or from the gorge. 9 Platoon held the lower slopes of the ridge looking into the gorge, 8 Platoon faced the river and 7 Platoon deployed west on the flat facing the river.[19]

Macky established his headquarters in a deep ditch behind 9 Platoon,

90 metres (98 yards) south of the road.[20] He deployed the Bren gun carrier platoon south-east of Tempe and the men of Mortar Platoon, lacking essential parts, became riflemen. The four 2-pounder guns of L Troop established anti-tank positions to cover the approaches against the panzers. L1 initially guarded the roadblock near B Company. However, in the evening, the gun redeployed to a gully covering the crater near C Company because it was too far in front of the infantry. L4 defended the same gully behind C Company, covering the road behind the crater, while L3 protected the position from further back. L2 supported the Australians of C Company (2/2nd Battalion), covering the railway bridge and the road out of Tempe village.[21]

In the 2/2nd Battalion sector, Chilton placed C Company (Captain Buckley) on the south bank of the Pinios River, south of Tempe village next to the New Zealanders. He positioned A Company (Captain Caldwell) further south-west to defend the approaches to Evangelismos and B Company (Captain King) with his battalion headquarters south of the village, next to the railway line. The three Australian anti-tank guns of A Troop defended the flats between the A and B Company positions against panzers exiting the gorge. D Company (Captain Hendry) guarded the left flank of the Allied line on the south bank west of Evangelismos. Chilton also placed two platoons — one from A Company and one from B Company — on Hill 1005 at the summit of the ridge south of Ampelakia.[22] After the 2/2nd Battalion's tools arrived, the men dug weapon pits, but they had no barbed wire or anti-tank mines. The Australians used Italian telephone cable captured in Libya to link battalion headquarters with Macky's headquarters.

The artillery formed a gun line, camouflaged among trees and bushes, south of Evangelismos from where they could dominate the high ground on the north bank near Gonnos and target any movement across the Pinios River. The Allies established three observation posts to direct the artillery: one in the hills above the gorge near C Company (21st Battalion), another south of Tempe near A Company (21st Battalion) and the third south of Gonnos. The artillery was well-placed to target German mountain soldiers approaching from Gonnos, but the topography made it difficult for the field guns to support the New Zealanders inside Tempe Gorge given the trajectory the shells would have to travel over vertical cliffs.[23]

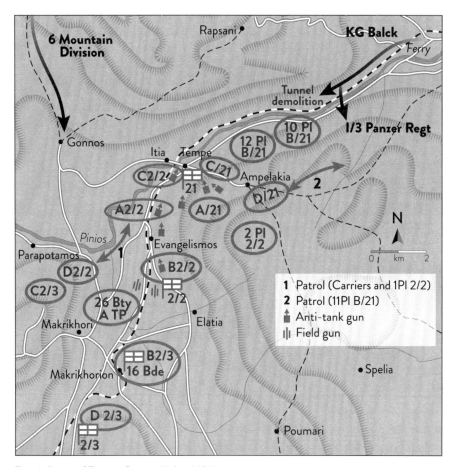

The defence of Tempe Gorge, 17 April 1941.

As the Allies prepared their positions, the Greek inhabitants of Itia village evacuated their homes using mules and donkeys to carry their possessions.[24] After midday, Brigadier Allen arrived and took over the defence. He informed Chilton that the bulk of the 2/3rd Battalion and eleven Bren gun carriers from the 2/5th and 2/11th Battalions would soon arrive to reinforce their defence. Allen, fearing the imminent arrival of the Germans, kept the battalion deployments largely in place but extended the 2/2nd Battalion's flank by moving D Company further west along the river to the high ground east of Parapotamos at Hill 156. He also sent a platoon from D Company and the Bren gun carriers from the 2/2nd Battalion to patrol the 1500-metre

(1640-yard) gap of wheat fields between D Company and A Company.

After the bulk of the 2/3rd Battalion arrived in the afternoon, Allen placed C Company (Captain Murchison) on the high ground south of Gonnos next to D Company (2/2th Battalion), which he placed under Chilton's command.[25] Allen placed the two other companies from the 2/3rd Battalion in reserve further south with B Coy north of Makrikhorion village and D Company at Hill 214 to delay the Germans if they exited Tempe Gorge. As the 2/3rd Battalion had hastily redeployed from the Veria Pass, it had left behind much of its equipment including barbed wire, anti-tank mines and most of its signal wire, forcing Lieutenant Colonel Lamb to rely upon runners to communicate with his company commanders.[26] Allen also established his brigade headquarters at Makrikhorion railway station.

In the late afternoon, the Allied commanders decided to move the Australian anti-tank guns slightly forward to make room for two 25-pounder field guns, which would now be used in an anti-tank role.[27] The three Australian anti-tank guns were repositioned further north with one guarding the road to Tempe village near A Company (2/2nd Company), one in Evangelismos guarding the road further south and one with B Company (2/2nd Battalion) on the same road further south.[28] At night, the two field guns established anti-tank positions south of Evangelismos — the gun from F Troop west of B Company (2/2nd Battalion) and the other from A Troop east of the road.

KAMPFGRUPPE BALCK APPROACHES TEMPE GORGE

On 16 April, after forcing the 21st Battalion from Platamon, Balck attempted to pursue the New Zealanders, but his panzers could not descend the southern slope of the ridge and the demolished railway tunnel would take five days to repair.[29] A panzer company attempted to move around the ridge along the coast but failed because heavy rain had made the path a quagmire. Balck ordered his engineers to create a path for his panzers, but their work progressed slowly:

> The descent from the ridge was even harder than the ascent. Time and time again tracks came off on the narrow mule path. Projecting rocks tore

Tanks from the 3rd Panzer Regiment in front of Platamon Castle prepare to advance towards Tempe Gorge.
(© IWM)

sprockets and tracks, and engineers had to knock off or blow these rocks. Then the descent became easier, but was still slow.[30]

At midday on 17 April, the panzers finally descended Platamon Ridge, and Balck lamented that it took twenty-four hours 'before we managed to get anything across that damned mountain'.[31] Although numerous tanks still had to have damaged suspension, gears and tracks repaired, 1st Company, with around thirty tanks supported by panzer grenadiers in armoured personnel carriers led by Lieutenant Colonel Karl von Decker, reached the coast and advanced south along the railway line to Tempe Gorge.

After advancing to a rail bridge 6 kilometres (3.7 miles) north of Tempe Gorge, Decker encountered the Cycle Squadron from the 112th Reconnaissance Unit (6th *Gebirgsjäger* Division) commanded by Lieutenant Count zu Eltz. The bicycle soldiers had climbed over Mount Olympus before being detached from the rest of the division and sent on a mission to investigate the eastern entrance to the gorge. Eltz had discovered that the bridges and ferry had been demolished and the railway line was blocked halfway through

German cycle soldiers in Greece.
(AWM)

the gorge.[32] Decker attached the squadron to his command and continued south. 'On we went with no opposition,' Balck recalled. 'Left and right cavalry, cyclists and mountain troops followed the procession of tanks, all inspired with the urge to get at the English.'[33]

In the afternoon, the panzer company reached the Pinios River at the entrance of Tempe Gorge. As the Allies had demolished the bridges and could not cross the river, the men of *Kampfgruppe Balck* advanced towards the gorge along the railway line on the north bank.

THE DESCENT FROM MOUNT OLYMPUS

As *Kampfgruppe Balck* advanced towards Tempe Gorge, the 6th *Gebirgsjäger*, commanded by Major General Ferdinand Schörner, approached the Pinios River. On 14 April, the mountaineers, having left their vehicles behind, began climbing the northern slopes of Mount Olympus with their mules carrying artillery and equipment. Schörner, an experienced soldier who had won the *Pour le Mérite* in 1917, well understood his mission: 'The division was to push towards Larissa south of Olympus and break this resistance, and to inflict heavy losses on the enemy by cutting his withdrawal route from the NW. The division was faced with a hard but magnificent task.'[34] He also sent a special patrol on a propaganda mission which reached the summit of Mount Olympus and hoisted the swastika flag during a heavy snowstorm.

At midday on 17 April, the 2nd Battalion (143rd Regiment), Schörner's vanguard, descended the southern slopes of Mount Olympus on the Leptokaria track and reached Gonnos. The exhausted mountaineers had completed an epic journey of endurance with inadequate supplies, having been sustained by airdrops from Junkers 52 transport planes. Greek villagers informed the Germans that British patrols had been seen on the south bank of the Pinios. In the afternoon, Schörner arrived at Gonnos and noted the 'good view towards Larissa' which 'gave an increasingly good idea of the division's future battleground'.[35] The other battalions of the 143rd Regiment continued their march towards Gonnos, followed by the 141st Regiment.[36]

In the evening, Schörner ordered two battalions from his 143rd Regiment, with support from the 1st Battalion (118th Artillery Regiment), to 'attack and destroy' the enemy on the south bank of the river 'opposite Gonnos on a wide front' who 'seem to intend to resist'.[37]

The 1st Battalion (143rd Regiment) would attack the river south-east of Gonnos with a feint at 0800 h at the river bend. At 0830 h, the 3rd Battalion (143rd Regiment) would launch the main attack and cross the river west of Parapotamos village to flank the Australian left wing held by D Company (2/2nd Battalion) and C Company (2/3rd Battalion). Schörner predicted that these attacks would lead to 'the destruction of the enemy on the south bank, the opening of the Tempe Gorge and the Elason–Larissa road'.[38] The 1st Battalion would later cross the river and attack the Australian right flank near A Company (2/2nd Battalion). Schörner also ordered the 2nd Company from the 1st Battalion (143rd Regiment), with engineer support, to cross the Pinios further west and advance over rough terrain to block the Tempe–Larissa road.[39]

THE ROADBLOCK IN THE GORGE

In the afternoon, *Kampfgruppe Balck* reached the eastern entrance of Tempe Gorge. Balck decided to enter the gorge with one panzer company, one rifle company and the cycle squadron because 'the effects of artillery are increased tenfold in rocky mountainous terrain because of the stone fragments. If one went in there with lots of people, the losses would be very high.'[40] As the small German force entered the gorge, Balck observed the jagged terrain:

> To our left and right the rock walls went straight up for three hundred meters, and the Pineios River raged through the middle of the valley. On the opposite side of the river there was a road, but it was out of our reach.[41]

After *Kampfgruppe Balck* entered Tempe Gorge, Major General Rudolf Veiel, commander of the 2nd Panzer Division, signalled Headquarters 18th Mountain Corps to update General Boehme on the progress:

> At first light Balck Gp began to bring up its tracked vehicles, and pushed the enemy back through Egani. A strong force of tracked vehicles thrust along the railway and reached the Tempe Gorge at 1600 hrs, but as there were no bridges available it had to push on SW on the north side of the gorge. Wheeled vehicles cannot yet get through the pass SE of Kuneri, and infantry and tanks are entirely without supplies. The enemy is withdrawing through the gorge and we are pursuing him. . . . At present the fighting troops of Balck Gp in the Tempe Gorge are not receiving supplies.[42]

Although Balck had overextended his main supply line, his men received some additional supplies from airdrops and small boats hugging the Aegean coast.[43]

The panzer company headed west along railway tracks on the north bank of the river screened by the cycle squadron. After progressing halfway through the gorge, the Germans reached the demolished railway tunnel which stopped the panzers and frustrated Balck:

> We were able to get through the first tunnel, but just short of the second tunnel the track bed had been blown up, and the tunnel entrance was

damaged as well. A freight car sat trapped between the two positions. The Tommies sat on the far side, shooting into the tunnel. That was as far as we could go.[44]

Decker ordered the cycle squadron forward to pass through the blocked tunnel on foot.

A platoon-sized patrol from the 2/2nd Battalion, led by Lieutenant Arnold and Sergeant Tanner, entered the gorge and moved through the road on the south bank. After passing the New Zealand roadblock, the men stopped directly opposite the tunnel entrance. In the late afternoon, the patrol observed German soldiers moving through the tunnel and a panzer which could not navigate around the obstacle. A burst of German machine gun fire from the north bank hit four men, seriously wounding Corporal Lyon and another soldier while lightly wounding others.[45] The Australians took cover as the New Zealand soldiers of 10 Platoon at the roadblock engaged the German infantry with rifles and Bren guns. The panzer opened fire on the New Zealanders as bullets ricocheted harmlessly off its armour. Although Allied artillery opened fire, the forward observer could not establish a good radio signal with the gun line because the cliff walls interfered with the transmission and the bombardment failed to disrupt the Germans.[46]

The cycle squadron on the north bank engaged the Australians and New Zealanders with machine guns and mortars, but the men could not move beyond the tunnel entrance. The fire from the panzer forced Second-Lieutenant Rose to withdraw 10 Platoon, which retreated 180 metres (196 yards) up the ridge.[47] The Germans in the tunnel pressed forward and, as Decker explained, their 'advance had to be made along the railway embankment on the enemy's strong MG positions. Casualties were considerable.'[48] The squadron's after-action report similarly noted:

The squadron came under heavy MG and shellfire from prepared positions. It immediately advanced to the attack. The country was almost devoid of cover. One platoon was sent round through the rocks to the right flank, and succeeded in pushing the enemy back about 800 metres [875 yards]. The enemy shellfire increased and went on all night. We had no artillery

support, and the attack was halted about 1900 hrs. During the night Lt
Col von Decker pulled the squadron back into the tunnel.[49]

At dusk, Lieutenant Arnold and Sergeant Tanner led their patrol back
through the gorge and the New Zealanders helped carry the wounded
Australians. Chilton reported that his patrol 'had encountered the enemy at
the road block' and had 'been pinned to the road in the floor of the Gorge
by fire from a tank' but after dark the patrol had 'succeeded in getting away
losing 3 killed and some wounded'.[50] Major Le Lievre ordered the exhausted
men of 10 Platoon to withdraw to the main defensive position and he sent
Second-Lieutenant Rose to Battalion Headquarters to get some sleep.[51]

THE RIVER CROSSING

As the Germans in the railway tunnel engaged the Allied soldiers near the
roadblock, Balck wanted to locate a spot where his panzers could ford the
Pinios and ordered Second-Lieutenants Brunnenbusch and Schmitthemmer
to wade through the river to find a suitable location. After both men dived
into the torrential river, they came back, having found a possible crossing
location, and Balck decided to risk one panzer:

> A Mk II tank drove determinedly down the high, steep embankment
> into the water. It struggled through the river like a walrus, with nothing
> showing except its turret; it appeared to be swimming. But the driver
> carried on calmly, although he was sitting up to his middle in water and
> the waves completely prevented him from seeing anything. Finally the tank
> clambered out on the other side amid loud cheers from the spectators and
> pushed on forward.[52]

Balck sent five more panzers across and, although two tanks sank into the
Pinios, the crew swam to safety. Four tanks had successfully crossed the river,
but their path was blocked as Decker explained: 'The Panzers couldn't
advance along the south road because a deep gap had been blown in the
road. Detouring in the water resulted in three Panzers stuck in the mud.'[53]
Balck sent a rifle battalion across the river to repair the damaged road and

A German panzer crossing the Pinios River.
(Author's Collection)

also brought four 105-mm guns forward by tractor. He placed Decker in command of all German troops in Tempe Gorge with orders to launch an all-out assault the next day. After sunset, the panzers halted. 'Night fell

German panzers crossing the Pinios River.
(Author's Collection)

and stopped our advance,' Balck recalled. 'Again the crews slept exhausted beside their tanks, for the going had demanded enormous exertions from everybody. The drivers in particular had accomplished miracles.'[54] A panzer column several kilometres long waited behind the tunnel for the morning.

THE VALLEY AT NIGHT

In the afternoon, Australian soldiers observed small bodies of men with pack animals on the ridges above Gonnos firing flares when German aircraft flew overhead. After dark, Captain Hendry sent a platoon led by Lieutenant Colquhoun across the river in a boat to investigate north of the river. The patrol observed Germans in Gonnos and small bodies of mountaineers with their pack animals moving west towards Elia.

During the night, German patrols searched for favourable routes towards the Pinios and locations to cross the river as the assault regiments from the 143rd Regiment moved towards their assembly areas.[55] One hour before midnight, a German patrol attacked three of Colquhoun's men who had remained behind to guard the ferry and, after a brief firefight, the Germans withdrew after one soldier had been killed.[56] After the patrol returned,

Colquhoun reported to Chilton that the Germans had occupied Gonnos, Rapsani and Ampelakia villages.[57] Other patrols from the 2/2nd Battalion moved along the south bank and exchanged fire with German troops across the river in the darkness.[58]

Allied artillery fire targeted German lights in the hills above Gonnos and disrupted the men of *Kampfgruppe Balck* inside Tempe Gorge, slowing down the repair work at the road block. In the darkness, Balck heard the explosion of shells echoing between the vertical cliff walls:

> As night came on, the air was full of balsamic spring fragrances, a nightingale was singing beautifully, and the English artillery was firing full force into the pass. Rock avalanches fell from both sides of the valley, increasing the effect of each round tenfold. Thank God I had halted my main body at the valley entrance.[59]

The artillery fire resumed every hour and, after Balck established his headquarters in a chapel near the tunnel, a shell hit the roof but caused no damage. Decker reported that the artillery had killed three of his men and wounded seventeen others. The medical officer, as Balck noted, 'had a lot of work to do, for there were dead and wounded on both sides of the Pinios'.[60]

The Allied soldiers spent an anxious night knowing the Germans would attack in the morning. Lieutenant O'Neill from 13 Platoon (21st Battalion) recalled the final preparations:

> Digging was impossible but by working throughout the night, when not on patrol, we built up forward of us just enough protection to get by. The spoil was camouflaged by weed. I know that my night's work with a pen knife and finger nails just raised the parapet high enough to lie behind it. For an hour or so we had shared a crow-bar between us but with darkness came sounds of German infiltration on the other side of the river so that noiselessness had to be our watchword in our labours.[61]

The German soldiers of *Kampfgruppe Balck* in Tempe Gorge and the mountaineers of the 6th *Gebirgsjäger* near Gonnos knew that their actions the next day would determine the fate of British Empire forces in Greece.

CHAPTER SEVEN
THE BATTLE OF TEMPE GORGE

CROSSING THE PINIOS

In the darkness before dawn on 18 April 1941, the assault units of the 6th *Gebirgsjäger* Division, the 1st and 3rd Battalions (143rd Regiment), moved into their assembly areas. The 1st Battalion had orders to conduct a feint attack on the Pinios River east of Parapotamos to divert Allied attention from the main attack, which would be launched later by the 3rd Battalion further downstream, west of Parapotamos.[1] After sunrise, the darkness gave way to a bright clear day.

At 0530 h, the New Zealand 25-pounder field guns from the 26th Battery opened fire on Gonnos village and the 1st Battalion's assembly area, disrupting German preparations. Half an hour later, forward observers from the 2/2nd Australian Battalion spotted German soldiers descending the high ground from Gonnos advancing towards the river. The Allied artillery bombardment intensified as D Troop targeted infantry and machine guns north of the river and E Troop shelled the Germans above Gonnos.[2] Captain Hendry, commander of D Company (2/2nd Battalion), observed mountain troops moving west from Gonnos along the goat tracks and, because no forward observer had been established near his location, he directed the artillery fire.[3]

The twelve 75-mm mountain guns from the 1st Battalion (118th Artillery Regiment) returned fire. An artillery duel erupted across the Pinios which lasted all morning and increased in ferocity as additional guns and mortars joined the action. German artillery concentrated on counter-battery fire before targeting the river bank, and their gunners established dominance along the front as more of their guns came forward and commenced firing. The 118th Artillery Regiment's after-action report described the engagement:

> The battle developed as an artillery duel, and it would have been desirable to have had more artillery in position. I/118 fired mainly on English MT convoys with marked success. It was hard to engage the enemy artillery, some of which was beyond our range. . . . The enemy artillery, which obviously had very good Ops, was very watchful, and particularly engaged our Ops, and 2 Bty's positions, with very accurate fire, which caused casualties in 2 Bty. But the enemy did not fire for real effect.[4]

At 0800 h, the 1st Battalion (143rd Regiment) commenced its feint attack at the river bend east of Parapotamos between A and D Companies (2/2nd Battalion) which was thinly held by patrols. The mountain troops moved forward as heavy mortars and a machine gun platoon suppressed the Australian troops on the south bank. The battalion commander noted that 'enemy shelling increased, and as our troops approached the river they came under heavy MG fire from the hills east of Parapotamos'.[5]

The Australian soldiers of the 2/2nd Battalion engaged the mountaineers approaching the north bank with machine guns and mortars while New Zealand artillery continued to shell the area. Lieutenant Colonel Chilton, commander of the 2/2nd Battalion, ordered the Bren gun carriers from the 2/5th and 2/11st Australian Battalions to race to the river bend to engage the enemy from across the river.[6]

One hour after the 1st Battalion commenced the feint attack, its soldiers were 500 metres (546 yards) from the river. As the German approached the river, Chilton reported: 'Enemy attack increasing in intensity — supported by Mortars. Their infantry clearly visible approaching river bank in large numbers.'[7] A Company (2/2nd Battalion) harassed the Germans and the 3-inch mortar platoon targeted the enemy troops, but Chilton remained unaware that this attack was a feint designed to distract his attention from the upcoming main assault.[8]

Frederick Chilton, commander of the 2/2nd Australian Battalion.
(AWM)

Lieutenant Love, in command of six Bren gun carriers, led his force to the river and concealed his vehicles beside the track before sending a section forward on foot on a reconnaissance mission. The patrol observed German soldiers and enemy mortars on the north bank before returning to the carriers. Love ordered his carriers forward and the platoon engaged the enemy at the river bend.

Chilton asked Lieutenant Colonel Macky, commander of the 21st Battalion, for his Bren gun carriers in order to repulse the anticipated crossing at the river bend. Macky sent nine carriers commanded by Lieutenant Dee, who rushed to the sector and deployed to the right of the Australian carriers already in combat. The New Zealanders opened fire at 1000 metres (1093 yards), killing several German soldiers crossing the river. As Macky had no means of communicating with his Bren gun carriers, they remained under Australian command.

The Germans returned fire with mortars, killing Private Sullivan, mortally

Allied Bren gun carriers in Greece.
(© IWM)

wounding Lieutenant Love and wounding four other soldiers. Sergeant Stovin and Private MacQueen silenced a mortar with Bren gun fire. After Corporal Lacey exposed himself to enemy fire to allow the others to rescue the wounded, the carriers withdrew to safety. At 1130 h, the 1st Battalion stopped its feint attack, which had successfully deceived the Australians as Chilton incorrectly believed he had repulsed a determined river crossing.[9]

Before dawn, the 3rd Battalion (143rd Regiment) left Gonnos and advanced towards the Pinios near Parapotamos village. As the mountain troops approached the river, German artillery suppressed the Australian soldiers defending the south bank as the 6th *Gebirgsjäger* War Diary noted:

The divisional commander ordered the artillery to be used as assault guns. So far it had been engaged in a hard artillery duel with the enemy from positions north and west of Gonos. The accuracy of its fire contributed materially to the decisiveness of our success.[10]

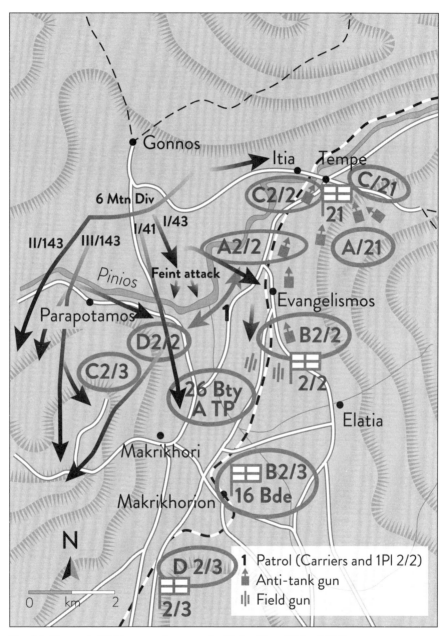

The 6th Mountain Division assault across the Pinios River, 18 April 1941.

At 0645 h, a platoon led by Sergeant Denk crossed the river in a captured boat and, as the battalion commander explained, the patrol was 'engaged in Parapotamos by English troops who had come up from Makii Chori on trucks'.[11] As the battalion continuously ferried reinforcements across the river, the Germans occupied Parapotamos.

D Company (2/2nd Battalion) had watched the Germans moving down from Gonnos but had not observed the patrols crossing the river. Although Captain Hendry sent Lieutenant Watson's 2 Platoon to investigate Parapotamos and destroy the ferry, enemy fire mortally wounded Corporal Baker and wounded two other soldiers, halting their advance.

The Australian forward observers called in artillery fire on German troops moving south of Gonnos for the rest of the morning. Captain Porter (2/2nd Battalion) directed the artillery using a field telephone with effective results. Lieutenant Clark from D Troop left the artillery position and established an observation post in the high ground near Parapotamos with excellent visibility. He directed artillery fire onto enemy mortars, machine guns and infantry, inflicting heavy casualties on the 3rd Battalion.[12]

By 0930 h, the Australian defence near Parapotamos village had collapsed and the men retreated southwards to high ground. As the German commander noted, 'The accuracy of our shellfire on Parapotamos and the sudden burst of fire from Patrol No 1 forced the English . . . to withdraw.'[13]

The 3rd Battalion advanced south and east, threatening C Company (2/3rd Battalion) and D Company (2/2nd Battalion) near Hill 156 east of Parapotamos with encirclement. One hour later, the Australian left flank was virtually surrounded on three sides. The 2/2nd Battalion's Bren gun platoon raced to clear the river in front of D Company, engaging the German infantry at the river near Parapotamos, but the crews sustained casualties from mortar fire and could not halt the enemy advance. As the mountain troops consolidated their bridgehead near Parapotamos, they also planned another crossing, closer to Tempe village.

As the Germans fought the Australians at Parapotamos, Major General Ferdinand Schörner ordered the 1st Battalion (143rd Regiment) to launch a full-scale assault across the river south-west of Tempe, opposite Evangelismos. The battalion commander sent a patrol forward in search of a crossing point west of the village which found a suitable location at the sandbank west of

Major General Ferdinand Schörner, commander of the 6th *Gebirgsjäger* Division, in Greece.
(Bundesarchiv, Bild 183-L29176)

Evangelismos: 'I decided at once to cross at the spot recced, and to attack the enemy at Evangelismos and on the hills SE of it.'[14] At 1400 h, the 1st Battalion commenced its river assault:

As soon as the enemy at and SE of Evangelismos recognized our attack he opened heavy shell, mortar and MG fire on our bank and the river itself. But before the fire could have any effect 1 Coy (which had been directed to establish a bridgehead) had reached the other bank, thanks to the speed of the advance, which took the enemy by surprise.[15]

As the German troops crossed the river, an Australian soldier, Charlie Green, observed the enemy:

They had our position pinpointed from our fire earlier in the day, and then began a rain of mortar and machine gun fire on our positions. From our position we could see thousands of German troops moving down from the mountains on the opposite side of the river.[16]

A Company (2/2nd Battalion) engaged the mountaineers with intense Bren gun fire as Sergeant Geoff Coyle's two 3-inch mortars rained down bombs on the 'enemy troops amassing to cross the river' who 'presented an irresistible target'.[17] Corporal Evans' mortar team lobbed 350 bombs at Germans crossing the river, but they kept moving forward as their dead floated downstream. Frank Delforce, another Australian soldier, recalled: 'Our lads mowed the bastards down like sheep, but they kept coming, wave after wave.'[18]

Despite considerable artillery, mortar and machine gun fire, the mountain company crossed the river and formed a beachhead, allowing the rest of the battalion to cross while Australian infantry and mortar fire harassed their movement. After the battalion reorganized on the south bank, the men attacked Evangelismos at 1600 h, as the 6th *Gebirgsjäger* War Diary noted:

The enemy offered stubborn opposition and some of our heavy weapons were casualties, so the attack made very slow progress. Not until 1730 hrs did we break into the enemy positions after hand-to-hand fighting.[19]

The battalion suffered twelve killed, one missing and sixty-nine wounded.[20] As the Germans approached Evangelismos, they could hear the noise of battle coming from Tempe Gorge as *Kampfgruppe Balck* assaulted the New Zealand defence.

ASSAULTING TEMPE GORGE

As the German mountain troops clashed with the Australians along the Pinios, *Kampfgruppe Balck* prepared to attack the 21st New Zealand Battalion inside Tempe Gorge. The Germans would attack through the gorge, along both banks of the river, under the tactical command of Lieutenant Colonel Karl von Decker. On the north bank, the battlegroup consisted of the 1st Company (1st Panzer Battalion) and the Cycle Squadron of the 112th Reconnaissance Unit. On the south bank, the German force included six panzers, the 7th Company of the 2nd Battalion (304th Infantry Regiment) and two elite special forces patrols from the 800th *Brandenburg* Regiment.[21]

At dawn, the cycle squadron, which had left their bicycles behind, advanced west along the northern bank of the gorge. As the soldiers emerged from the safety of the railway tunnel, they met light resistance and made significant progress, advancing 2 kilometres (1.2 miles) until New Zealand machine gun fire from the south bank stopped their advance opposite the valley between B and C Companies (21st Battalion). Major Barth noted this setback in his after-action report:

> The squadron advanced under aimed rifle fire and reached the shrine on the railway embankment . . . where it was halted by heavy enfilade fire from MGs, mortars and artillery from the hills south of the river.[22]

Although the Germans returned fire with mortars and machine guns, New Zealand small-arms fire and artillery prevented progress and, as Decker explained, 'their further advance wasn't possible until the occupation of the south side was pushed forward'.[23]

The cycle squadron on the north bank posed little threat to the 21st Battalion and Macky was more worried about the prospect of German mountain troops attacking the rear of his battalion. In the morning, he told his subordinates in a conference 'that if completely cut off and overwhelmed, those left would make out in small parties to Volos'.[24] Macky had earlier ordered his company commanders to hold their positions for as long as possible before falling back to a second defensive line, but this new order now empowered his company commanders to decide when to withdraw.

As the cycle squadron attacked along the north bank, the infantry from the 7th Company and the *Brandenburger* patrols, having crossed the river on kapok floats, continued clearing the abandoned roadblock. The panzer crews which had crossed the river the previous day waited anxiously for the obstacle to be cleared before they could commence their attack along the south bank road. Decker believed that as soon as his six panzers rolled forward and attacked the New Zealand positions, the cycle squadron currently pinned down on the north bank would be able to resume its advance.

The Allied artillery had concentrated its fire on the mountain troops attacking from Gonnos and the cycle squadron on the north bank without realizing the presence of enemy armour and infantry inside the gorge on the south bank.[25] As 10 Platoon had retreated from the roadblock the previous evening, the New Zealanders could no longer observe the obstacle or the river crossing and no patrols had been sent forward to investigate. The 21st Battalion, therefore, had no advance warning of the impending assault and its forward observers could not direct artillery fire at the Germans preparing to attack. Macky later acknowledged his critical error: 'The major mistake at Pinios was the siting of the road block in the gorge. The defending platoon became defiladed. The block was rendered unobserved when this platoon had to be withdrawn.'[26]

At midday, after the roadblock had been cleared, the six panzers moved forward, supported by the men from the 7th Company and the *Brandenburger* troops. German fire from the cycle squadron on the north bank intensified as the panzers advanced west along the road towards B Company's position on the New Zealand right flank.

As the soldiers of 12 Platoon — the forward element of B Company — continued engaging the cycle squadron across the river, six panzers suddenly approached their position along the south bank road. The New Zealanders opened fire on the tanks as mortar fire rained down on their own position. The panzers bypassed the men of 12 Platoon who could not stop the tanks with their inadequate weapons as they endured heavy suppressive fire. Major Le Lievre, after observing the panzers pass 10 Platoon, moved B Company further up the ridge towards D Company's position near Ampelakia village in accordance with Macky's order which authorized company commanders to independently withdraw. Once the soldiers of B Company reached the high ground, they had an excellent view of the Germans but were too far away to engage them.

The panzers halted to fire at the men of B Company while they climbed the ridge towards Ampelakia. As Allied artillery fire targeted the tanks, the infantry from the 7th Company and the *Brandenburger* troops advanced over the ridges while fire from the panzers and German artillery supported their movement. Decker noted that the 'attack went forward. About 80 prisoners were taken that were pulled out of the mountains'.[27] Balck observed that his infantry 'climbed like goats and cleared out the enemy positions, under cover of the fire of the leading tanks'.[28]

Decker, believing the incoming artillery fire was covering an Allied withdrawal, ordered the cycle squadron to resume its advance along the north bank. The squadron, as Balck noted, 'advanced 4 km, under shellfire and flanking MG fire from the south bank all the way. The road forward was not easy even for old soldiers.'[29] Decker informed Balck that the assaults on both sides of the river were making slow progress because the panzers had difficulty advancing along the narrow road on the south bank. Balck, however, bluntly replied, 'I don't want to hear from you until you have taken Tempe. I can't give you any more troops.'[30]

The panzers slowly approached the ridge held by C Company and the anti-tank guns of L Troop. The New Zealand gunners, who had only expected panzers to appear on the north bank, were astonished to see enemy tanks on the south bank. Captain Nolan attempted to direct artillery fire on the tanks from his observation post, but the field guns could not properly target the south bank because the steep cliff walls protected the Germans from the flat trajectory of the shells.[31] As the panzers approached the ridge held by 13 Platoon, they fired ineffectively uphill at the men in pits. Although 14 and 15 Platoons in the higher ground withdrew up the ridge, the soldiers of 13 Platoon in the lower ground 90 metres (98 yards) from the tanks were trapped in their pits.[32]

As the New Zealand defence collapsed, Captain Robert McClymont, commander of A Company, reported to Battalion Headquarters. Macky ordered him to delay the enemy as long as possible, before retreating up the ridge and forming a rearguard to cover the withdrawal of the battalion towards Volos.

At 1300 h, the panzers cautiously resumed their advance towards Tempe village and, as German infantry advanced over the ridge, Lieutenant Mervyn O'Neill surrendered 13 Platoon, which had suffered one fatality and two wounded. Balck observed that the New Zealand prisoners 'acted with dignity, refused to make any statements, and firmly believed in the victory of the Empire'.[33] 11 Platoon (B Company) watched the panzers advancing towards Tempe from the high ground further up the ridge, but they could not direct artillery fire against the tanks because they did not have a radio.[34] After Second-Lieutenant Yeoman received Major Le Lievre's orders to withdraw, he pulled back his forward sections, which were engaging German infantry, and his men retreated to the hills above Ampelakia.

As the panzers approached the anti-tank guns, they reached the crater created by the Australian engineers in front of the spur near C Company as Decker explained: 'the road was again destroyed by detonation. The second lead Panzer had to halt and the Pioneer-Zug of the Abteilung [battalion] pulled forward. After scouting, it turned out that this barrier was crossable.'[35]

The crew of gun L4, camouflaged behind the spur under the command of Sergeant Cavanagh, had observed the panzers reach the crater. After the first panzer rounded the spur, he held his fire waiting for more tanks to come within range. The panzers halted and their crews climbed out to wait for the other tanks to arrive. After the third tank appeared, Cavanagh opened fire at 90 metres (98 yards).[36] Decker witnessed two panzers burst into flames:

As both lead Panzers (Leutnant Brunnenbusch and Feldwebel [Sergeant] Weber) drove forward to attack the village of Tempi, each was hit twice by anti-tank gun fire that knocked them out of action. Of all of the crew members, only Feldwebel Weber was unscathed. Three of the crew were killed and the fourth severely burned. Four including Leutnant Brunnenbusch were severely wounded and one lightly wounded.[37]

Balck also observed the destruction: 'In a moment both point tanks were burning. Some of the crews, including 2/Lt Brunnenbusch, escaped into the thick scrub seriously wounded' and the medics 'came up quickly and had plenty to do'.[38] Sergeant Grzeschik, a panzer driver, battled the flames with a fire extinguisher until the ammunition exploded.

As the infantry from the 7th Company engaged the New Zealanders of C Company, the four remaining panzers on the south bank resumed their advance. Balck watched his tanks engage the defenders and 'some of them got direct hits too. Finally one tank fought its way forward alone, defending itself with great difficulty against the direct fire of the artillery and A Tk guns.'[39] The Germans could not pinpoint gun L4's location, but after the troops of C Company retreated, Cavanagh realized his gun position was isolated and decided to withdraw. The crew retreated to their truck 90 metres (98 yards) away and drove to the lines held by the 2/2nd Australian Battalion, only to later be captured by the Germans.[40]

German infantry located gun L1, commanded by Sergeant Quinn, at the foot of the ridge and opened fire, as Decker reported: 'An enemy anti-tank gun was positioned about 50 meters behind the barrier. Its crew was pinned down by machine gun fire from the northeast of Itis.'[41] Soldiers from the 7th Company probably destroyed gun L3 as a lieutenant earned a Knight's Cross in the action and his citation stated 'he personally destroyed with hand grenades an A Tk position which fought to the last'.[42] As the panzers approached Tempe village and the exit of the gorge, the Germans on the south bank had suffered three killed, six wounded and two tanks destroyed.[43]

After the surviving panzers resumed their advance, artillery fire halted their further progress for two hours. The New Zealanders withdrew as the remaining 21st Battalion positions on the high ground became untenable. As each platoon retreated through the gullies and ravines of Mount Ossa, Macky lost contact with his men as his battalion fragmented and only A Company and a section of Bren gun carriers remained effectively under his command.[44]

As *Kampfgruppe Balck* approached A Company and the exit of the gorge, the Bren gun carriers kept the infantry at bay but the panzers, supported by mortar fire, broke into their position. After German fire knocked out the Australian anti-tank gun, the New Zealand infantry could no longer offer effective resistance. Warrant Officer Lockett, in a desperate exploit, rammed

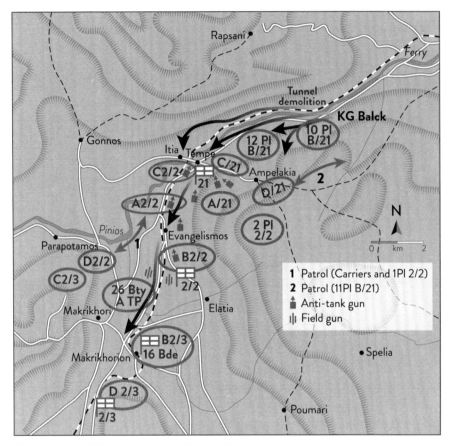

Kampfgruppe Balck's assault through Tempe Gorge.

his Bren gun carrier into the lead panzer, knocking it off the road in an act of valour which earned him the Military Medal.[45] Lockett tragically died the following month in Crete, on 27 May 1941. After the Germans had knocked out four of the six carriers, the others withdrew under the cover of artillery fire. With the New Zealand defence routed, Decker could now turn his panzers south along the road to Evangelismos.

Macky had ineffectively attempted to command his companies from battalion headquarters and failed to maintain situational awareness or influence the battle.[46] He effectively delegated command to each of his company commanders who fought individual battles without being able to support each other. In contrast, Balck placed Decker firmly in charge of all German forces inside the gorge who co-ordinated the two groups on both sides of the river, which mutually supported each other's operations.

CRISIS AT TEMPE

As the Australians fought the German mountain troops crossing the Pinios River, Macky informed Chilton by radio that Tempe village was under heavy mortar fire and his men were engaging enemy troops inside the gorge from across the river. Chilton did not realize the Germans had overrun the 21st Battalion: 'During all our conversations he [Macky] never indicated that his position was at all serious or that he intended to withdraw.'[47] After midday, contact over the radio abruptly ceased and Chilton remained ignorant of the collapse of the 21st Battalion's defence.

One group of fleeing New Zealanders passed through Chilton's headquarters and Major Paul Cullen remembered that efforts were made 'to stop them and persuade them to stay with us, but we mostly failed'.[48] One New Zealand platoon commanded by Lieutenant Southworth rallied and Chilton placed the troops in 'the centre of the position' and they carried out their duty 'in a very creditable manner during the remainder of the day'.[49]

Balck's panzers meanwhile advanced towards Tempe, followed by soldiers in trucks and marching infantry, and the Germans reached the village in the early afternoon. After advancing along the north bank, the cycle squadron also reached the village, as Major Barth noted, 'Tempe was reached at 1530 hrs, and the enemy was thrown back out of the houses in Tempe along the railway embankment. At 1645 hrs the blown railway bridge was stormed.'[50] The squadron had suffered four killed and ten wounded, including its commander Lieutenant Count zu Eltz.[51]

After the New Zealand withdrawal, the men of the 2/2nd Battalion experienced a two-hour lull in the battle, although intermittent mortar and machine gun fire continued to harass their positions. By this time, the Australians had suffered around forty killed and wounded.[52]

In the C Company (2/2nd Battalion) position south-west of Tempe village, Captain Buckley waited for the inevitable German attack: 'Throughout the morning small arms fire was coming from NZ Bn on our right. Could not see what they were shooting at.'[53] After a group of 21st Battalion soldiers passed through the company's lines, Buckley learned that German tanks had passed the roadblock and that the New Zealand anti-tank gunners had been overwhelmed.

As the panzers moved south from Tempe village towards C Company, Chilton ordered Buckley to warn his anti-tank gunners to expect the enemy and defend the road from the village. Buckley, however, reported to Chilton that the New Zealand crew from gun L2 had fled, taking the breech-block with them.[54] The Australians of C Company engaged the advancing panzers from the slopes above the road, but without anti-tank support they could not stop the enemy.

After a tank drove through Lieutenant Lovett's platoon, 365 metres (400 yards) in front of Buckley's headquarters, most of the platoon fell back across the road to the southern slopes. Lovett had been wounded and was later captured by the Germans. Three panzers advanced south along the road and fired on the Australian anti-tank gun, preventing the crew from shooting back, making the infantry position untenable. Buckley informed Chilton that tanks had broken into his position and German infantry were firing on his troops from the high ground previously held by the New Zealanders. After Buckley lost contact with battalion headquarters, he independently ordered his men to withdraw, a decision Chilton later agreed with: 'In the light of all facts now known to me Capt. Buckley's decision was justified.'[55]

In the late afternoon, as the men of C Company withdrew up the ridges, the Australian and New Zealand Bren gun carriers covered their withdrawal. The panzers halted and fired on the retreating Australians with cannons and machine guns. As *Kampfgruppe Balck* overwhelmed the right flank of the Australian defence, the German mountain soldiers threatened to overrun Chilton's left flank.

COLLAPSE OF THE AUSTRALIAN LEFT FLANK

As the Australian and New Zealand soldiers fought the Germans along the Pinios, Major General Bernard Freyberg ordered Brigadier Arthur Allen, in command of all Allied units around Tempe, to hold the road to Larissa until 0300 h the next day to allow the rest of W Force to pass through the crossroads. The 6th New Zealand Brigade was scheduled to pass through the town at 0100 h and Allen Force had to keep the Germans at bay until then. Allen accordingly planned a rearguard action and placed Lieutenant Colonel Lamb, commander of the 2/3rd Battalion, in command of the force. The rearguard was based around Lamb's B and D Companies, which had been placed in reserve near Makrikhorion railway station. The New Zealand Divisional Cavalry Regiment despatched a squadron to Allen Force to reinforce his defence of the Tempe–Larissa Road.

The Allied troops fighting at the Pinios were to withdraw and rendezvous at the rearguard to strengthen its defence. As C Company (2/3rd Battalion) and D Company (2/2nd Battalion), under Chilton's command, continued fighting the German mountain troops near Parapotamos on the Allied left flank, Lamb despatched orders to C Company to withdraw to the rearguard at dusk and to pass that order on to D Company.[56]

At 1400 h, thirty-five German aircraft circled Makrikhorion railway station near Allen's headquarters for half an hour, dropping bombs, and one smashed the railway station.[57] After the air raid, General Freyberg arrived at Allen's headquarters, hoping to find out what had happened to the 21st Battalion. As Macky could not be reached, Freyberg phoned Chilton who explained that contact with Macky had ceased. After Chilton described the situation and assured the general that he would collect any New Zealand stragglers, Freyberg told Allen, 'You've a fine man up there, he's as cool as a cucumber.'[58] After this conversation, Allen lost contact with Chilton.

As Allen and Lamb planned the rearguard, the soldiers of D Company (2/2nd Battalion) and C Company (2/3rd Battalion) continued to resist the mountain soldiers. Although D Company near Hill 156 held its ground, around 1500 h Captain Hendry reported to Chilton over the field telephone that the enemy was moving round his left flank and digging in south of Parapotamos. Chilton ordered Hendry to withdraw his patrol from the river bank and to counter-attack with Sergeant Stovin's Bren gun carriers at the flats to the west.[59] After Hendry received this order, the phone line went dead.

Hendry withdrew his patrol from the river and prepared the counter-attack until Captain Murchison arrived with an order signed by Captain Walker, the 2/3rd Battalion's adjutant. Walker's order stated that

C Company (2/3rd Battalion) was 'now withdrawing' and Murchison must co-ordinate the withdrawal of C and D Companies.[60] Hendry questioned the misinterpreted order but ultimately obeyed it and in the afternoon, the men of C and D companies fell back towards Makrikhorion railway station, covered by Bren gun carriers, while German mortars and infantry harassed their movement. After the men reached Makrikhorion, Lamb ordered them to join the rearguard.[61]

Although the premature withdrawal of C and D Companies left a wide gap in the Australian defence, Chilton knew nothing about Lamb's order or its misinterpretation. When German fire on the 2/2nd Battalion's left flank ceased, he incorrectly assumed that both companies on the left flank had been overrun. Chilton's A and B Companies remained the only Allied force left defending the Pinios near Evangelismos and the men now found themselves in an impossible position, threatened by *Kampfgruppe Balck* from the east and the mountain soldiers of the 6th *Gebirgsjäger* from the west.

THE FALL OF EVANGELISMOS

In the late afternoon, Balck reached Tempe village and ordered his men south towards Evangelismos on the road to Larissa with the 2nd Company (1st Panzer Battalion), commanded by Lieutenant von Nostitz-Wallwitz, and the 7th Company (304th Infantry Regiment) in the lead while the battle-scarred 1st Company (1st Panzer Battalion) followed behind the vanguard. 'It was a marvellous feeling to advance with 2 Coy,' Balck declared, 'with a wide valley ahead and abandoned enemy guns by the roadside.'[62] The 1st Battalion (143rd Regiment) also advanced south-east towards the village from its bridgehead on the Pinios.

The Allied artillery could not disrupt the German advance because the gunners had too many targets for their small number of field guns to cope with. After the panzers entered Tempe village, Lieutenant Hanna suggested moving the guns to positions better suited for an anti-tank role, but permission was refused. The artillery observers withdrew to their guns while a Stuka dive-bombing raid caused confusion and delay but no casualties.

A Company (2/2nd Battalion), which had been engaging the Germans crossing the river, also faced attack from *Kampfgruppe Balck* along the Tempe–

Evangelismos road. The company — supported by eleven Bren gun carriers and an Australian anti-tank gun — was now the only Allied force between the Germans and Evangelismos. After learning that panzers had overrun C Company on the outskirts of Tempe, Captain Caldwell prepared to defend his position and German small-arms fire soon harassed 7 Platoon on the right rear of his position.[63] At 1655 h, two panzers approached Caldwell's right flank:

> . . . the first enemy tank came in from the right flank and was knocked out, in flames, by a 2 lb anti-tank gun fwd of Coy HQ. A second tank was also hit but withdrew. These were approaching along the road. This line of advance was then abandoned and tanks came between the road and river.[64]

After another ten German armoured vehicles with infantry support arrived, Decker pressed his attack with his 2nd Panzer Company, supported by the infantry of the 7th Company marching on foot. The tanks and riflemen soon broke into A Company's position so Caldwell ordered a withdrawal up the ridge. From the high ground, he witnessed panzers and infantry advancing south, followed by more tanks and motorized infantry. As the panzers advanced, the Bren gun carriers covered the infantry's withdrawal. Decker, cautious after the losses on the road, halted his panzers and the stationary armour fired on the carriers and forced them to withdraw.

After A Company retreated, *Kampfgruppe Balck* exited Tempe Gorge and moved west into the open ground on the road to Larissa. The panzers spread out across the western flats and, as they advanced, the two New Zealand 25-pounders commanded by Second-Lieutenant Brown opened fire. Sergeant Franklin's gun from A Troop (5th Field Regiment), positioned east of the railway on the southern outskirts of Evangelismos, engaged the panzers, hitting the first two tanks which burst into flames. The third tank, however, returned fire and hit a truck loaded with petrol and explosives, creating a fireball which forced Sergeant Franklin to withdraw.[65] The gun crew headed south down the road and joined an Australian convoy.

Sergeant Gunn's 25-pounder from F Troop (4th Field Regiment), positioned further south, knocked out two panzers, but another tank came

Hermann Balck in his command tank and a New Zealand prisoner of war.
(Bundesarchiv, Bild 146-1994-009-17)

forward and searched for the camouflaged gun. The crew manhandled their
gun 90 metres (98 yards) and re-engaged the Germans from a slight hollow.
After firing the last armour-piercing shell, Gunner Kelly attempted to collect
more ammunition as Warrant Officer Tasker kept the German infantry at
bay with a Bren gun. After a tank shell burst below the gun, wounding three
crewmen, the others attempted to withdraw the gun, but their vehicle could
not be backed into the hollow and the uninjured men could not pull the
gun out on their own. The gunners had little choice but to withdraw in
their vehicle back to the artillery line. Balck praised the courage of the field
gunners who 'scored hits which caused casualties both to the infantry and
to us'.[66]

After *Kampfgruppe Balck* captured Evangelismos and continued south,
the men linked up with the mountain soldiers from the 1st Battalion (143rd
Regiment) advancing from the Pinios. By this time, the battalion had suffered
twelve killed, sixty-nine wounded and one missing. Major General Schörner

ordered the entire 6th *Gebirgsjäger* Division to cross the river and pursue the retreating enemy towards Larissa.[67]

The 1st and 2nd Battalions (143rd Regiment) advanced towards Makrikhorion railway station while the 3rd Battalion moved up the high ground south of Parapotamos towards Hill 591. The 141st Regiment advanced from Gonnos towards the Pinios and Captain Maile, commander of the 1st Battalion, noted:

> When the battalion arrived there was considerable noise of fighting going on. The enemy was still offering opposition and trying to prevent us from crossing the Pinios in order to avoid being surrounded and to be able to carry out an orderly withdrawal.[68]

The 1st Battalion crossed the river under artillery fire and advanced towards Makrikhorion village, west of the railway station.

Meanwhile, B Company (2/2nd Battalion), near battalion headquarters south of Evangelismos, defended the Tempe–Larissa road alone after A, C and D Companies had withdrawn. As *Kampfgruppe Balck* approached, the crew of the last Australian anti-tank gun, 70 metres (76.5 yards) from battalion headquarters, fled and Chilton explained: 'No orders for its withdrawal were given and it had not been in action.'[69] Smoke from the burning panzers drifted south-west, creating a screen hiding the German tanks and infantry moving on the flat west of the road. As stray bullets began landing around battalion headquarters, Chilton talked to stragglers passing through his headquarters:

> I halted some of troops on right flank and ascertained they were A Coy men. They informed me that enemy tanks had reached their forward area and that their O.C. (Capt. Caldwell) had given them instructions to scatter and take to the hills — every man for himself. They informed me that C Coy was withdrawing — no news of B Coy.[70]

As German troops attacked from the north and north-west, Lieutenant Gibbins' platoon from the 2/3rd Battalion and Lieutenant Southworth's platoon from the 21st Battalion withdrew into the hills. The men of

B Company resisted and Balck observed their valiant defence:

The Australians defended themselves desperately, but they had no tanks, and their antitank capabilities were limited since they had counted on the rough 'No-Go' terrain. The enemy was caught totally by surprise, wondering where we had come from. . . . We broke through line after enemy line. Their trucks went up in flames left and right, and we destroyed what few antitank guns they had.[71]

After panzers and infantry engaged the battalion headquarters staff at close range, Chilton ordered B Company to retreat. The wounded in the regimental aid post withdrew first, followed by battalion headquarters and B Company. Lieutenant Adrian Wilson, the battalion transport officer, formed a line of logistics troops and engaged several Panzer IV medium tanks with rifle and pistol fire.[72] The signallers destroyed their radios and moved south down the road. A section, commanded by Corporal Kentwell, covered the withdrawal of Chilton's headquarters by firing anti-tank rifles and Bren guns at the tanks, before withdrawing to another position further up the hill.[73]

Meanwhile, a patrol led by Second-Lieutenant Mittinger from the 1st Battalion (141st Regiment) attacked Makrikhorion village, north-west of the railway station, held by Australian soldiers who had retreated from the Pinios:

We carried on through orchards, and were again fired on from Pt 326. L/Cpl Ricko definitely destroyed this post, using tracer ammunition. Enemy snipers and MH fire from Makrihori prevented us advancing directly on Makrihori. We moved to our left and wiped out the snipers with MG and machine-pistol fire. We broke into Makrihori with hand grenades and machine pistols and took possession of the SE exit of the village.[74]

After the mountain soldiers had captured Makrikhorion village, the men observed panzers advancing south from their vantage point. As darkness fell, small parties of Australians climbed nearby hills east and west of the road to Larissa. As *Kampfgruppe Balck* and the mountain troops advanced south, Lamb's rearguard near Makrikhorion railway station was the only force between the Germans and Larissa and the fate of W Force hung in the balance.

CHAPTER EIGHT
ATHENS AND ESCAPE

RETREAT TO LARISSA

On 17 April 1941, Major General Rudolf Veiel, commander of the 2nd Panzer Division, frustrated by a 'stubborn and gallant withdrawal action', ordered his western battlegroup to pursue the 5th New Zealand Brigade through Olympus Pass.[1] After the 22nd Battalion had demolished the road in the pass, the brigade retreated from the mountain along the Larissa–Lamia road to Volos.[2] The 23rd Battalion kept the Germans at bay until Brigadier James Hargest ordered his rearguard to withdraw and, in the afternoon, the brigade headed south in a convoy towards Larissa. The Germans at Mount Olympus, short of supplies, could not pursue the New Zealanders along the poor roads. After the 5th Brigade reached Larissa, the men witnessed a town heavily damaged from both air raids and a recent earthquake.

At Servia Pass, *Kampfgruppe Sponeck* and the 9th Panzer Division's vanguard probed the front but made no effort to cross the Aliakmon River. General Georg Stumme ordered his troops to 'tie down' the defenders while the 5th Panzer Division attempted to outflank the pass through Grevena and Elassona.[3]

The 4th New Zealand Brigade began withdrawing from Servia Pass. The 18th and 19th Battalions retreated south at night while the 20th Battalion formed the rearguard and planned to withdraw the next day. The 18th Battalion reached Larissa during the night and the trucks continued on towards Molos.[4]

German soldiers advance through the mountains of Greece.
(INTERFOTO/Alamy Stock Photo)

During the day, the Allied rearguard assembled at Domokos, south of Larissa, to defend the road to the Thermopylae Line. The 2/7th Australian Battalion arrived from Larissa in the morning and elements of the 2/4th and 2/8th Battalions from the 19th Australian Brigade arrived later that day. After nightfall, large bodies of W Force troops from Larissa began to pass through Domokos on their way to Thermopylae. Meanwhile, General Archibald Wavell's planning staff arrived in Athens to co-ordinate the evacuation.

On the morning of 18 April, as *Kampfgruppe Balck* and the 6th *Gebirgsjäger* Division attacked Tempe Gorge, the bulk of W Force had not yet passed through Larissa. During the day, seemingly endless columns of trucks drove south on narrow mountain roads towards the crossroads. The *Luftwaffe*, taking advantage of the clear skies, bombed the retreating columns but caused little damage because the aircraft dispersed their effort and attacked in small groups.[5]

Meanwhile, a detachment of panzers and motorcycle troops from the 2nd Panzer Division's western battlegroup, which had bypassed Olympus Pass by driving south along the Katerini road, attacked the New Zealand Cavalry Regiment. Three anti-tank guns destroyed two panzers before the cavalry withdrew towards the 6th Brigade's rearguard south of Elassona, which defended the road to Larissa. After the cavalry passed through the rearguard, panzers approached the position until artillery fire disrupted their advance. The battlegroup's advance guard moved through the abandoned Servia Pass and advanced towards the 6th Brigade's forward posts, but demolitions delayed further progress. At night, the rearguard departed as the brigade withdrew south from Elassona towards Larissa.

As fighting raged in Tempe Gorge, the 16th Australian Brigade's elements not committed to the battle withdrew from Zarkos and approached Larissa. The 4th Brigade reached the town and continued south towards Thermopylae and, by this time, most of W Force had passed safely through the crossroads. The Australians and New Zealanders at Tempe Gorge had saved these troops being encircled by *Kampfgruppe Balck*. Despite this achievement, Allen Force at Tempe Gorge, the 6th Brigade at Elassona and the 17th Australian Brigade in Kalabaka had not yet passed through the town.[6] Balck still had an opportunity to cut off and capture a significant portion of W Force.

Meanwhile, the SS *Leibstandarte* Adolf Hitler Regiment advanced west to cover the right flank of the 40th Panzer Corps and threatened to cut off the withdrawal of Greek troops from Albania. The Greek cabinet met in Athens and agreed that King George II and his government should soon evacuate to Crete. Later that day, Premier Koryzis, realizing the Germans could not be stopped, returned to his house and used a gun to commit suicide.

REARGUARD AT HILL 214

In the afternoon of 18 April, as the Allied defence of the Pinios River collapsed, two troops of Marmon-Herrington armoured cars from B Squadron (New Zealand Divisional Cavalry), commanded by Major John Russell, arrived at Brigadier Arthur Allen's headquarters near Makrikhorion railway station. The armoured cars joined Allen's rearguard alongside B and D Companies (2/3rd Battalion) and the Bren gun carriers which had retreated from Tempe Gorge. These soldiers had to defend the Tempe–Larissa road until 0300 h the next day to allow the last troops of W Force to withdraw through the crossroads. In the late afternoon, Australian soldiers from D Company (2/2nd Battalion) and C Company (2/3rd Battalion) began arriving at Allen's headquarters while New Zealand field guns moved through the area. As the 2/2nd Battalion's other companies and the 21st Battalion had been cut off and could not reach Makrikhorion, most of the survivors headed east through gullies and ravines hoping to reach the coast.

Allen formed the rearguard at the crossroads near Hill 214 and placed Lieutenant Colonel Lamb, commander of the 2/3rd Battalion, in charge of the force and ordered him to 'forcibly hold all guns particularly anti-tank guns — that tried to get through from the forward lines, and also to grab all other troops he saw and make use of them'.[7] As the New Zealand artillery tried to retreat through the rearguard, Lamb rallied the gun crews: 'I twice had to draw my Revolver to force N.Z. Guns into position.'[8] He deployed the artillery from D Troop (4th New Zealand Field Regiment) south of the rearguard.

After the 2/2nd Battalion withdrew from the Pinios, E and F Troops (4th Field Regiment) fought a delaying action against the panzers on the road to Makrikhorion with seven field guns, which covered the withdrawal of the infantry to the rearguard. The guns engaged advancing tanks and infantry from less than 900 metres (985 yards) and, as the Germans approached closer, one troop covered the withdrawal of the other as they leapfrogged south at intervals. During the fighting retreat, the gunners fired on the panzers using open sights, destroying two tanks and putting several others out of action.[9] The Germans advanced cautiously as the leapfrogging New Zealand field guns maintained a constant rate of fire, which an Australian infantryman witnessed:

> The officer stood out in the open directing the fire, the crews crouched behind the shields and fed and fired the guns while everything the enemy had was being pelted at them. . . . They looked like a drawing by someone who had never been to a war, but the whole thing was unreal. They got two tanks, lost one gun and pulled the other gun and their wounded out, having done what they could. There was nothing to stop the tanks then, and they formed up and came on.[10]

After E and F Troops reached the rearguard, some of the guns deployed forward to support the armoured cars while the remainder joined D Troop at the gun line.

Lamb's rearguard consisted of D Company (2/2nd Battalion) on the left, C Company (2/3rd Battalion) in the centre and B Company (2/3rd Battalion) on the right on the high ground east of the road. Lamb positioned most of the Bren gun carriers to extend both flanks, but he retained the remaining carriers and D Company (2/3rd Battalion), now only thirty men strong, as a reserve while the New Zealand cavalry formed a protecting screen in front of the rearguard. Allen felt confident that the rearguard would hold the Germans until after dark and he planned a fighting withdrawal as the men could fall back to other points on the road to Larissa to create successive rearguard positions. In the fading light of early evening, Lamb observed panzers moving south from Evangelismos entering Makrikhorion.

Kampfgruppe Balck, led by the 2nd Company (1st Panzer Battalion) and the 7th Company (304th Infantry Regiment), advanced south towards the rearguard followed by the mountain soldiers from the 1st and 2nd Battalions (143rd Regiment). The Germans halted while the *Luftwaffe* attacked Hill 214 as Lamb observed: 'The troops fought back vigorously to cover the intervening ground under cover of the fire from the planes and very quickly after we were in contact with the enemy.'[11] The *Luftwaffe* in Greece played little direct role during land battles and, as Balck explained, 'there was essentially no air-ground cooperation. I saw only one Stuka attack.'[12]

The panzers resumed their advance after the *Luftwaffe* departed, followed by the infantry. The Germans unleashed heavy mortar fire on the defenders prior to assaulting the rearguard. As dusk approached, the panzers engaged the New Zealand armoured cars, but Allied artillery disrupted their advance. The panzers slowly moved through the trees, forcing the cavalry screen troops to fall back to the main defensive position. Major Stewart, the 26th Battery commander, observed the action from the hills and witnessed Major Russell 'magnificently handling his squadron'.[13] After the Germans reached the rearguard at dusk, fierce fighting erupted as at least twelve panzers broke into the position while rounds from Bren guns and Boys anti-tank rifles bounded off their armour. Lamb witnessed the determined resistance of his troops:

> By this time darkness had fallen, and it was decided to let the tanks penetrate the line whilst the force lay in wait for the Infantry in rear; the

tank however after passing the first line of Infantry became aware of our presence and opened fire; our own troops replied vigorously with small arms and A/Tk fire, which caused him to withdraw. This tank stopped some short distance away, and was considered knocked out by our action.[14]

Captain Hendry, commander of D Company (2/2nd Battalion), also watched the desperate fight:

At one stage a group of fifteen to twenty men were round a tank firing rifles and L.M.G.s to no apparent effect. This tank crushed two men, Privates Cameron and Dunn. The feeling of helplessness against the tanks overcame the troops and they began to move back in small parties to the trucks.[15]

Corporal Bill Cameron climbed onto a panzer and set it alight with a can of petrol, but it suddenly moved and he fell, landing on soft ground. Although the tank rolled over Cameron, he survived and was carried to safety.[16] Fire from anti-tank rifles slowed the leading German vehicles and, after two panzer shells hit a Bren gun carrier commanded by Corporal White, 'the carrier still kept going, with the crew extinguishing a fire as they went'.[17]

Despite heroic resistance, the mechanized assault forced the soldiers of D Company (2/2nd Battalion) and C Company (2/3rd Battalion) to fall back. Lamb explained, they 'had withdrawn without orders from me, being forced out by tanks which had penetrated the position on the left flank'.[18] As the line broke, an Australian officer from brigade headquarters recalled 'suddenly, everybody seemed to become panic stricken'.[19]

Balck observed the fight for the high ground and noticed that his men 'were taking heavy fire from the decisive Hill 214, but we punched through it'.[20] The 1st Company (1st Panzer Battalion) intercepted a convoy of Allied trucks and destroyed them as the infantry surged forward. Karl von Decker's troops reached Hill 214 'in spite of the enemy resistance consisting of artillery and machine guns. . . . Only the Panzer of Leutnant Langhammer was hit which immobilized it.'[21] *Kampfgruppe Balck* captured eight 47-mm anti-tank guns, eight 105-mm guns and 120 prisoners.[22]

As the Allied troops withdrew from Hill 214, Allen and Lamb planned to stop the Germans at the second rearguard location, further south down the road to Larissa, while W Force continued to withdraw through the crossroads on their way to Thermopylae.

THE SECOND REARGUARD

After retreating from Hill 214, Allied infantry, trucks and artillery moved down the road to Larissa in the darkness. Lamb rallied his troops and deployed them 1400 metres (1530 yards) south where he established the second rearguard. The artillery and the remaining Bren gun carriers joined the new position and their trucks moved a few hundred metres further rearwards. After some Australian soldiers became separated from their platoon, Sergeant Arthur Carson shouted, 'Get down here and fire, there's no platoons here, we're soldiers and we've got to stop these bloody Huns.'[23]

As the lead panzer from *Kampfgruppe Balck* approached the rearguard, Australian soldiers opened fire, killing the tank commander who was standing in the turret. Lamb encouraged his soldiers to keep firing at the tanks which could not effectively return fire in the dark.[24] The panzers returned fire in the darkness with tracer rounds and shells seemingly aiming at random, and Allen witnessed 'a scene of colourful confusion' and a 'world of Very lights [flares], tracer bullets and blazing vehicles'.[25]

Balck realized that his panzer troops could not operate in the darkness because 'they could see so little from their vehicles'.[26] After unsuccessfully assaulting the second rearguard, his tank commanders protested and 'refused to attack at night' because they 'knew they were likely to suffer murderous losses'.[27] After German troops accidentally began to fire on each other in the pitch darkness, Balck cancelled the attack by firing flares which signalled his panzers to form a laager around him. He also realized that his men were running low on supplies:

The petrol position was bad. We had enough to reach Larissa, but we did not know how much farther. We were almost out of ammunition. All the ammunition was taken from the knocked out tanks, and ammunition was ferried across the Pinios in open wagons, for all other vehicles were waiting for a bridge to be built.[28]

Although the German infantry did not probe or pressure the rearguard during the night, patrols investigated the hills beside the road under the light of flares. The panzer crews found food in abandoned Allied vehicles and Balck studied maps by the light of burning Australian trucks while his troops slept.

Brigadier Allen had achieved his mission and he later recalled the surreal thrill of battle:

> It was a fantastic battle. Everybody was on top (no time to dig in), and all in the front line, including artillery, Bren carriers, infantry and various unit headquarters, with unit transport only a few hundred yards in rear. Some confusion could be expected with every weapon firing and aircraft strafing from above. If you saw it at the cinema you would say the author had never seen a battle.[29]

After the Germans halted, Lamb decided to withdraw his men further south to where the road crossed wet ground at the Nessonis swamp north of Larissa. As the men withdrew, the armoured cars covered their withdrawal. Around midnight, a New Zealand field gun became stuck in a ford, creating a temporary traffic jam, and the convoy resumed its journey south along the road to Larissa, but the withdrawal did not go according to plan.

AMBUSH AT THE LEVEL CROSSING

After dawn on 18 April, the 2nd Company from the 1st Battalion (143rd Regiment) separated from the rest of the 6th *Gebirgsjäger* on a special mission. Lieutenant Jacob, the company commander, explained the plan:

> The company . . . was to cross the Pinios river on the division's extreme right flank, cross the mountains (522 metres [1712 feet] high) west of Makrihori, block the Tempe–Larissa road and railway line behind the enemy's lines, hold them against any enemy force withdrawing or attacking from Larissa, and finally pushing forward to the northern entrance to Larissa.[30]

After crossing the Pinios west of Parapotamos, the mountain soldiers marched south and remained unseen by Allied eyes. In the early evening, the men tried to rescue a downed *Luftwaffe* pilot, but Allied troops in trucks arrived first and captured the man. After the mountaineers reached the railway, they followed the tracks toward the Tempe–Larissa road. At 1900 h, the men reached the rail–road level crossing, 4 kilometres (2.5 miles) north of Larissa, after marching 150 kilometres (93 miles) across the mountains with only two-and-a-half hours of sleep.

Jacob's troops surprised two trucks from the 21st Battalion heading south along the road after opening fire with machine guns, wounding three New Zealanders and forcing the group to surrender. The Germans used the captured trucks to create a roadblock and formed an all-round defence position in a natural redoubt. Second Lieutenant Roemmer noted: 'Before dark the MGs were sited and trained on the road and the block.'[31]

At 2130 h, the first convoy of Lamb's withdrawing rearguard, consisting of around ten trucks, approached the level crossing and Jacob initiated his ambush:

> The leading vehicle (a light tank) came up to the block at 40 to 50 m.p.h. and immediately opened fire. It was engaged with several LMGs, 2 HMGs and an A Tk rifle and destroyed. The rest of the convoy had stopped, and the troops took cover on either side of the road and opened a heavy fire with rifles and machine pistols.[32]

The convoy halted in confusion and Australian soldiers from the 2/3rd Battalion took casualties as they jumped from their trucks. A burst of fire killed or wounded nearly every man in the lead truck and, as the survivors took cover beside the road, the Germans threw grenades. The Allied troops returned fire before scattering in the darkness and, one hour later, two Bren gun carriers tried to force the roadblock as Jacob witnessed:

> In the darkness they came forward with no lights along the railway embankment (which was higher than the road) and stopped. . . . In the first pause in the firing the rest of the Australians left the vehicles and made a determined attempt to overrun the positions on the embankment by coming in to very close range. Our accurate defensive fire inflicted heavy casualties on the enemy.[33]

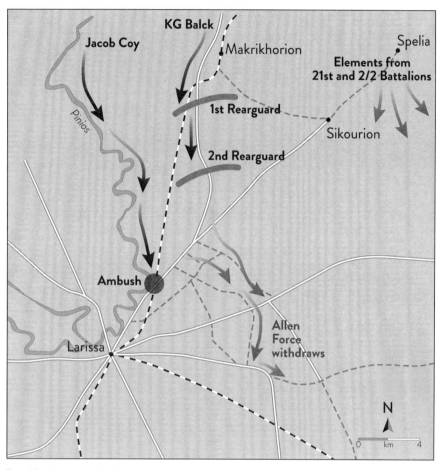

The Allied rearguard at Larissa, 18–19 April 1941.

The mountain troops repulsed unco-ordinated assaults for over two hours. 'My platoon was on the embankment,' Roemmer recalled, 'and we helped to repel the attack by firing over the heads of the foremost troops of Jacob Coy'.[34]

As the firefight continued, four New Zealand Bren gun carriers attempted to force the roadblock as Lieutenant Johnson observed: 'Upon proceeding 100 yards the leading carrier ran into what I presume was a land mine, slewed across the road and blocked any further movement forward.'[35] Johnson rallied a small group of New Zealand soldiers who overran a

German machine gun nest before withdrawing to the flat ground with several wounded. He decided against further assaults and instead attempted to bypass the roadblock and reach Larissa.

After Roemmer's platoon resisted another assault, the ambush site went quiet for the rest of the night and Jacob reported: 'The attack collapsed. About 30 Australians came in to surrender, and the rest ran in all directions across the fields trying to escape SE.'[36] The Allies left behind around ten dead and twenty wounded while Jacob's company had suffered two killed and two wounded.

Another convoy further north along the road halted after observing the tracer fire and flares from the ambush site and rumours spread that the Germans had captured Larissa. Lamb, believing that the town had fallen, diverted the convoy east along what he incorrectly believed was the Volos Road but was actually a dead-end road to a village near Mount Ossa.[37] The Allied survivors of Tempe Gorge dispersed into small groups as men and vehicles headed east along dirt tracks towards the coast and, in the darkness, many of them became lost.

THE FALL OF LARISSA

At sunset on 18 April, three W Force formations remained north of the Larissa crossroads — Allen Force retreating from Tempe, the 6th New Zealand Brigade from Elassona and the 17th Australian Brigade from Kalabaka. As Lamb's rearguard held *Kampfgruppe Balck* at bay, the 6th New Brigade passed through the town and its last troops cleared the crossroads shortly after midnight.

As the fighting raged along the Pinios during the day, Brigadier Stanley Savige kept the 17th Brigade in place until he received orders to immediately withdraw.[38] The 2/5th Battalion accordingly headed to Larissa in trucks at dusk and the 2/11th Battalion followed after midnight. The last convoy of the 2/11th Battalion passed through Larissa at 0300 h.[39] The defenders of Tempe Gorge had saved W Force as Wavell acknowledged:

> The defence of the gorge was carried out with such spirit that when
> at last on the evening of 18th April the Germans were masters of the

gorge, the main body of the Anzac Corps had successfully withdrawn past its western exit.[40]

At dawn on 19 April, Jacob's company advanced towards Larissa from the ambush site while the panzers advanced south towards the town. Balck observed the devastated landscape:

> Now for the first time we could really see what a hiding the enemy had taken. As in France, trucks in convoy stood on the road and in the bushes. All round were guns and A Tk guns, shell-shattered or manned only by corpses, and among them Bren carriers and two tanks. We were hungry and had no field kitchens with us, but we found wonderful food and drink to cool our throats.[41]

As the mountain troops neared Larissa, the advance guard of *Kampfgruppe Balck* overtook them and entered the town at 0615 h. Balck praised the mountain troops 'who had performed terrific feats in marching over the hills from the north in an attempt to win the race. But we beat them.'[42] Although the Germans had finally captured the crossroads, they had narrowly missed the last withdrawing troops and Balck lamented: 'Unfortunately, the main body of the English forces escaped.'[43] However, he did note that his men 'dealt the English a decisive blow at Olympus and opened the way to Athens'.[44]

In Larissa, Balck witnessed a devastated town. Most buildings were destroyed or damaged, but he saw 'from those ruins the lavish splendor of a southern spring bloomed forth, accompanied by swarms of Eurasian Hobbies [falcons] feeding on the insects'.[45] After the strained German logistics system in Greece collapsed, Balck found it virtually impossible to evacuate his wounded or bring fuel forwards, but his men captured British supply dumps and found ten truckloads full of rations and fuel as 'German soldiers stood with astonishment in their eyes in front of this rich haul of best quality goods'.[46]

After the Germans secured the airfield, Junkers 52 transport planes flew in additional supplies to sustain the offensive. Balck ordered his Panzer II light tanks to pursue W Force, but they ran out of fuel 40 kilometres (25 miles) down the road. As the Germans now prepared for the final phase of the Greek campaign, Major General Rudolf Veiel praised his men:

> The enemy has been completely defeated and has fled south. Battle
> Gps 1 and 2 by the violence of their onslaught have thrashed and
> partly destroyed their opponents. . . . I wish to express my thanks and
> appreciation to the troops for their unique achievements and their
> valiant deeds.[47]

After Veiel disbanded *Kampfgruppe Balck*, the 3rd Panzer Regiment's two
battalions reformed in Larissa and the men provided work parties at the
airfield to help bring in fresh supplies.[48] Although the campaign continued
with battles raging further south on the Thermopylae Line, the war in
Greece had come to an end for Balck and his soldiers.

ESCAPE FROM GREECE

On 19 April, as Balck's troops entered Larissa, small parties from the 2/2nd
and 2/3rd Battalions began arriving in the Brallos area. In the afternoon,
Lamb reached the 6th Australian Division Headquarters near Gravia and
reported that most of his battalion had scattered. Major Edgar, second-
in-command of the 2/2nd Battalion, established a straggler post between
Amfiklia and Livadia and 304 soldiers from the battalion arrived there
during the day. Meanwhile, the bulk of the 2/2nd Battalion marched east
through the mountains in isolated parties, hoping to reach the coast. The
majority of the 2/3rd Battalion had travelled east in trucks from the Tempe–
Larissa road during the night and had arrived at Lamia or joined the main
road to Thermopylae south of Larissa.

After being overwhelmed by *Kampfgruppe Balck*, the New Zealanders from
the 21st Battalion withdrew south from Tempe Gorge. Lieutenant Colonel
Macky had established a rendezvous point where trucks could collect his
men. Major Harding, the battalion second-in-command, organized a
twenty-truck convoy which arrived in the afternoon and found 150 waiting
men, mostly from Headquarters Company. After fifty more men arrived,
the convoy departed under the command of Captain Sadler, and Harding
remained behind with two vehicles in case any more stragglers arrived.[49]

During the night, Harding's trucks departed the rendezvous point and joined a 2/3rd Battalion convoy withdrawing southwards and the group continued south towards Volos.

Captain Sadler's convoy drove down the main road towards Larissa and ran into Jacob's ambush. After the men in the first trucks jumped out and scattered in the darkness, the remaining vehicles made a wide detour eastwards and eventually reached Molos with 114 men.[50] After the ambush, Sergeant Crowley and seven men took to the hills and found their way to the coast and used small Greek boats to reach Allied lines.

W Force meanwhile consolidated the Thermopylae Line, at the neck of the Attica Peninsula, where King Leonidas and his 300 Spartans had made their last stand against the invading Persians. Wavell arrived in Athens and General Alexandros Papagos agreed that all Anglo forces should leave Greece, but British planners pessimistically believed that they would be lucky 'to get away with 30 per cent of the force'.[51]

By the night of 20 April, 250 men from the 2/2th Battalion and 500 men from 2/3rd Battalion had reported to Allen's headquarters near Brallos. After 132 men from the 21st Battalion arrived at the Thermopylae Line, they began digging trenches in an olive grove while the *Luftwaffe* strafed and dive-bombed the area.[52] Although Macky and his four company commanders were still missing, a small group led by Sergeant Anderson found a boat at Volos and sailed down the coast before joining the other 21st Battalion survivors at Thermopylae.

Field Marshall Wilhelm List ordered the 5th Panzer Division to advance south towards Thermopylae with the 6th *Gebirgsjäger*. As the Germans advanced, the Greek Government in Athens lost control of the country as Lieutenant General Georgios Tsolakoglou, commander of the Western Macedonian Army, surrendered to the Germans.

King George II and most of the Greek Cabinet departed on a plane to Crete and Papagos later resigned, declaring to Prince Peter, 'I've done my duty, which is to defeat the Italians in Epiros and Albania, and to fight the Germans. I will stay and share the fate of the army and people.'[53] Papagos also told Lieutenant General Henry Wilson, 'We are finished. But the war is not lost. Therefore, save what you can of your army to help win elsewhere.'[54] Although the Germans arrested Papagos in 1943, he survived the war and was reinstated as commander-in-chief and later fought against the communists during the brutal Greek Civil War.

On the morning of 22 April, the 5th Panzer Division probed the Thermopylae Line, initiating an artillery duel which lasted the rest of the day. Harding, who had assumed command of the 21st Battalion in Macky's absence, ordered the men to destroy all surplus gear as they would be the first troops to head to the embarkation beach near Athens where the Royal Navy would evacuate them under Operation Demon. After dark, the survivors withdrew from Thermopylae and reached Restos in the morning, 8 kilometres (5 miles) outside Athens. The men rested under olive trees before moving towards Rafina at night where the guides led them to the dispersal areas.

On 24 April, the 5th Panzer Division and the 6th *Gebirgsjäger* attacked the Thermopylae Line, defended by the 6th New Zealand Brigade and the 19th Australian Brigade. The 55th Motorcycle Battalion engaged the 2/11th Australian Battalion without artillery support and the men came under heavy shellfire and became pinned down in a ravine. Meanwhile, a reinforced panzer company advanced directly towards Thermopylae Pass, but New Zealand artillery destroyed twelve tanks and disabled seven others. The 6th *Gebirgsjäger* attempted to outflank the line from the north, but the Allied defenders repulsed their attack.

At night, the remnants of the 21st Battalion and the 5th Brigade moved to the evacuation beach near Porto Rafti where barges ferried them to the transport ship *Glengyle*. Once the New Zealand soldiers were on board, sailors gave them mugs of hot coffee and biscuits, and they found quiet places to lie down and sleep as their Greek odyssey came to an end. The *Glengyle* embarked 4000 men that night and the cruiser HMS *Calcutta* rescued 700 others from the beach.[55] The Royal Navy also evacuated 6500 W Force men from Nafplion that night.

By dawn on 25 April, most Allied troops had withdrawn from the Thermopylae Line and passed through the rearguard at Erithrai while the 5th Panzer Division and the 6th *Gebirgsjäger* advanced towards Thebes and Athens. During the night the Royal Navy evacuated 5900 men, including the 19th Australian Brigade, from Megara.

On 26 April, 6000 men from Allen Force arrived at Kalamata in the

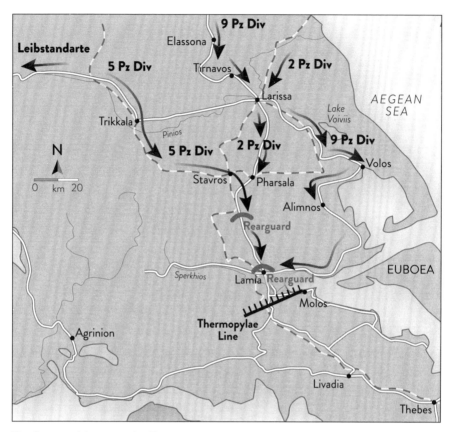

The German Advance to the 'Thermopylae Line', 19–21 April 1941.

Peloponnese and found the town and beach full of exhausted troops.[56] During the day, over 16,000 soldiers assembled around Kalamata and waited for nightfall. Brigadier Allen ordered 'active measures' to stop any man not under his command from embarking on the ships allocated to his troops.[57] In the afternoon, the Australians marched to their beach and Allen posted guards at the wharf. The Royal Navy arrived after dark and the men embarked on the transport ships *Dilwarra*, *City of London* and *Costa Rica*. Lamb noted 'we had our first cup of tea in many days'.[58]

A group of Auxiliary Military Pioneer Corps soldiers tried to force their way onto a destroyer allocated to Allen Force, only to be beaten back with rifle butts by soldiers from the 2/2nd Battalion. After Allen learned that no more destroyers would arrive that night, he knew that small groups of his men would be left behind but he ordered two staff officers to remain behind to embark these troops the following night before boarding that last destroyer, joining the 8600 men evacuated from Kalamata that night.[59] During the night, the Royal Navy also rescued 8200 men from beaches near Athens and 5200 men from the Peloponnese.

Allen Force steamed away from Greece in a convoy escorted by one cruiser and six destroyers. The next day, the *Luftwaffe* attacked the ships and the Germans lost seven aircraft, but two bombs hit the water near the *Costa Rica* and, after the ship began taking on water, all troops were ordered on deck for an evacuation. The men transferred to the destroyers HMS *Hero*, *Defender* and *Hereward* before the *Costa Rica* sank. On 29 April, the convoy reached Alexandria and the men disembarked in Egypt.

On the morning of 27 April, German troops entered Athens and soldiers from the 2nd Motorcycle Battalion, which Balck had commanded at Platamon, reached the Acropolis and hoisted a German flag over the ruins. As the Germans consolidated their hold on Greece, the 4th New Zealand Brigade withdrew to Porto Rafti and the Royal Navy evacuated 3800 soldiers from the beach that night.[60] As the last elements of W Force north of Corinth departed Greece, the 5th Panzer Division and the *Leibstandarte* advanced through the Peloponnese to capture the last Allied troops before they could evacuate. The next day, Allied troops near Tolos beach waited as an Australian rearguard dug in on the high ground just north of the town. In the afternoon, the Germans overran the rearguard and most troops in the area soon surrendered, but during the night, the Royal Navy rescued 4320 men, including Major General Bernard Freyberg, from Monemvasia.

The Royal Navy returned to Kalamata after dark where 8000 soldiers awaited evacuation, but after German troops entered the town, the destroyers HMS *Kandahar*, *Kingston* and *Kimberly* departed after only rescuing the wounded and 332 other soldiers. The destroyers signalled 'Many Regrets' to the 8000 men trapped on the beach.[61] The next day, the Germans captured 7500 men at Kalamata which accounted for almost half of W Force's losses during the Greek campaign.[62] Although Operation Demon had ended, numerous small groups of Allied soldiers remained in Greece and, by December 1941, over 1400 of these men had escaped on their own.

A German Panzer IV medium tank in Athens.
(Bundesarchiv, Bild 101I-175-1270-36)

After the battle of Tempe Gorge, the majority of the 21st Battalion could not link up with the rest of W Force and the New Zealanders scattered along the ridges near Ampelakia and marched towards the coast in small groups along different routes. Most Australians from the 2/2nd Battalion, similarly cut off, also headed towards the coast in small groups, hoping to find boats to sail to Crete or Turkey. As Lieutenant Colonel Chilton explained, each group 'independently came to the conclusion that the only course open was to attempt to get to the coast'.[63]

Macky led a group of eight officers and around thirty-five soldiers from the 21st Battalion across the snowline of Mount Ossa in the bitter cold before descending through a forest towards the Aegean coast. After acquiring a small boat, the group sailed south towards Thermopylae. At Skopelos, local Greeks warned the New Zealanders that the British had withdrawn from Thermopylae so Macky decided to instead to head for Andros Island. At dawn on 24 April, after the group had sailed off course, they headed east to Chios, off the Turkish coast. From there, they sailed south until the boat foundered at Siros. Macky's men joined a group of Greek officers with another boat and they reached Crete on 2 May.

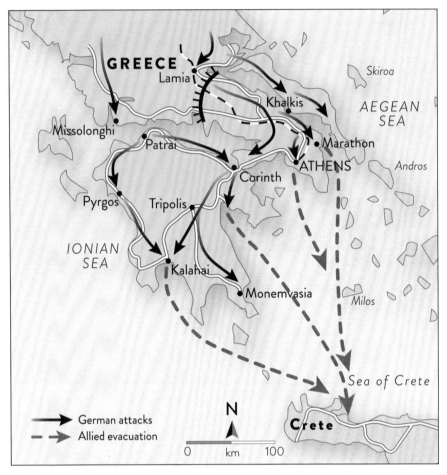

The Allied evacuation from Greece, 22–28 April 1941.

After withdrawing from Tempe Gorge, Captain Trousdale from D Company (21st Battalion) led his men south-east over the mountain forests towards the coast. During the march, they linked up with a group of forty-one New Zealanders and thirty Australians led by Lieutenant Yeoman before chancing upon Major Paul Cullen and 100 Australians at Spelia. On the night of 20 April, the group found Captain Tongue, Second-Lieutenant Mason and seventeen soldiers. After several smaller parties arrived, the men decided to split into smaller groups because it would be impossible for Greek villages to feed all of them.

Trousdale and Yeoman led a group of around sixty Australians who reached the coast at Keramidi and, after island hopping, they reached Crete on 10 May. Captain Tongue's group reached the coast south of Volos in a hired boat. After arriving at Euboea Island, they stole three small boats and eventually reached Turkey and were later repatriated to Egypt. Cullen's group reached Chios where Greeks civilians gave them food and the men arranged passage on a small vessel bound for Crete carrying 400 Greek soldiers. On 29 April, the ship departed and two days later rendezvoused with a vessel containing around 280 Allied soldiers led by Captain Jackson, who had seized a steamer at gunpoint. The two ships eventually reached Crete on 5 May.[64]

Captain King from the 2/2nd Battalion and 133 men had remained on Chios and later sailed to Cesme in Turkey where the locals warmly welcomed them. The men obtained the Greek yacht *Kalamara* and, after embarking another group of survivors led by Lieutenant Harkness which had also reached Turkey, they arrived in Cyprus on 7 May.[65]

After the 2/2nd Battalion's headquarters had been overrun by *Kampfgruppe Balck*, Chilton lead a small group of three soldiers south-west from Tempe Gorge. After passing Sikourion, they came across abandoned Australian and New Zealand trucks bogged in the plain east of Larissa and found tins of bully beef. Chilton's party joined other groups and the men marched to the coast at night with the help of Greek guides while avoiding German convoys on the roads. The group eventually sailed to Skyros where they came across sixteen Australian soldiers and the enlarged group later reached the Turkish coast near Smyrna. Turkish and British officials arranged for their passage to Egypt and, after arriving, Chilton learned that his men had kept the Germans out of Larissa until W Force had withdrawn through the crossroads.[66]

AFTERMATH

As the Royal Navy evacuated the bulk of W Force from Greece, the 3rd Panzer Regiment joined the German advance towards Athens in the second echelon. Balck moved through the fields of Pharsalus 'where the decisive battle between Caesar and Pompey had been fought'.[67] After arriving in Athens, the men enjoyed themselves and Balck noted that 'just as in France, days of endless pleasure followed the exertion of combat. Every man in the regiment got a chance to go to Athens and see the Acropolis, where I arranged for expert guided tours.'[68] Balck, with his deep interest in antiquity, became intoxicated with the sites from Greek history:

> Previously, I had an image of the Acropolis as an unplanned cluster of beautiful buildings, but what I finally saw was quite different. Nowhere had I seen a finer use of space as there and later at Delphi. The visitor's eye is led consciously through the architecture, from building to building, from highlight to highlight. The master accomplishment was the positioning of the Temple of Athena Nike oblique to the axis of the Propylaea.[69]

Balck also visited other ancient sites in Greece including Delphi and Acrocorinth where 'the two Greek goddesses met, Pallas Athena coming from the north, and the erotic cult of the Middle Eastern Aphrodite. All the old tales from mythology came to life for me here in this country.'[70]

Although Balck enjoyed his triumph in Greece, not all his men lived to see the German conquest of the country. The 1st Battalion (3rd Panzer Regiment) had suffered four deaths and thirty-seven wounded in the Platamon and Tempe battles while two Panzer IV and four Panzer III medium tanks and thirteen Panzer II light tanks had been destroyed or knocked out of action. The German 12th Army in Greece had 1160 men killed, 3755 wounded and 345 missing. During Operation Marita, the *Wehrmacht* had won a comprehensive victory in twenty-two days, expelling the British from the Balkans and securing the Romanian oil supply and southern Europe before Operation Barbarossa.[71]

Karl von Decker, for his brave conduct at Tempe Gorge, was awarded the Knight's Cross on 13 June 1941. After succeeding Balck as commander of the 3rd Panzer Regiment, he led the men on the Eastern Front during the late phase of Barbarossa and during the battle of Moscow. After being promoted to colonel on 1 February 1942, Decker continued to command the 3rd Panzer Regiment on the Eastern Front until January 1943. After working in Heinz Guderian's Panzer Inspectorate, Decker returned to the Eastern Front on 20 June 1943 to command the 21st Panzer Brigade and later commanded the 5th Panzer Division. After being promoted to lieutenant general on 1 June 1944, he was awarded the Knight's Cross with

Oak Leaves. Shortly afterwards, he fought the Red Army during Operation Bagration while commanding the 39th Panzer Corps. Decker fought in Courland and East Prussia before being promoted to General of Panzer Troops on 27 December 1944. He later fought in the Battle of the Bulge in January 1945. After being surrounded by American forces in the Ruhr Pocket, Decker committed suicide in his headquarters in Brunswick on 21 April 1945. He was posthumously awarded the Knight's Cross with Swords.[72]

Major General Rudolf Veiel later commanded the 48th Panzer Corps on the Eastern Front in 1942 and the Replacement Army in September 1943. After the July 1944 plot against Hitler's life, Veiel was arrested for complicity but was not executed. After being liberated by the Allies in 1945, he retired to Stuttgart and died in 1956.[73]

After the Greek campaign, the 3rd Panzer Regiment refitted in Bavaria before arriving on the Eastern Front in September 1941. After heavy fighting in the Russian winter, the regiment advanced towards Moscow before the Red Army's counter-offensive forced the men to withdraw. The regiment suffered heavy casualties in the fierce fighting at Klin, Karmanowo, Bjeloje and Rzhev in 1942. In the following year, the unit participated in fighting at Kursk, Orel, Kiev and Gomel. During the winter of 1943–44, the regiment sustained heavy casualties in the Dnieper battles before leaving the Eastern Front in January 1944. After D-Day, the unit fought the British 7th Armoured Division in Normandy and recaptured Villers-Bocage only to be virtually destroyed while breaking out of the Falaise Pocket. The rebuilt regiment later spearheaded the German offensive during the Battle of the Bulge only to be nearly destroyed again during the American counter-attack. In 1945, the 3rd Panzer Regiment defended the Rhine with its handful of surviving tanks before surrendering to the Americans in April 1945.

After occupation duties in Greece, the 6th *Gebirgsjäger* arrived in Norway in September 1941 and fought in Arctic Russia during the failed offensives towards Murmansk on the Finnish Lapland front. The division remained in far north Russia until late 1944 when the Finns signed a separate peace with the Soviet Union and the men withdrew into Norway, later surrendering to the British at the end of the war.[74] Major General Ferdinand Schörner, who commanded the division in Greece, was later imprisoned in the Soviet Union for war crimes and then in West Germany for atrocities committed against his own soldiers.[75] He died on 2 July 1973 and is remembered as 'Bloody Ferdinand'.

Of the 62,611 W Force troops sent to Greece, around 50,000 were evacuated although much equipment had been lost including tanks, artillery, truck and weapons. During the campaign, 320 Australians had died and 2065 became prisoners while 291 New Zealanders had been killed and 1614 captured. British casualties had been 256 deaths, 132 wounded and 6508 prisoners. The Italians had lost 13,755 men killed and 25,067 missing, but the Greeks suffered the most with 80,000 soldiers killed, wounded or missing.

At Tempe Gorge, four men from the 21st Battalion had been killed or wounded and the unit's total casualties in Greece were 14 deaths, 26 wounded and 235 prisoners, although eight of the wounded later died. Although the battalion regrouped in Crete, it played only a small role in the campaign but Second-Lieutenant Southworth and Captain McClymont both died during the German invasion.[76] After being evacuated from Crete, the battalion rebuilt in Egypt before fighting at Sidi Rezegh, El Alamein and Tunisia. The unit spent the rest of the war fighting in Italy, including the battle at Monte Cassino, and was disbanded on 2 December 1945.

After the 21st Battalion arrived on Crete, Lieutenant Colonel John Allen commanded the unit in Macky's absence. Although Macky later arrived in Crete, Freyberg had deep misgivings concerning his performance at Tempe Gorge and did not reappoint him to command. Macky returned to New Zealand in September 1941 and, although he never commanded a battalion again, he did command the fortress troops in the Bay of Islands region. After the war, he resumed his legal career and devoted much time to charitable causes and educational work. Neil 'Polly' Macky died in Auckland on 4 October 1981.

The 2/2nd Battalion at Tempe Gorge suffered 14 men killed, 16 wounded and 112 taken prisoner. After departing Greece, 189 soldiers from the unit fought in the 16th Brigade Composite Battalion on Crete.[77] The battalion reformed in Palestine and garrisoned Syria between October 1941 and January 1942. After departing the Middle East, the unit fought the Japanese on the Kokoda Trail and elsewhere in New Guinea, suffering heavy casualties from combat and jungle diseases before returning to Australia. The battalion later fought the Japanese in the Aitape-Wewak region of New

Guinea between December 1944 and August 1945. After the war, the unit was disbanded in Brisbane on 15 February 1946.[78]

Chilton received the Distinguished Service Order in May 1941 for his fine conduct during the Greek campaign. He later commanded the 18th Brigade in New Guinea and Borneo. After the war, he worked in the Joint Intelligence Service, established the Defence Signals Inspectorate and helped to expose a Soviet spy ring during the Cold War. Chilton became the Assistant Secretary of the Defence Department and later became Chairman of the Repatriation Commission, responsible for the welfare of veterans. He was later appointed an Officer of the Order of the British Empire and knighted in 1969. Sir Frederick Chilton died on 1 October 2007.

During the battle of Tempe Gorge, the 2/3rd Battalion suffered 12 deaths, 31 wounded and 62 taken prisoner. After departing Greece, most of the men reached Egypt, although 141 soldiers fought German paratroopers in Crete as part of the 16th Brigade Composite Battalion. The battalion reorganized in Palestine and fought the Vichy French in Syria and Lebanon. After Pearl Harbour, the unit fought the Japanese in New Guinea. After the war, the 2/3rd Battalion disbanded on 8 February 1946.

Lamb later commanded the 2/3rd Battalion in Syria and was wounded in a Vichy French counter-attack at Fort Sarrail on 20 June 1941. After returning to Australia, he commanded the 2/2nd Guard Battalion in the Pacific for the rest of the war. On 6 March 1947, he was appointed an Officer of the Order of the British Empire for highly meritorious service in the Middle East and New Guinea. Donald James Lamb died on 21 May 1969.

THE CAMPAIGN IN RETROSPECT

Balck's success in Greece in part reflected his preference to lead from the front as 'the essence of the forward command idea is for the leader to be present personally at the critical place'.[79] Macky, on the other hand, had commanded from his headquarters through his field telephone and failed to impose his will on the fighting, as the historian Peter Wood explained:

Having won an MC [Military Cross] in the First World War, he was a brave man, but he does not appear to have been energetic in the defence at

Platamon, and this was reflected in his unit's reactive response. On the other hand, the energetic and hard driving Balck was able to call forward additional units, plan and orchestrate attacks and impose his character on his battlegroup.[80]

During the battle of Tempe Gorge, Chilton and Lamb displayed forward presence in the same vein as Balck. 'Chilton and Lamb led their men from the front,' historian Peter Ewer explained, 'rallying their troops under fire to stand against tank attacks.'[81] Chilton later condemned Macky because he had 'given the game away before the fight started'.[82]

After the Greek campaign, Allied commanders explained away their defeat by claiming that W Force faced an overwhelmingly superior enemy. Freyberg, for example, declared that 'there could be no adverse criticism of the actions of the 21st New Zealand Battalion. They were overwhelmed by a greatly superior enemy force.'[83] Wavell similarly announced that 'our troops were completely on top whenever they met the Germans under reasonable conditions' but a 'great numerical superiority' of the panzers 'gave the Germans the advantage'.[84] However, the Germans never massed tanks in Greece and the campaign was instead characterized by the reconnaissance and advance guard elements of panzer divisions fighting Allied troops in narrow mountain corridors.[85] Australian and New Zealand soldiers in Greece never faced entire German divisions in battle.

The lead elements of *Kampfgruppe Balck* never possessed overwhelming numbers and relied upon surprise, combined arms co-operation and better leadership to win. Chilton's 2/2nd Battalion was attacked by only two battalions from the 6th *Gebirgsjäger* while the rest of the division descended Mount Olympus.

Despite post-war myths that Australian and New Zealand troops in Greece fought the panzers with nothing but rifles, Allied soldiers were capable of repulsing German armoured attacks, as Freyberg acknowledged: 'At Olympus the Artillery, firing a phenomenal number of rounds, smashed the German tank advance, the infantry beating off heavy attacks made through the woods under cover of mist.'[86] The historian Craig Stockings provided another example:

In fact, the German tank company that attacked the 6th NZ Brigade at the Thermopylae Pass was the second time in two weeks that a German armoured thrust, the likes of which had already gained a fearsome reputation, was stopped in its tracks by dug-in infantry well-supported by artillery. On 11 April, a similar attempt on Tobruk in North Africa left 17 destroyed German tanks behind. This was to be repeated at Tobruk again on 1 May.[87]

At times Allied soldiers in Greece engaged panzers with nothing but rifles; however, these occasions resulted from a failure to properly employ combined arms tactics because infantry appropriately supported by artillery, anti-tank guns and mines can stop tanks. Despite tactical shortcomings, Allied soldiers fought bravely and displayed fierce resistance as a 2nd Panzer Division after-action report made clear:

> . . . the English soldier is a good fighter, and the Australian and New Zealand soldiers fought an outstanding defensive battle in the craggy wooded country in which they had to fight. Their choice of ground, use of ground, adaption of the ground and construction of positions were good and made things very hard for the attackers. The siting and use of the British artillery was also very skilful. The shellfire was heavy and accurate. The British made great use of anti-tank weapons, which were always sited in good, well-camouflaged positions.[88]

The panzers of *Kampfgruppe Balck* did not independently triumph in Greece and depended upon support from infantry, artillery and engineers. Balck only captured Platamon Ridge after dismounted motorcycle troops flanked the defence through the mountains. The 21st Battalion at Tempe Gorge fled from an attack by only six tanks but only after infantry overran its anti-tank guns. Balck's panzers had to overcome incredibly difficult terrain and often faced long delays due to obstacles and demolitions, such as the descent from Platamon Ridge, which took an entire day. Despite these challenges, Balck expertly moved small armoured forces through extremely difficult mountainous terrain, which surprised the Allies who were not expecting to face tanks:

Through their incredible efforts we had overcome obstacles that the English had considered impassable. As one of their captured intelligence reports later read, 'The 3rd Panzer Regiment knows how to cross terrain which we consider "No-Go" for tanks'.[89]

Balck assigned dismounted motorcycle soldiers and infantry flanking missions through steep terrain normally considered only suitable for alpine troops, surprising the defenders of W Force. The *New Zealand Official History* even praised the remarkable endurance of German soldiers during the campaign:

Seldom in war, however, were tanks forced through such difficult country, or had foot soldiers, already with over 500 kilometres' marching behind them, pushed forward so rapidly under such punishing conditions; it was a record of which any soldier could be proud.[90]

Balck commanded a flexible combined arms battlegroup according to the *kampfgruppe* principles he had formulated in France. Lieutenant Colonel George Soldan echoed this sentiment in a German report on Operation Marita:

. . . our superiority in leadership, in tactical mobility and adaptability, in the art of exploiting the terrain, in readiness to shoot, in elan and presence of mind and complete expertise in collaboration of arms were brought to bear in Yugoslavia and Greece.[91]

List similarly concluded that in Greece 'this very model of co-operation between mountain and armoured troops, presenting an unprecedented feature'.[92]

The German victory in Greece had been won despite a completely inadequate logistics system which struggled to provide essential supplies such as food, ammunition and fuel to frontline soldiers. After *Kampfgruppe Balck* reached Tempe Gorge, it had overextended its supply lines and faced critical shortages until the Germans captured Allied depots at Larissa. After experiencing the failure of a logistics pipeline, Balck certainly understood the importance of functioning supply lines:

The troops have to be taken care of — you have to attend to their food, their clothing, their shelter, their medical care — and all these logistics arrangements must function. For this reason, good combat leaders cannot ignore the resupply and administrative functions. And to really get these functions to operate well, you can do it only from the front — by constantly checking that the troops at the *front* are actually receiving what the logisticians claim they're providing.[93]

The *Wehrmacht*'s victory in Greece, however, masked its inherently weak logistics system, the flaws of which soon became all too obvious in the vast distances of Russia. Operation Barbarossa failed after the Red Army halted the German invasion at the gates of Moscow during the winter of 1941–42. One year later, as the German 6th Army faced annihilation in the frozen hell of Stalingrad, Balck won a series of armoured battles along the Chir River which established his reputation as one of the greatest panzer generals in history.

CHAPTER NINE
CASE BLUE

THE EASTERN FRONT

After the Greek campaign, Balck briefly commanded the 2nd Panzer Brigade before being assigned to the equipment directorate in the Army High Command in July 1941, where he was responsible for replacing vehicle losses sustained on the Eastern Front. Germany had invaded the Soviet Union on 22 June 1941 but Balck, stuck in Berlin, experienced frustration: 'I was not happy being left out of it, sitting around passively, just patching up tanks.'[1] Nevertheless, he had a philosophical approach to dealing with the various duties military officers must perform:

> One day you may be dealing with close combat, the next day you will be involved in an artillery duel, and the day after that you have to be commanding economic warfare. You simply have to adapt and use the means at hand.[2]

After Balck arrived in Berlin, he learned that his son, Officer Cadet Friedrich-Wilhelm Balck, had died in Russia: 'my oldest son had died a hero's death. He had been killed leading his platoon in a most exemplary manner, from the front.'[3] Over the next four months, Balck swallowed his grief and threw himself into work, transferring 100,000 vehicles from rear units to the front line.[4]

On 1 November 1941, Balck was appointed Inspector of Mobile Troops within the Army High Command, Heinz Guderian's former post. As Balck had to inspect panzer units on the Eastern Front, he visited German-occupied Russia and, as a man used to the high culture of Europe's great cities, found something different in the Soviet Union:

> There was absolutely no décor in the living areas. The art was gigantic kitsch. Everywhere there were the same stucco statues of Lenin and Stalin. The architecture was a poor imitation of American styles. Russian family life, however, was completely different from what we had imagined. There was no prostitution. Discipline and morality within the family were highly valued.[5]

In Russia, Balck met with Guderian, now commander of the 2nd Panzer Army, at Orel and both men toured the front near Tula where they inspected abandoned Russian tanks. A horrified Balck realized the new Soviet T-34 medium tank completely outclassed the panzers:

> The T-34 was completely impervious to our weapons, and it mounted a first-rate main gun. Nearby we saw one of our own PzKpfw14 IIIs, which had been torn apart by just one Russian tank round.[6]

The *Wehrmacht* began to erode in the Russian winter as the weather and fierce Red Army resistance stopped the Germans before Moscow. Balck realized the German invasion of Russia had culminated as the men reached the limit of their endurance. On 27 November, he bade Guderian farewell and promised to inform the high command of the bleak conditions at the front.

On 5 December, the Red Army, commanded by General Georgy Zhukov, counter-attacked at the gates of Moscow, forcing the *Wehrmacht* onto the defensive. As the winter crisis threated disaster, Hitler took direct control of the German Army after firing the commander-in-chief, Field Marshal Brauchitsch. The Army High Command dispatched its officers to the front to improve morale, and Balck returned to Russia and arrived at Gzhatsk near Moscow on Christmas Eve, where he inspected General Erich Hoepner's 4th Panzer Army:

The troops were totally spent. The individual divisions were mere shadows of their former selves. The 160th Division, for example, had eighty riflemen left. Everything was drowning in snow.[7]

On Christmas Day, Balck visited the 7th Corps and witnessed a shattered force in the bleak landscape. The disintegration of a once proud army reminded him of Napoleon's retreat from Moscow:

Slowly I drove through the Russian winter landscape, past the 1812 battlefields of Borodino. I could still see the heaps of earth from the Russian positions. There was sunshine but no wind in the -5 to -20 degrees Fahrenheit weather. The smoke from the villages rose straight up in long, solid columns, high into the sky. It was a picture that could have been inspirational, were it not for our desperate situation and the Napoleonic memories.[8]

Balck returned to Gzhatsk the next day where he learned that Hitler had sacked Guderian: 'It hit us all very hard. He was made the scapegoat for the disaster.'[9] However, despite fondness for Guderian, Balck agreed with Hitler's decision:

Psychologically, Guderian leads masterfully, however, he increasingly depends on the moods and weaknesses of his troops in making his decisions. The troops like this situation. They feel understood. This is not, however, conducive to the tough decisions that a field commander who demands the most must make.[10]

Balck would always remain somewhat detached from his men, never allowing sentiment to influence 'tough decisions'.

On 31 December, Balck reported to Hitler and pleaded with him not to allow the army in Russia to withdraw because large-scale operations could not be carried out in the harsh weather:

Front lines were being held wherever we could manage to get just one tank and twenty men to one decisive point after days and days of trying.

The demand to hold under such conditions might sound brutal, but in reality it was the greatest clemency.[11]

Hitler agreed with Balck's assessment and the dictator's subsequent 'no retreat' order saved the *Wehrmacht* during the Russian winter. The Germans held the line and no other option was viable as Balck explained: 'Considering the conditions of the Russian winter, any withdrawal on our part would result in a catastrophe of Napoleonic dimensions.'[12]

As Inspector of Mobile Troops, Balck also briefed Hitler on German tank production and stressed the critical need to increase productivity as industry only produced thirty tanks per month. Hitler bluntly replied, 'No, I just had a report that it's 60 this month.'[13] Balck, however, disputed the *Führer*'s statistic: 'In that case, you've been lied to.'[14] Field Marshal Wilhelm Keitel, Chief of the *Wehrmacht*, interrupted: 'If so, then I am the liar.'[15] Balck held his ground and defended his figure, 'My number is right. Your numbers have both the December and January production combined.'[16] Balck's courageous insistence and defiance of the bureaucrat Keitel earned Hitler's respect and they developed a good rapport: 'I apparently got Hitler's attention, because he immediately summoned Minister for Armaments Fritz Todt.'[17]

After returning to Berlin, Balck longed to once again command troops in the field. 'I had always considered myself a soldier first and not a pencil pusher', he explained. 'During wartime I did not want to be the latter.'[18] Balck accordingly requested a frontline command and the *Wehrmacht* obliged.

THE 11TH PANZER DIVISION

On 16 May 1942, Balck took command of the 11th Panzer Division. The unit had been formed on 1 August 1940 and first saw action in Yugoslavia where it helped capture Belgrade. The division later participated in Operation Barbarossa as part of Army Group South, fighting at Zhitomir, Uman and Kiev before participating in the battle of Moscow near Vyazma as part of Army Group Centre. After suffering heavy losses defending Gzhatsk during the Red Army's winter counter-offensive, the division fought partisans east of Smolensk. Balck realized the unit desperately needed rebuilding as it 'really only existed as remnants, although it once had a good reputation'.[19] The division's main combat power consisted of the 15th Panzer Regiment and the mechanized infantry of the 110th and 111th Panzergrenadier Regiments but, as Balck understood, attrition on the Eastern Front had taken a toll:

> Despite all the efforts some areas still looked dismal. Personnel and weapons were at 100 percent. Motorized vehicles were still 40 percent short. I had to initiate emergency measures. Artillery batteries were formed with six guns each, and thus the number of batteries was reduced.[20]

Despite these equipment shortfalls, Balck was particularly impressed with Lieutenant Colonel Paul Freiherr von Hauser, commander of the 61st Motorcycle Battalion:

> I had a superb armored reconnaissance battalion, mostly because it was led by a very, very skillful reconnaissance combat leader, an Austrian who was one of the best soldiers that ever served me. This officer was able to do phenomenal things with the relatively poor materiel that was available.[21]

After taking command, Balck developed a routine of practising English for an hour before dinner as it 'was a good way to balance out the often hectic, exciting, and physically challenging events of the day'.[22] He also developed a strict custom of having dinner with his staff officers, which reduced administrative work as problems could be informally resolved over a meal.

As Balck rebuilt the 11th Panzer Division, the *Wehrmacht* planned Case Blue — its major Eastern Front offensive for 1942 — in which Army Group South would advance to the Volga River and seize the Soviet oilfields in the Caucasus. The plan developed from Hitler's Directive No. 41 dated 5 April 1942, which assessed the Soviet Union was close to exhaustion and aimed to defeat the Red Army through a sequence of encirclement operations. The first operation would involve a double envelopment of Kursk and Belgorod before a rapid advance towards the city of Voronezh on the Don River. Army Group South would then split into two new army groups: Army Group B would establish a defensive screen along the Don River's great bend while

CASE BLUE + 191

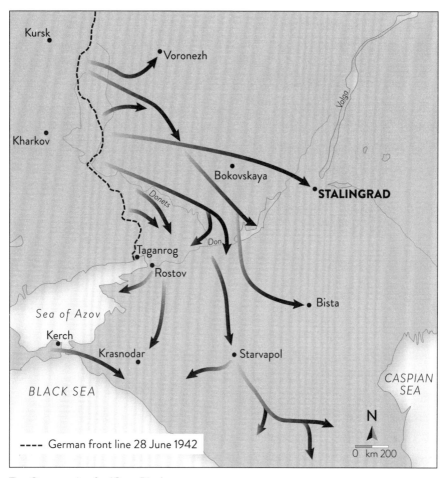

The German plan for 'Case Blue'.

Army Group A secured Rostov before advancing into the Caucasus.[23]

The 11th Panzer Division would support Case Blue by protecting Army Group South's left flank during the advance to Voronezh alongside the 9th Panzer Division as part of General Willibald von Langermann's 24th Panzer Corps, which was attached to General Maximilian von Weichs' temporary army group. The Red Army's defence in this sector was split between Lieutenant General Filipp Golikov's Briansk Front and Marshal Semen Timoshenko's Southwestern Front. The *Wehrmacht* planned an

German soldiers advancing on the Eastern Front.
(Bundesarchiv, Bild 101I-748-0099A-20)

envelopment, aiming to encircle the Briansk Front's 40th Army and the
Southwestern Front's 21st Army.[24] Army Group Weichs' 24th and 48th
Panzer Corps would form the northern pincer of the envelopment and
strike the vulnerable boundary between both Red Army fronts.

The 40th Army, commanded by Lieutenant General Mikhail Parsegov,
defended the northern sector with five rifle divisions in his first echelon,
supported by the 14th and 170th Tank Brigades with around 70 tanks while
Major General Mikhail Pavelkin's 16th Tank Corps with around 180 tanks
deployed behind the 40th Army.[25]

On the eve of the campaign, Balck's division fielded 155 panzers — 15
Panzer II light tanks, 124 Panzer III medium tanks, 13 Panzer IV medium
tanks and 3 command tanks.[26] As Case Blue approached, he oversaw detailed
preparations for the operation:

After several days of thorough reconnaissance, questioning prisoners,
and meeting with the artillery and the adjacent units, everything was set.
I did not issue a written order, but rather oriented all the commanders
using a detailed map exercise and a terrain walk. That technique had the

advantage that all doubts could be cleared up immediately and wrong interpretations and misunderstandings came to light right away.[27]

Balck, in his command post, relished the calm before the storm. 'The world was quiet and peaceful,' he remembered. 'Not a single sound interrupted the silence. The blooming pastures gave off a nice aroma.'[28]

At 0215 h on 28 June 1942, German artillery initiated Case Blue by bombarding Red Army positions and Balck witnessed 'an artillery barrage of incredible force' as 'dust, smoke, and thunder covered everything'.[29] As Balck's regiments engaged the Soviet 15th Rifle Division, belonging to the Briansk Front's 13th Army, he left his command post and moved forward:

I walked along the forward lines while the troops were being engaged. Every officer and NCO jumped up and while standing at attention reported to me under enemy fire, just like during a peacetime inspection. From that moment on I had control of the division.[30]

Balck advanced with the 15th Panzer Regiment in his *Kübelwagen* staff car towards Mikhaylovka as a Stuka squadron flew overhead.

After encountering determined Red Army resistance, Balck halted the attack as Russian infantry, hidden in fields of grain, fired at them as artillery landed nearby. After a shell fragment hit Major von Webski's head, Balck treated his wound:

Instinctively I pulled his hand away from his wound and bandaged him. He fought me and said, 'Sir, you have more important things to do right now. I can take care of myself.' Then he lost consciousness. I handed him off to my aide, who took him back to the rear. A few days later this marvelous man passed away without ever having regained consciousness.[31]

On the first day of Case Blue, the 11th Panzer Division had advanced 10 kilometres (6 miles) as the *Wehrmacht* smashed through the junction between the Briansk and Southwestern Fronts, pushing back Parsegov's 40th Army.[32]

The next day, Soviet aircraft strafed Balck's *Kübelwagen* and, although a bullet hit the map he was studying, he escaped injury. After the air raid, the advance resumed and Balck followed his panzers:

> My 15th Panzer Regiment moved forward with unbelievable speed,
> disappeared over the horizon, and was not to be seen anymore. I drove
> after them for two lonely hours along the clearly marked tracks. I caught
> up with them as they were establishing a strongpoint six kilometers in
> front of the Olym sector. . . . Naturally the infantry divisions lagged far
> behind the Panzers on the left and on the right.[33]

The 11th Panzer Division, with strong artillery and Stuka support, advanced to the Kshen' River where Balck encountered Pavelkin's 16th Tank Corps supported by the 11th and 119th Rifle Brigades.[34]

Golikov reacted to Balck's advance by reinforcing the 16th Tank Corps with the 106th Rifle Brigade. In the evening, he ordered a counter-attack against the 11th Panzer Division. Major General Mikhail Katukov's 1st Tank Corps would strike from the north while Pavelkin's 16th Tank Corps attacked from the east. Fortunately for Balck, Katukov and Pavelkin lacked the expertise to properly co-ordinate their corps and each tank brigade would fight isolated battles against veteran German troops. At this stage of the war, most Red Army tank generals struggled to command armoured forces larger than brigades and, therefore, their attacks were not effectively synchronized.[35]

Katukov's 1st Tank Corps struck the 11th Panzer Division's left flank but soon ran out of steam while Pavelkin's 16th Tank Corps attacked the division's forward troops along the Kshen' River. Balck's troops repulsed this onslaught, destroying around 15 per cent of the 16th Tank Corps.[36] After this bloody failure, a Red Army after-action report concluded that this attack 'was not smoothly controlled' and that 'artillery preparation was not organized'.[37]

On 30 June, Pavelkin resumed his counter-attack and Balck's troops knocked out fourteen Soviet KV heavy tanks. Meanwhile further south, General Friedrich Paulus's 6th Army broke through the Soviet 21st Army's lines and formed the second German pincer advancing towards Voronezh.[38]

On 1 July, Balck ordered his panzers to cross the Olym River and consolidate the bridgehead on the opposite bank. As the 15th Panzer Regiment approached, seven Red Army tanks, which had been cut off by

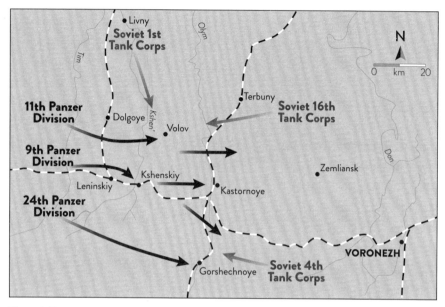

The 11th Panzer Division's attack towards Voronezh, 28 June 1942.

the German advance, attacked their rear in an attempt to reach their own lines. 'Six of them broke down under our fire,' Balck witnessed. 'The seventh raced forward at high speed and did not notice the twenty-meter drop at the bank of the Olym. It flipped over in the air and dropped into the torrents of the river.'[39]

As Army Group South advanced towards Voronezh, the 11th Panzer Division guarded its left flank. At this time, the Red Army's 17th Tank Corps launched a series of counter-attacks. During these battles, Balck established a command system in which his chief-of-staff remained with the division's headquarters, slightly behind the front line, to maintain communications with corps headquarters and adjacent units and to direct reinforcements to the front, while Balck remained mobile and led from the front, giving verbal orders in person or over a field radio. 'I was always at the respective key spot and could shift my position quickly', he explained. 'I continued that command technique throughout my tenure as a division commander and never regretted doing so.'[40] As Balck preferred to be at the front, battles often raged around him:

A destroyed Red Army KV heavy tank on the Eastern Front.
(Bundesarchiv, Bild 101I-216-0412-07)

At one time the tank battle was circling around my command car just like a carousel. From the vehicle's roof I had a grand view, and I was able to direct the battle from there. Gradually the adjacent units came up and we moved into a defensive line. One Russian tank attack after another rolled up against us every day. We shattered them one attack at a time before they even reached our front line. The area looked like a tank cemetery.[41]

The 11th Panzer Division had destroyed 160 Red Army tanks since the beginning of Case Blue. Balck realized that upgraded Panzer IIIs and Panzer IVs, with their new 50-mm and 75-mm cannons, could stand up to Red Army T-34s, but he also noticed improved Soviet craftiness:

. . . the Russians were good at setting up traps. Some of their light tanks would pretend to bolt in front of us. If we followed carelessly we would end up in a minefield and caught in a crossfire from the left and the right by camouflaged antitank guns and heavy tanks.[42]

On 3 July, Soviet resistance near Voronezh collapsed and the Red Army retreated across the Don River.[43] By the end of the day, the 11th Panzer Division approached the town of Zemliansk, halfway to Voronezh, as Weichs' two panzer corps advanced in *kampfgruppe* columns towards the Don.[44] Pavelkin's shattered 16th Tank Corps, which had suffered heavy losses at the hands of Balck's troops over the past two days, withdrew from the front line.

On 4 July, Langermann's 24th Panzer Corps advanced north-east as the 11th and 9th Panzer Divisions protected the northern flank of the German thrust to Voronezh. Meanwhile, the Soviet dictator Joseph Stalin ordered the Briansk and Southwestern Fronts to immediately counter-attack and placed Lieutenant General Aleksandr Lizyukov's 5th Tank Army under Golikov's command, ordering him to personally direct the counter-attack from a forward command post at Voronezh.

On 5 July, the 5th Tank Army counter-attacked with 640 tanks west of Voronezh. Lizyukov had previously fought the Germans at Smolensk and Moscow in 1941 but lacked experience in conducting large armoured operations. He accordingly failed to co-ordinate his forces and his three tank corps subsequently engaged the Germans piecemeal.[45] The 5th Tank Army's brigades fought independent engagements after separately arriving at the front. The *Luftwaffe* maintained air superiority over the battlefield and German planes struck Lizyukov's troops as they moved by train and road to their assembly areas, further hampering his attempts to concentrate his army.[46]

After the 4th Panzer Army captured Voronezh that day, Golikov lost his ability to control his soldiers and fled his forward command post to seek safety across the Voronezh River.[47]

On 7 July, the 4th Panzer Army and the 6th Army's pincers met south of Voronezh. Lizyukov ordered Major General Pavel Rotmistrov's 7th Tank Corps to attack at 0600 h, with only four-and-a-half hours' warning. Rotmistrov had earlier led a tank brigade with distinction during the battle of Moscow the previous year.

Rotmistrov's corps attacked with the 67th and 87th Tank Brigades forward — with around 120 tanks — followed by another fifty tanks from the 59th Tank Brigade and a battalion from 12th Motorized Rifle Brigade from Major General Aleksei Popov's 11th Tank Corps. The Red Army surprised a *kampfgruppe* of around fifty tanks from the 11th Panzer Division near the village of Krasnaya Polyana, 55 kilometres (34 miles) north-west of Voronezh, and the battlegroup swiftly retreated across the Kobylia Snova River.[48]

To counter the Soviet thrust, the 9th Panzer Division moved north with 120 tanks to support Balck's right flank and encountered Rotmistrov's lead tank brigades. The Germans held the Red Army at bay along the Kobylia Snova River for the remainder of the day.

On 8 July, Popov reinforced Rotmistrov's attack with the rest of the 11th Tank Corps, forcing the 11th and 9th Panzer divisions to withdraw 6 kilometres (3.7 miles) south to the Sukhaya Vereika River. The Soviet offensive, however, faltered after Stuka airstrikes disrupted the advancing Red Army troops and nearby marshes halted their progress. At 1830 h, Lieutenant General Nikandr Chibisov, the Briansk Front's deputy commander, informed Lizyukov:

Comrade Stalin orders you to seize Zemliansk today at all cost. In no circumstances bring 2nd Tank Corps forward, but instead keep it in second echelon. Penetrate farther with individual tanks and smash the enemy's rear and transport.[49]

Despite such encouragement, *Luftwaffe* bombers, German artillery fire and the marshes prevented forward movement.

At 0400 h on 9 July, Lizyukov's 5th Tank Army resumed its offensive as 100 tanks from Rotmistrov's 7th Tank Corps and 163 tanks from Popov's 11th Tank Corps advanced. Rotmistrov's 19th Tank Brigade broke through the 9th Panzer Division's defence along the Sukhaya Vereika River, but Stuka dive-bombing attacks forced his tanks to withdraw. Meanwhile, Popov, in a sign of improving Red Army co-ordination, deployed all four of his brigades in a single line during the attack. Balck, however, immediately counter-attacked Popov's corps south of the Kobylia Snova River, causing a battalion from the 12th Motorized Brigade to retreat in panic as airstrikes and artillery halted the rest of the brigade. Although Rotmistrov and Popov failed to achieve a breakthrough, they had forced two panzer divisions to withdraw, demonstrating increased Soviet skill at corps-level operations.[50]

Case Blue entered a new phase after Army Group South split in two: Army Group A under Field Marshal Wilhelm List would advance south towards the Caucasus while Army Group B commanded by Field Marshal Fedor von Bock would protect the northern flank along the Don and Volga rivers.

On 10 July, the 340th Infantry Division relieved the 11th Panzer Division and Balck's men rested and refitted the next day. At dawn on 12 July, the 11th and 9th Panzer Divisions conducted a well-synchronized counter-attack at the boundary between 7th and 11th Tank Corps. Balck manoeuvred his division 5 kilometres (3 miles) into the Soviet rear before outflanking the 7th and 2nd Tank Corps, forcing them to withdraw.[51] Lizyukov ordered the 193rd Rifle Division to bolster the defence, but Stuka attacks inflicted mass casualties, rendering the division combat ineffective. By the next day, Pavelkin had lost 136 of his original 181 tanks.[52] Lizyukov's 5th Tank Army had failed to stop the 11th Panzer Division.

Aleksandr Lizyukov later died on 23 July, after commandeering a KV heavy tank in a brave attempt to rescue two encircled brigades. Mikhail Pavelkin became commandant of Moscow Tank Centre in October and later commanded tank and mechanized forces in the 3rd Ukrainian Front in 1945. He survived the war and later became the Soviet military adviser to the Czechoslovakian Army.

Stalin meanwhile permitted the Southwestern and Southern Fronts to withdraw and ordered five new Soviet armies to defend the Don's eastern bank.[53] Balck confirmed that most Russian troops successfully withdrew:

> The Russian tanks had suffered heavily during their counterattacks, but the bulk of their divisions opposing us had evaded us masterfully. Using the fields of high grain and the countless deep ravines, they had managed to withdraw.[54]

On 19 July, the 11th Panzer Division advanced north-east and, as the panzers approached Rechitsa village, several T-34 medium tanks appeared from deep gullies and attacked the vanguard's left flank before vanishing into the gullies. Soviet heavy tanks, dug into the ground with only their turrets visible, appeared further north and inflicted significant casualties. Balck responded with artillery fire and brought his anti-tank guns forward, but after these measures failed, he ordered air strikes which forced the Russian tanks to withdraw.[55]

Balck later submitted an after-action report on the recent fighting, which noted that while medium tanks dominated the battlefield, light tanks were no longer effective on the front line. He accordingly recommended that light tanks should only be used to guard supply lines. Balck also noted that his troops had 'destroyed 256 tanks, despite being the target of very heavy enemy air raids from [Sturmovik] ground-attack aircraft'.[56] The *Wehrmacht* acknowledged Balck's leadership and promoted him to major general on 1 August.

Balck expected the 11th Panzer Division to head south towards the Caucasus as part of Army Group A, but he instead was ordered north to support the 2nd Panzer Army near Orel. During the winter battles, the Red Army had created a great bulge at Sukhinichi which threatened the nearby German position. The 2nd Panzer Army planned to eliminate this threat as Balck explained:

> Since then the Sukhinichi Bulge had been depleting our strength. Our intent was to attack it from three sides, destroy the forces inside it, and establish a shorter, less exhausting front line.[57]

On 11 August, the 2nd Panzer Army launched the offensive, codenamed Operation Whirlwind, led by the 11th and 9th Panzer Divisions. The troops attacked well-developed fortifications defended by the Soviet 16th Army as the 11th Panzer Division's war dairy explained:

> Every gorge must be taken by riflemen in heavy fighting . . . every height, with a deep, organized defense system must be stormed, numerous bunkers must be reduced. The difficulty of the struggle is made plain by the high level of casualties.[58]

The 11th Panzer Division made slow progress, fighting its way through the bulge, but by 17 August it had killed 2095 Red Army soldiers, captured 1692 prisoners and destroyed or captured 123 enemy tanks.[59] However, by this time the offensive had stalled as General Franz Halder, Chief of the General Staff, noted: 'Operation WHIRLWIND has made gains, but is approaching its objective only slowly in very difficult, fortified terrain and against very strong opposition.'[60] After Balck faced protests from an exhausted subordinate officer, he attempted to justify the failing operation:

A troop leader under these circumstances must be hard, and in regard to the particular situation demand the utmost from the Truppe. It must be made clear to the troops that clearing the Shisdra crossings is the last difficult task, and that the terrain north of the Shisdra is more open with fewer ravines.[61]

The continued lack of progress in the Sukhinichi Bulge prompted General Rudolf Schmundt, Hitler's adjutant, to assemble Balck and other commanders for a dressing down: 'the Führer wants to express to you through me his displeasure that the battle is stalemated!' The 11th Panzer Division repulsed a series of Red Army counter-attacks, and Balck recalled the seemingly pointless struggle:

The heavy fighting continued, during which we made daily gains against newly committed Russian units, but only painfully so. For days the heavy fighting raged without decision in the primal forests of the Zhizdra.[62]

On 21 August, Balck noted in his journal: 'The Russians are attacking from everywhere. Suddenly they have a lot of artillery.'[63] After the 11th Panzer Division repulsed more assaults over the next two days, Balck recorded in his journal: 'Again endless attacks. Prisoners are telling us that the slogan "Victory or death!" has been put out. But the victory belonged to us and death belonged to them.'[64] The Army High Command meanwhile cancelled Operation Whirlwind and further operations in the Sukhinichi Bulge would only be a containing action.[65]

On 24 August, the 11th Panzer Division once again defeated strong Red Army attacks and the following day Balck's artillery destroyed yet another

Russian offensive: 'My superbly led 119th Artillery Regiment proved to be a wonderful main effort weapon.'[66] On 29 August, Balck's troops repulsed an attack from the 9th Tank Corps supported by two infantry divisions, destroying ninety-one tanks:

> We were lucky that we had been able to separate the Russian infantry from their tanks immediately with machine gun fire and artillery and then destroy them both separately. In the evening I could see that my division had achieved a huge success.[67]

Since the beginning of Case Blue, the 11th Panzer Division had destroyed 501 Soviet tanks and Balck boasted that this number 'was never equaled by any other division during the war'.[68] However, he also noted that this tactical success had not resulted in wider operational gains:

> The division can be proud of itself. The equipment of six enemy tank brigades is scattered along our route of march, as well as in front of and even in our positions. We simultaneously destroyed the same number of enemy infantry divisions. Unfortunately, none of this translated into an operational success.[69]

On 3 September, the 11th Panzer Division devastated a large Russian attack, destroying twenty-eight Soviet tanks while losing eight Panzer III tanks, but Balck became increasingly detached from the slaughter:

> The action is still going on as I write this. Slowly one reaches a state of psychological equilibrium that cannot be shaken by anything. Today during the height of the crisis we were laughing and bantering in our command vehicle. Hopefully, the Russians will soon stop these senseless attacks.[70]

As 11th Panzer Division attacked Kolosovo, twenty T-34s engaged Balck's vanguard and fought a delaying action. After the panzers rolled through Kolosovo, Red Army anti-tank guns opened fire from the woods north of the town. Most of the panzers turned towards the enemy and, as the tanks neared the forest, a brigade of T-34s attacked from the flank and rear, forcing the Germans to withdraw. Kolosovo changed hands several times during the savage tank battle but, after Balck committed all his artillery and anti-tank guns to the struggle, he secured the town.[71]

By 5 September, the recent heavy fighting had exhausted the 11th Panzer Division. 'My troops are pretty worn out', Balck recorded in his journal. 'I would like to take them back to the winter positions as soon as possible. But higher headquarters does not want to pull back yet.'[72] Five days later, the division was finally pulled from the front line and the exhausted men rested. Balck noted that his men had 'left the field as a battle-hardened unit that had not known failure, only victory'.[73] However, he was clearly downplaying the failure of Operation Whirlwind in the Sukhinichi Bulge.

The 15th Panzer Regiment had only nine operational Panzer IV medium tanks left. Freiherr von Hauser's 61st Motorcycle Battalion had experienced near continuous combat for three weeks and had conducted eight attacks, repelled forty-two attacks and launched twenty-three counter-attacks, destroying eighty-five Russian tanks including fifteen in close combat. Balck accordingly praised Hauser's exceptional leadership:

. . . he was not only tough, he was also caring and skillful. He led from the front, conducting numerous, rapid, and unpredictable counterattacks, so that his unit was never taken under flanking fire and his soldiers were always able to counterattack from secure positions.[74]

The 11th Panzer Division rested and refitted at Bryansk, billeted in pleasant workers quarters. Although the men expected to hold a winter defensive position, a disaster further south would soon propel them once more into fierce combat as the *Wehrmacht* in southern Russia faced catastrophe.

ENCIRCLEMENT AT STALINGRAD

As the 11th Panzer Division guarded Army Group South's left flank, Paulus' 6th Army reached the Volga River and fought a merciless war in the streets of Stalingrad. Meanwhile, List's Army Group A invaded the Caucasus and advanced towards the Soviet oilfields. Although the Russian winter would soon commence, the Army High Command was confident of holding the Russians along the Volga and Don while List's troops secured the Caucasus — the ultimate objective of Case Blue. The Red Army, however, had its own grand strategy to seize the strategic initiative from the *Wehrmacht*.

In October 1942, Stalin and the *Stavka* (Soviet High Command) planned the 'planetary' series of counter-offensives. Operation Uranus, the first offensive, aimed to encircle and destroy German forces in the Stalingrad region. Operation Saturn would later strike north of Stalingrad and capture Rostov to isolate and eventually destroy Army Groups A and B. Operation Mars would simultaneously attack Army Group Centre's salient at Rzhev, north-west of Moscow, to prevent German reinforcements reaching the critical sectors in southern Russia.[75] General Georgy Zhukov, the mastermind of these operations, realized 'the Nazis had not achieved their strategic objectives' and were overextended 'from the Black Sea through the Northern Caucasus, Stalingrad, the Don area and up to the Barents Sea'.[76] Therefore, he sensed a great opportunity to turn the tide of war in favour of the Soviet Union.

Planning Operation Uranus involved the creation of the new Southwestern Front, commanded by Colonel General Nikolai Vatutin, to conduct the northern pincer surrounding Stalingrad. Vatutin had earlier defended Novgorod on the road to Leningrad in 1941, where he delayed Army Group North's advance and bought time for the Red Army to develop the city's defence. During the winter counter-offensive, he surrounded two German corps in Demyansk and later commanded the Voronezh Front during Case Blue.

Vatutin's 5th Tank Army and the 21st Army, supported by the Don Front's 65th Army, planned to overrun the vulnerable Romanian 3rd Army before advancing south-east to encircle Stalingrad. Further south, the Stalingrad Front's 51st and 57th Armies would attack the Romanian 4th Army and link up with the 5th Tank Army near Kalach on the Don. Once Operation Uranus surrounded Stalingrad, the *Stavka* would unleash the 1st Guards Army in Operation Saturn to liberate Rostov.[77]

On 19 November 1941, the Red Army launched Operation Uranus by attacking the Romanian armies defending the northern and southern flanks of the 6th Army in Stalingrad. After the Soviets overwhelmed the

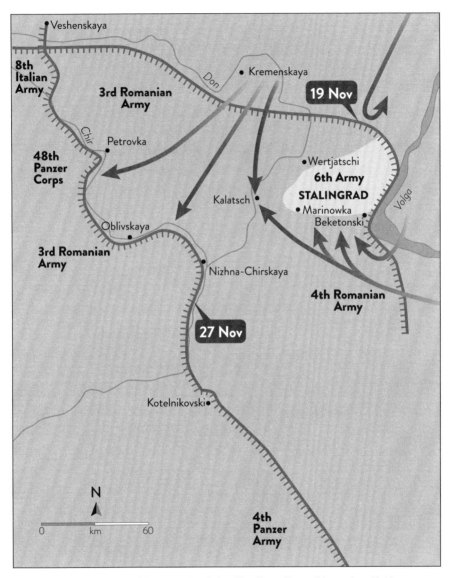

The Soviet encirclement of Stalingrad and the Chir River Front, November 1942.

Romanians, the Soviet pincers met at Kalach on the Don four days later, completely surrounding 22 divisions, totalling 330,000 men, including the 6th Army and one corps from the 4th Panzer Army.[78] The next day, Field Marshal Erich von Manstein took command of the hastily assembled Army

Colonel General Nikolai Vatutin, commander of the Southwestern Front.
(Author's Collection)

Group Don and the Stalingrad front. As the *Luftwaffe* airlifted an inadequate amount of supplies to the besieged city, Manstein planned Operation Winter Storm, a counter-attack designed to save the 6th Army.

On 25 November, the 11th Panzer Division joined Army Group Don and moved by rail to its assembly area south-west of Morozovsk near Tormosin and prepared for Winter Storm, after being assigned to the 48th Panzer Corps, as Balck recalled:

> I had no illusions. The positive side was that the 11th Panzer Division was combat experienced and confident of victory. Personnel and equipment were at 100 percent strength. We were fully mobile.[79]

Colonel Friedrich von Mellenthin became the 48th Panzer Corps' chief-of-staff two days later. He had previously served on Guderian's staff during the

Red Army Soldiers during the Stalingrad campaign.
(INTERFOTO/Alamy`Stock Photo)

French Campaign and been Rommel's operations officer in North Africa before being evacuated from El Alamein in September. Mellenthin flew to Rostov and reported to the headquarters of Army Group Don where he learned that *Luftwaffe* field formations and rear-echelon personnel were building up defensive positions along the Chir River, a tributary of the mighty Don River. The 48th Panzer Corps had been encircled north-west of Stalingrad near Kalach. However, the panzer corps had fought its way out and had taken up defensive positions on the Chir River.

Mellenthin flew to his new headquarters in a *Storch* light plane. 'The landscape recalled the North African desert,' he observed, 'but with snow instead of sand. As we came down on the small frontline airfield, I realized that I had entered a new and very grim phase of my military career.'[80]

Manstein planned Operation Winter Storm as a two-pronged attack — the 48th Panzer Corps including the 11th Panzer Division would assemble across the Don at the Rychkovskii bridgehead near Nizhna-Chirskaya and attack from the north while the 57th Panzer Corps would attack further south from Kotelnikovo. As Balck prepared for Winter Storm, he recorded in his journal: 'Yesterday the storm was howling across the steppes and today there was a marvelous sky across the wide, beautiful land.'[81]

CHAPTER TEN
THE CHIR RIVER BATTLES

SOVCHOS 79

On 4 December 1942, the 48th Panzer Corps' headquarters moved to Nizhna-Chirskaya, where the Chir River flows from the Don, 100 kilometres (62 miles) west of Stalingrad. General Otto von Knobelsdorff, the corps commander, planned to assemble the 11th Panzer Division, the 336th Infantry Division and the 7th *Luftwaffe* Field Division to support the drive to Stalingrad during Winter Storm.[1] The 336th Division and the 7th *Luftwaffe* Field Division would defend the west bank of the Chir north of Nizhna-Chirskaya to protect the 11th Panzer Division's flank as it advanced towards Stalingrad.

The 336th Infantry Division defended the Chir River from Ostrovskii to Lissinski while Group Adam, further south, defended the Rychkovskii bridgehead near Nizhna-Chirskaya. *Kampfgruppe* Schmidt and the 7th *Luftwaffe* Field Division guarded the left flank near Surovikino while Group Heilmann's light outposts protected the right flank from Nizhna-Chirskaya to Biriuchi.

The *Stavka* realized that Army Group Don could launch relief operations to rescue the 6th Army trapped in Stalingrad with the 48th Panzer Corps from the Rychkovskii bridgehead and further south with the 57th Panzer Corps from Kotelnikovo. General Georgy Zhukov correctly assessed that, as the 48th Panzer Corps was only 52 kilometres (32 miles) from Stalingrad, it represented the greater threat as the 57th Panzer Corps was 140 kilometres (87 miles) from the city. The *Stavka* accordingly ordered the Stalingrad Front's 51st Army to defend the approach from Kotelnikovo while Colonel General Nikolai Vatutin's Southwestern Front would launch an unrelenting offensive across the Chir River with 5th Tank Army to unhinge and defeat any German relief operation from the Rychkovskii bridgehead. Zhukov ordered Vatutin to commence the Chir River offensive on 7 December.

The 5th Tank Army had earlier fought Balck's 11th Panzer Division near Voronezh in July but after sustaining heavy casualties, the shattered unit needed to be reconstituted. The reorganized 5th Tank Army, now commanded by Lieutenant General Prokofy Romanenko, participated in the encirclement of Stalingrad during Operation Uranus. Romanenko had earlier commanded the 3rd Tank Army during the unsuccessful Kozelsk Offensive against the 2nd Panzer Army in August 1942.

For the upcoming Chir River operation, Vatutin reinforced the 5th Tank Army with the 5th Mechanized Corps and the 1st Tank Corps.[2] Major General Vasily Butkov's 1st Tank Corps had 146 tanks — five KV heavy tanks, seventy-five T-34 medium tanks and sixty-six T-70 light tanks. Romanenko had reinforced Butkov's corps with the 216th Tank Brigade, giving him a total of around 200 tanks. Butkov planned to cross the Chir, penetrate the German line and advance south to Sovchos 79 (State Farm 79) before turning south-east towards Nizhna-Chirskaya, aiming to unhinge the entire German defensive position along the lower Chir River.[3]

Major General Mikhail Volkov's 5th Mechanized Corps contained three mechanized brigades and five tank regiments with 200 tanks — two T-34s and seven T-70s as well as 114 MK III Valentines and 77 MK II Matildas — British infantry support tanks acquired through lend-lease. Romanenko ordered the 5th Mechanized Corps to conduct another attack across the Chir and advance south toward Tormosin, west of the initial offensive near Nizhna Kalinovski, to commence on 9 December.[4] As such, Romanenko planned a two-stage operation involving more than 400 tanks.

The 5th Tank Army's assault units — the 1st Tank Corps, the 216th Tank Brigade, 333rd Rifle Division and 8th Guards Tank Brigade with 38 KV heavy tanks — moved into their assembly areas on the night of 6 December. Romanenko had received reports indicating the presence of the 336th Infantry Division in the Chir area, but Red Army intelligence had failed to detect the arrival of the 11th Panzer Division in the Tormosin area.[5]

Lieutenant General Prokofy Romanenko, commander of the 5th Tank Army.
(Author's Collection)

Colonel Shaposhnikov, the 5th Mechanized Corps chief-of-staff, explained the operational plan:

> The mission of destroying the enemy's Tormosin grouping was entrusted to the forces of 5th Tank Army. Our corps [5th Mechanized] was designated to operate along the main axis. . . . The corps had the mission to cross the Chir River and capture the Chuvilevskii and Nizhniaia Kalinovka line in cooperation with the rifle divisions by day's end.[6]

As the Soviet commanders made their final preparations for the Chir River offensive, the first elements of the 11th Panzer Division detrained near Morozovskaya airfield and moved into its assembly area north-east of Tormosin. The 15th Panzer Regiment, commanded by Colonel Theodor Graf Schimmelmann, fielded about seventy operational tanks — nine Panzer II light tanks, fifty-four Panzer III and six Panzer IV medium tanks, and three command tanks.[7] After Balck arrived at Nizhna-Chirskaya, he reconnoitred the sector where his division would cross the Don at the Rychkovskii bridgehead during Winter Storm.

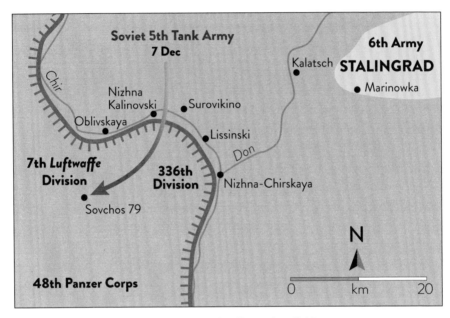

The 5th Tank Army's advance to Sovchos 79, 7 December 1942.

On 7 December, before the 11th Panzer Division could cross the Don, Romanenko's 5th Tank Army — led by the 1st Tank Corps, the 3rd Guards Cavalry Corps and two rifle divisions — attacked various points along the Chir River. Although the 336th Division held its ground, the 5th Tank Army broke through the boundary between *Kampfgruppe* Schmidt and the 336th Infantry Division, south-west of Ostrovskii.

The 117th, 159th and 216th Tank Brigades from Butkov's 1st Tank Corps advanced south-west. The 89th Tank Brigade rolled west while Butkov held the 44th Motorized Rifle Brigade in reserve. The three lead tank brigades overran *Kampfgruppe* Buddenbroch, on the right of the 7th *Luftwaffe* Field Division before bypassing the 336th Infantry Division. The three brigades advanced 10 kilometres (6 miles) and liberated Sovchos 79 around 1030 h. The men then established a defensive ring around the farm and Butkov planned to advance south-east the next day.[8]

Meanwhile, the 89th Tank Brigade on Butkov's right wing advanced 2 kilometres (1.2 miles) west and captured Hill 129 from the 7th *Luftwaffe* Division. The 333rd Rifle Division advanced past Hill 129 and moved

2 kilometres north of Sovchos 79 before advancing east to a position north of the 336th Infantry Division. The 8th Motorcycle Regiment simultaneously moved south-west, intending to conduct raids deep in the German rear area near Tormosin to disrupt enemy supply lines.

The 11th Panzer Division assembled near Tormosin and after the Soviet offensive commenced, the 48th Panzer Corps signalled the divisional headquarters: 'Enemy tanks from vicinity Soyevski have broken through towards the southwest. Prepare Pz.Rgt.15 for possible counterattack.'[9] As Balck was conducting reconnaissance of Nizhna-Chirskaya, his headquarters relayed the order to Schimmelmann and his regiment departed northwards fifteen minutes later. In the afternoon, the panzers, supported by anti-aircraft guns and engineers, engaged a large Red Army tank force near Sovchos 79, stopping its further advance.[10] The regiment also halted the 8th Motorcycle Regiment before establishing blocking positions 4 kilometres (2.5 miles) south of Sovchos 79.[11]

As the first day of the Chir River offensive had proceeded smoothly, Romanenko signalled Butkov at 1915 h: 'I order you to continue fulfilling your mission . . . on the morning of 8 December. The enemy's Nizhne-Chirskaia grouping must be liquidated by day's end of 8 December.'[12] At Sovchos 79, Butkov deployed the 117th, 159th and 216th Tank Brigades in an arc to defend the approaches from the west, south and east. He also ordered the 44th Motorized Rifle Brigade to march to the farm at dawn.[13]

As the 336th Division had no armour and inadequate anti-tank guns, the 1st Tank Corps at Sovchos 79 posed a serious threat to the entire German position in the Chir sector. Therefore, General Knobelsdorff ordered Balck to restore the situation by pushing the Red Army back across the river.

After apprising himself of the new threat, Balck immediately moved his headquarters to the 336th Division's command post at Verkhne-Solonovskii to enable both divisions to better co-ordinate operations. 'The 336th Infantry Division was positioned solid as a rock on the Chir River,' he noted. 'Everything depended on it holding fast, even in the most desperate situations. It was the shield and the pivot for all of the operations of the 11th Panzer Division.'[14] The division's piecemeal deployment continued while the 110th and 111th Panzer Grenadier Regiments and the 61st Motorcycle Battalion arrived in the area.

Balck planned to attack Sovchos 79 at dawn and Lucht asked him to conduct a sudden frontal attack against the farm. Balck, however, wanted to destroy the Soviet tank force and instead planned an envelopment operation to block all escape routes.[15]

Balck gave his regimental commanders verbal orders over the radio. He deployed the 110th Panzer Grenadier Regiment, commanded by Colonel Albert Henze, 88-mm anti-aircraft guns and an engineer battalion south of the farm to prevent an enemy advance from that direction overrunning the 336th Division. Schimmelmann's 15th Panzer Regiment and 111th Panzer Grenadier Regiment, commanded by Colonel Alexander von Bosse, would surprise the Russians by enveloping the farm from the north-west. The 110th Panzer Grenadier Regiment would shortly afterwards conduct a direct attack from the south while Balck's 209th Pioneer Battalion and his 88-mm guns would prevent encircled forces escaping.

The 15th Panzer Regiment only had around thirty operational tanks, mostly Panzer III medium tanks armed with 50-mm guns, which would face fifty-three Russian tanks, mostly superior T-34s with 76-mm guns. Although the gullies and dry streams around Sovchos 79 could conceal Russian tanks camouflaged in the snow, Balck reasoned the low hills in the western sector would also hide the movement of his panzers.[16]

During the night, Schimmelmann's 15th Panzer Regiment and Bosse's 111th Panzer Grenadier Regiment moved north and passed west of Sovchos 79 without being detected by the Soviet reconnaissance screen. 'When the Russians got ready to attack the next morning we were right there,' Balck explained. 'They did not suspect our presence.'[17] Schimmelmann would wheel right at dawn and attack with the 111th Panzer Grenadier Regiment in support. At 1000 h, Henze's 110th Panzer Grenadier Regiment would commence its northward attack while a battalion from 336th Infantry Division would advance east on the regiment's right flank.

At dawn on 8 December, the 11th Panzer Division attacked Sovchos 79 before the Red Army launched its own attack against the 336th Division and, as Balck stressed, it 'was critical to be an hour earlier than the Russians at the decisive point'.[18]

At 0650 h, the 15th Panzer Regiment encountered the 44th Motorized Rifle Brigade moving south-west in column. Schimmelmann's panzers

A Red Army T-34 tank during the Russian winter.
(Sueddeutsche Zeitung Photo/Alamy Stock Photo)

attacked the surprised column 2 kilometres (1.2 miles) north of the state
farm, inflicting heavy casualties and destroying most of the trucks.[19] As the
Red Army survivors attempted to flee, Schimmelmann secured a blocking
position along the road and sent a panzer column south towards the farm
while another panzer column linked up with the 336th Division, encircling
three Soviet tank brigades. Balck's attack caught the Russians off guard
because they had not established a proper defensive position.

After reaching Sovchos 79, the 15th Panzer Regiment attacked the Soviet
T-34 and KV tanks from the rear, supported by the armoured personnel
carriers and infantry from the panzer grenadier regiments, causing panic
to erupt among the surrounded Red Army soldiers as the three Soviet tank

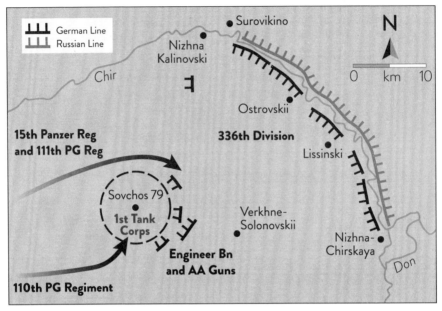

The 11th Panzer Division's counter-attack at Sovchos 79, 8 December 1942.

brigades attempted to fight their way out of the farm in multiple directions. Balck witnessed his troops assault the farm:

> Both of my regiments hit the Russians in the rear, just at the moment they were starting to advance to the East. First they annihilated a long column of mechanized infantry, and then the mass of the Russian tanks that were attacking the 336th Division. I positioned my approaching 110th Panzergrenadier Regiment toward Sovkhos 79, where another significant number of Russian tanks were cut off in the valley. We could see tanks, trucks, and Russians running back and forth nervously.[20]

By 1400 h the battle of Sovchos 79 had ended. The 11th Panzer Division had destroyed fifty-three enemy tanks — a third of Butkov's corps — while only sustaining around ten tanks destroyed or damaged.[21] The surviving tanks of 117th, 159th and 216th Tank Brigades reached the 333rd Rifle Division's lines further north near Ostrovskii.

Although Balck had been surprised by the Soviet attack at Sovchos 79 the previous day, he had quickly seized the initiative, despite being forced to commit his division piecemeal, and had completed his mission within twenty-four hours.[22] Balck set a rapid tempo of operations with short verbal orders, giving his regimental commanders sufficient information for the operation to be co-ordinated.

A Red Army General Staff summary of the action at Sovchos 79 noted:

> 5th Tank Army defended its current positions on its right wing and conducted offensive fighting and repelled enemy counterattacks with infantry and tanks on its left wing. . . . 1st TC [Tank Corps] beat back several counterattacks by enemy infantry and tanks continued to fight, while widening penetration sector.[23]

Romanenko did not report that the Germans had surprised the 1st Tank Corps and that three of its tank brigades had suffered heavy losses.

In the afternoon, the 111th and 110th Panzer Grenadier Regiments repulsed counter-attacks by the 333rd Rifle Division while the 336th Infantry Division defeated an attack near Lissinski by the 6th Guards Cavalry Division supported by one regiment from the 258th Rifle Division.

After the 11th Panzer Division captured Sovchos 79, the men found the bodies of soldiers from the 336th Division's supply units who had been executed by the Soviets, and an enraged Balck addressed his troops:

> The Bolshevist cruelties at Sovkhos 79, where several hundred German soldiers were slaughtered by the Russians, will remain in our memories forever. . . . Comrades, the tough days of fighting that are behind us now show us anew that this is about the existence or nonexistence of our people. If in the future you waver in your courage, should you grow weak during the bitter fighting, always remember . . . the horrible sights at Sovkhos 79 that prove to us without a doubt the fate that will await us if we do not win this fight.[24]

The *Stavka*, in response to the battle of Sovchos 79, ordered the 5th Tank Army to continue its planned offensive and committed General Volkov's 5th Mechanized Corps to attack at dawn the next day. The *Stavka* also ordered the 1st Tank Corps, which still possessed over one hundred tanks, to renew its attack. After midnight, Major General Aleksei Danilov, the 5th Tank Army's chief of staff, signalled Butkov:

> 1st Tank Corps, with 8th Motorcycle Regiment, will destroy the enemy's 336th Infantry Division by an attack in the general direction of Surovikino in cooperation with 333rd Rifle Division, and subsequently capture Surovikino together with 119th Rifle Division.[25]

The *Stavka* believed it could destroy the 11th Panzer Division or, at the very least, prevent it from conducting a relief operation towards Stalingrad. However, the *Stavka* now lacked confidence in the 5th Tank Army and ordered the creation of the 5th Shock Army to reinforce Romanenko's operations in the Chir region. The 5th Shock Army, commanded by Lieutenant General Markian Popov, contained the 7th and 23rd Tank Corps, the 4th Mechanized Corps, the 3rd Guards Cavalry Corps and five rifle divisions.[26] Popov had commanded the Leningrad Military District in 1941 before participating in Zhukov's winter counter-offensive while commanding the Leningrad Front.

The veteran 7th and 23rd Tank Corps provided the armoured nucleus of Popov's shock army. The 7th Tank Corps, commanded by Major General Pavel Rotmistrov, had fought Balck in the Voronezh region in July 1942. The 23rd Tank Corps, formed on 12 April 1942, had been destroyed during the battle of Kharkov in May 1942, but a new force commanded by Major General Efim Pushkin reorganized in early June.

The *Stavka* ordered Popov to 'destroy the enemy's Nizhne-Chirskaia and Tormosin groupings in cooperation with 5th Tank Army' and 'prevent at all cost an enemy penetration from the Tormosin and Nizhne-Chirskaia region to link up with the enemy grouping encircled in the Stalingrad region'.[27]

THE CHIR 'FIRE BRIGADE'

As Field Marshal Erich von Manstein, commander of Army Group Don, prepared Winter Storm, the 6th Army's position inside Stalingrad became critical as the *Luftwaffe*'s air supply only delivered one-fifth of the supplies required by the besieged German soldiers each day. Balck and the 48th

Lieutenant General Markian Popov, commander of the 5th Shock Army.
(Author's Collection)

Panzer Corps remained preoccupied with restoring the Chir River front and would not be able to participate in Winter Storm.

On 9 December, the 11th Panzer Division in the Ostrovskii region bypassed and encircled Soviet forces east of Sovchos 79 to compress the shrinking Soviet bridgehead across the Chir. Balck deployed Hauser's 61st Motorcycle Battalion to his left wing and moved most of Bosse's 111th Grenadier Regiment and half of Henze's 110th Grenadier Regiment north to the outskirts of Ostrovskii. Meanwhile, the remainder of the 110th Regiment cleared Soviet forces west of Savinskii. By nightfall, the 11th Panzer Division had completed its clearing operations and expected to rest the next day.[28]

On the morning of 10 December, the 5th Tank Army recommenced operations. At 0730 h, several regiments of 47th Guards Rifle Division supported by fifty tanks from the 159th Tank Brigade attacked from the Ostrovskii bridgehead at the boundary between the 110th Panzer Grenadier Regiment and the 336th Infantry Division. The attackers advanced almost 2 kilometres (1.2 miles) before heavy German artillery fire from the 336th Division halted their advance and forced their withdrawal.[29] Meanwhile, Volkov's 5th Mechanized Corps crossed the Chir west of Surovikino and liberated the villages of Chuvilevskii and Nizhna Kalinovskii.

At 0900 h, the mechanized infantry of the 111th Panzer Grenadier Regiment, supported by fifty-eight tanks from the 15th Panzer Regiment, advanced north and attacked the 333rd Rifle Division before turning east to the outskirts of Ostrovskii, where elements of the 1st Tank Corps, the 8th Guards Tank Brigade and the 47th Guards Rifle Division halted their progress. By the end of the day, Balck's 11th Panzer Division had only reduced the Soviet bridgehead by 1 kilometre (0.6 mile).[30]

On 11 December, Romanenko ordered his forces to conduct limited attacks to pin down and exhaust the 11th Panzer Division and the rest of the 48th Panzer Corps. The 5th Tank Army launched two thrusts along the Chir River that day. Volkov's 5th Mechanized Corps attacked from its bridgehead at Nizhna Kalinovski while the 6th Guards Cavalry Division supported by a brigade from the 1st Tank Corps crossed the Chir and liberated Lissinski.

In the evening, Balck received a signal from the 48th Panzer Corps: 'Enemy broken through at Lissinski and at Nizhna Kalinovski, the one breakthrough 22 km as the crow flies away from the other.'[31] The 11th Panzer Division had been reducing the Soviet bridgehead at Ostrovskii, which was no longer an immediate threat but had not been completely cleared.[32] Balck decided to first deal with the new enemy threat at Lissinski and ordered half of the 15th Panzer Regiment to counter this threat, leaving the 111th and 110th Grenadier Regiments to contain the Ostrovskii bridgehead.

Balck's assault force raced south-east towards the decisive point after sunset:

'Night marches save blood' became the slogan in the division. I often yelled to the men, 'What do you want to do, bleed or march?' 'Let's march, Sir,' came the answer from the tired and worn-out faces.[33]

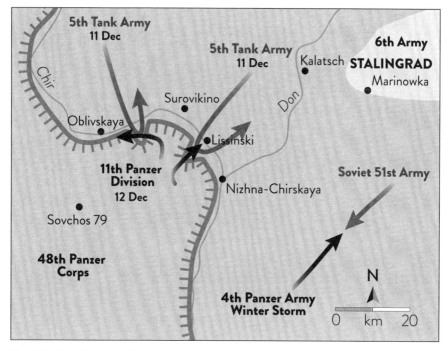

The Chir River Front, 11–12 December 1942.

By this time, Balck's gifted abilities as a commander had been noticed by the Red Army, as a 5th Tank Army intelligence report revealed following the interrogation of a prisoner from the 11th Panzer Division:

A prisoner, who was seized 2 kilometers west of Ostrovskii on 11 December . . . indicated his division bears the name of 'Leading' [*Privedenie*]. It received this designation because the division moves mostly at night, goes on alert by surprise, and shifts rapidly from place to place to appear unexpectedly.[34]

On 12 December, Manstein launched Winter Storm and Colonel General Hoth's 4th Panzer Army achieved initial success, breaking through the Soviet 51st Army's defences and, within a few days, the panzers advanced 50 kilometres (31 miles).[35] Balck hoped that his actions along the Chir would support Manstein's effort:

With delight we followed the initial successes of Colonel General Hermann Hoth's Fourth Panzer Army. The more enemy forces we drew toward us, the easier would be the mission of the Fourth Panzer Army. 'Is our adversary the Fifth Tank Army still there, or did they march off against Hoth's army?' That was the daily critical question. Then a report would arrive: 'Tanks broken through at X,' and the reaction would be, 'Thank God, they are still here.'[36]

At dawn, Balck's panzer force approached Lissinski and annihilated advancing Soviet tanks with the support of the 209th Pioneer Battalion. Although the 1st Battalion (110th Panzer Grenadier Regiment) lost two company commanders in the brutal fighting, the 336th Division recaptured Lissinski in the afternoon. Balck next ordered the 111th Grenadier Regiment and most of the 15th Panzer Regiment north-west to contain Volkov's 5th Mechanized Corps at Nizhna Kalinovski.[37]

Volkov had earlier committed the 50th Mechanized Brigade, supported by the 168th Tank Regiment, into combat from his second echelon which engaged Balck's 61st Motorcycle Battalion and the 7th *Luftwaffe* Division south of Nizhna Kalinovski. In the early afternoon, Volkov's force repulsed a counter-attack by a battalion from the 15th Panzer Regiment south of Chuvilevskii. Around 1600 h, the 111th Panzer Grenadier Regiment and 15th Panzer Regiment's main force approached Nizhna Kalinovski, halting the 50th Mechanized Brigade and 168th Tank Regiment's further advance and reducing the bridgehead.

Meanwhile further east, Henze's 110th Grenadier Regiment defended against the 5th Tank Army's breakout attacks from the Ostrovskii bridgehead. The 333rd and 47th Guards Rifle Divisions, supported by at least fifty tanks from 1st Tank Corps and 8th Guards Tank Brigade, attacked the 110th Panzer Grenadier Regiment and 336th Infantry Division near Ostrovskii, encircling one of the regiment's battalions.

Balck could not support the 61st Motorcycle Battalion and the 7th *Luftwaffe* Division near Nizhna Kalinovski and cancelled his planned attack on the bridgehead. He instead sent Schimmelmann's 15th Panzer Regiment and Bosse's 111th Panzer Grenadier Regiment back to the Ostrovskii bridgehead to rescue the encircled battalion. At 1400 h, these

Hermann Balck (front left) and Friedrich von Mellenthin (front right) on the Eastern Front.
(Author's Collection)

regiments, supported by two battalions of 7th *Luftwaffe* Division, fought the Soviets near Ostrovskii as Colonel Friedrich von Mellenthin, the 48th Panzer Corps' chief-of-staff, explained:

> Eleventh Panzer discontinued its assault on the [Nizhna Kalinovski] bridgehead and turned against the attacker, the encircled battalion was freed, and the battle ended with an indubitable German defensive success. Unfortunately it was not possible to liquidate the Russian bridgehead at Nizhna Kalinovski.[38]

By the end of the day, the Germans and Soviets had fought to exhaustion and although Balck failed to capture the bridgehead, he could not fault his men: 'My troops were outstanding. During those days I saw nothing that did not make me proud of them. Even the attitudes of the wounded at the aid stations were exemplary.'[39]

The 11th Panzer Division's operational tank strength continued to decrease as the attrition of combat and the frozen terrain took a heavy toll on equipment.[40] Balck only had thirty operational tanks left while the 1st Tank Corps and 8th Guards Tank Brigade had at least sixty tanks.[41] Balck, nevertheless, planned to destroy the Soviet positions around Nizhna Kalinovski in the morning before returning to Ostrovskii the following day to deal with the lesser threat. During this time, he perfected his 'fire brigade' tactics:

The Russian forces would break through at location X. We would counterattack, and in the evening everything was back to normal. Soon, another report would come in of a deep breakthrough at the position of some rapid reaction force. We would turn around with lights blazing, tanks, riflemen, artillery driving through the winter night. We were ready the next morning at dawn. Positioned at the Russians' weakest point, we would bear down on them in surprise and destroy them. The following morning we would play the same game ten or twenty kilometers farther to the west or east.[42]

Balck also perfected his command system:

My General Staff officer . . . Major Kienitz, sat in one position a little toward the rear and maintained radio contact with me, the higher headquarters, and everyone else. I remained highly mobile, moving to all the hot spots. I usually was at every regiment several times a day. While still out on the line during the evening I drew up the basic plan for the next day. After communicating by phone with Kienitz, I drove to every regiment and gave them the next day's order personally. Then I drove back to my own command post and spoke by phone with the chief of staff of the XLVIII Panzer Corps, Colonel von Mellenthin. If the commanding general Knobelsdorff concurred, the regiments received the short message: 'No changes!' If changes were necessary, I drove at night one more time to all the regiments so that there would not be any misunderstandings. At daybreak I was always back at the decisive point.[43]

During this time Balck developed an 'exceedingly harmonious relationship' with Mellenthin 'that would last throughout the rest of the war'.[44] Mellenthin found himself in awe of Balck's command abilities and, in honour of his Scandinavian ancestry, referred to him as 'Cool Nordic'.[45]

As Balck's troops fought the 5th Tank Army and the 5th Mechanized Corps, Lieutenant General Popov's 5th Shock Army began its offensive further south towards the critical German bridgehead on the east bank of the Don River at Rychkovskii near Nizhna-Chirskaya. One day earlier, Rotmistrov discussed the upcoming operation with Popov:

Popov expressed concern that the Germans had pre-empted us. It turned out that, during the morning of this day, the enemy had launched an offensive [Winter Storm] . . .'And perhaps they will also strike from Rychkovskii?' said Markian Mikhailovich [Popov] as he anxiously looked at me. 'Today they have not struck, but we will strike in the morning,' I reassured the army commander.[46]

On 13 December, the 5th Shock Army surprised the Germans as Rotmistrov's 7th Tank Corps overran the strongpoints at Rychkovskii and Verkhne-Chirskii as Rotmistrov observed:

The snow-covered steppes were still cloaked in darkness. . . . We tensely peered into the distant spot where Colonel Vovchenko's tank brigade first went. And we suddenly noticed rising colored rockets. The enemy was clearly taken unawares. . . . 'The Germans in Rychkovskii are kaput!' I said to Markian Mikhailovich [Popov] as I observed through my binoculars how decisively events were developing along the axis of the main attack.[47]

By the end of the day, the 7th Tank Corps had liberated Rychkovskii while the 315th Rifle Division cleared the Germans from the woods east of Verkhne-Chirskii. Rotmistrov recalled the brutal fighting:

Verkne-Chirskii turned out to be a strong center of the enemy's defenses, which was saturated with a great number of antitank guns. To liquidate this centre of resistance of the Hitlerites required careful preparations. . . . The fighting was intense and lasted all day.[48]

Although the 5th Tank Army had failed to break out from the Ostrovskii and Nizhna Kalinovski bridgeheads or destroy the 11th Panzer Division, Romanenko had successfully pinned down the 48th Panzer Corp. Balck was therefore unable to intervene further south at Rychkovskii and Verkhne-Chirskii when the 5th Shock Army seized the German bridgehead across the Don — the more important objective — which ended any hope of the 48th Panzer Corps participating in Winter Storm.[49]

NIZHNA KALINOVSKI

On 15 December, Popov's 5th Shock Army continued clearing German forces from the eastern bank of the lower Chir River while Romanenko's 5th Tank Army faced the 11th Panzer Division along the Chir further north from the Ostrovskii and Nizhna Kalinovski bridgeheads.

The bulk of 11th Panzer Division in the Ostrovskii and Nizhna Kalinovski regions launched a strong attack against the eastern sector of the Nizhna Kalinovski bridgehead. In the evening, Balck withdrew his two grenadier regiments south to Nizhne-Solonovskii to rest and refit.

Balck planned to move his division south towards Nizhna-Chirskaya where the Chir branched from the Don. The division withdrew from its position covering the Russian bridgehead at Nizhna Kalinovski and handed the sector over to the 7th *Luftwaffe* Field Division. Balck planned to recapture the bridgehead across the Don at Rychkovskii and link up with Hoth's 4th Panzer Army. However, before he could commence this attack, the Red Army seized the initiative after launching Operation Little Saturn.

In the original plan for Operation Saturn, the 1st Guards and 2nd Guards Armies would have attacked the Italian 8th Army and seized Rostov, trapping Army Groups A and B. However, Operation Uranus had trapped far more German forces in the Stalingrad pocket than had been anticipated, resulting in more Red Army forces being required to contain the encircled enemy troops. After the 2nd Guards Army then redeployed to counter Winter Storm, the *Stavka* accordingly scaled down Operation Saturn into a smaller envelopment of the Italian 8th Army and Army Detachment Hollidt defending the southern banks of the Don and Chir rivers.

On 16 December, the Red Army launched Little Saturn and focused its

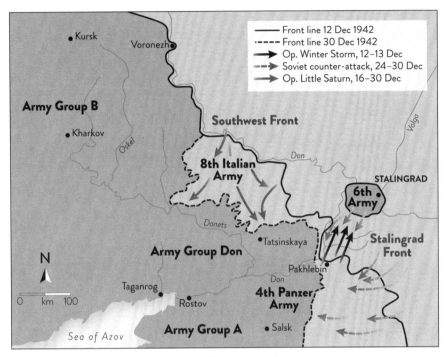

'Winter Storm' and 'Little Saturn', 12–30 December 1942.

attacks against the Italian 8th Army on the Don with the ultimate goal of reaching Rostov on the Black Sea, as Zhukov recalled:

> . . . the troops of the South-Western Front and the 6th Army of the Voronezh Front struck out to crush the German concentration along the middle reaches of the Don and emerge in the rear of the enemy's Tormosin grouping.[50]

The 1st Guards Army attacked on the right wing supported by the 6th Army while the 3rd Guards Army assaulted on the left wing.[51] Little Saturn completely unhinged German planning, as Mellenthin explained:

> At this juncture the Russian Command showed strategic insight of a high order. . . . Instead of concentrating their reserves to meet Hoth's thrust [towards Stalingrad], they unleashed a new offensive on a massive scale

against the unfortunate Italian Eighth Army on the middle Don . . . and
the positions of the 48th Panzer Corps on the River Chir.[52]

The Red Army during Little Saturn overran units of the 336th Division,
forcing Balck to abandon his plan to recapture the bridgehead across the
Don at Rychkovskii. Although Hoth's advance guard reached the Aksay
River the next day, less than 64 kilometres (40 miles) from the 6th Army,
Winter Storm failed because Manstein had to redeploy his forces to meet
the new threat to Rostov.

General Vatutin's plan for Little Saturn excluded large-scale operations
by the 5th Tank Army, which had transferred the 3rd Guards Cavalry Corps
and two rifle divisions to the 5th Shock Army. However, Vatutin ordered
Romanenko to launch an attack two days later, intending to keep the 11th
Panzer Division pinned down in the lower Chir region.[53] As Butkov's 1st
Tank Corps had already suffered heavy casualties, Romanenko's only
available force was Volkov's 5th Mechanized Corps supported by the 321st
Rifle Division. Romanenko ordered Volkov to attack south from the Nizhna
Kalinovski bridgehead and seize the sector west of Surovikino, recently
vacated by the 11th Panzer Division, defended by *Kampfgruppe* Wagner, a
battalion-sized force from the 7th *Luftwaffe* Division.[54]

On 17 December, the 5th Tank Army launched major attacks along the Chir
River between Ostrovskii and Lissinski, breaking through the 336th Division's
defences 10 kilometres (6 miles) north of Nizhna-Chirskaya, and Mellenthin
noted: 'There was nothing for it but to commit the 11th Panzerdivision.'[55]

On the morning of 18 December, the 5th Mechanized Corps attacked
from the Nizhna Kalinovski bridgehead. The 188th and 168th Tank
Regiments spearheaded the assault followed by the 45th, 49th and 50th
Mechanized Brigades. By evening, the 5th Mechanized Corps and the
321st Rifle Division had advanced 12 kilometres (7.5 miles) south of the
Chir, threatening the 7th *Luftwaffe* Field Division's right flank and the 336th
Infantry Division's left flank. Meanwhile further east, the 321st Rifle Division
attacked across the Chir, overwhelming *Kampfgruppe* Wagner.

Balck had planned to repulse the Soviet attacks between Ostrovskii and
Lissinski, but the 5th Mechanized Corps breakthrough at Nizhna Kalinovski
forced him to revert to his 'fire brigade' role. After proposing to first finish

off the Red Army at Ostrovskii before facing the new threat, Mellenthin interjected, 'No, General, this time it is more than critical. The 11th Panzer Division must go there immediately, every second counts.'[56]

Balck ordered the 11th Panzer Division on another night march and planned to attack the Nizhna Kalinovski bridgehead at dawn, just before the Russian offensive resumed. Henze's 110th Panzer Grenadier Regiment would block the line in front of the Soviet position while Schimmelmann's 15th Panzer Regiment attacked its rear and Bosse's 111th Panzer Grenadier Regiment protected the eastern flank of the division. The men quietly moved into their assembly areas after dark.

At 0500 h on 19 December, Volkov's 5th Mechanized Corps, which possessed around 200 tanks — mostly British Valentine and Matilda infantry support tanks — formed a column and prepared to resume its advance, unaware of Balck's nearby panzers. Schimmelmann accordingly delayed his attack and let the 50th and 49th Mechanized Brigades advance southwards before manoeuvring his twenty-five operational tanks to fall in behind the Russian columns. The panzers opened fire on the rear of the Valentine and Matilda tanks and Schimmelmann reported to Balck: 'over half of the enemy tanks destroyed. No friendly losses.'[57] Balck later praised Schimmelmann's perfectly executed attack:

[The Red Army] tanks and other formations were rolling past us toward the south. Then Schimmelmann released Captain Karl Lestmann's element. Just like in a training area, our tanks pivoted around and followed the Russians. The Russians had no idea that the tanks following their columns were German.[58]

The 15th Panzer Regiment destroyed forty-two Russian tanks without any casualties and Schimmelmann's panzers turned towards the second wave of enemy armour.

At 1315 h, Red Army tanks attacked the 110th Panzer Grenadier Regiment. Ten minutes later Henze reported that fifteen enemy tanks were overrunning his position.[59] Less than half an hour later, Schimmelmann's regiment arrived and, as the Soviet tanks crested a height exposing their soft underbelly, his panzers opened fire, destroying twenty-three tanks. After

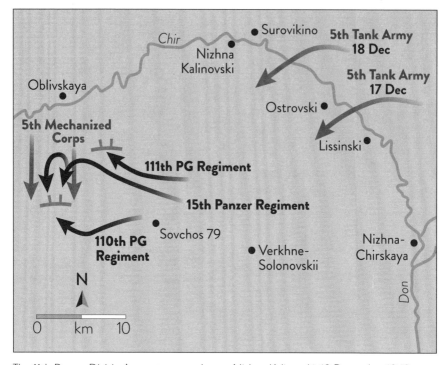

The 11th Panzer Division's counter-attack near Nizhna Kalinovski, 19 December 1942.

destroying the second wave of Russian armour, he signalled Balck: 'Enemy tanks destroyed. Count not yet clear.'[60]

The 11th Panzer Division had destroyed sixty-five Red Army tanks as Balck proudly recalled:

> Twenty-five German tanks had shot up sixty-five Russian tanks. . . . The accompanying Russian infantry escaped initially, but then a Russian relief attack broke down with heavy losses. . . . Shortly thereafter I moved among the still burning enemy tanks, thanking my courageous troops. Gone was the strain of the previous days, as the smiling faces of the unbeatable force peered out from their turrets.[61]

Balck, in his after-action report, noted that he had only lost three panzers as 'total write-offs' that day.[62] Mellenthin also noted that 'thanks to the activities of the 11th Panzer Division as a "fire brigade," the situation on the Chir

Hermann Balck (centre) and Colonel Graf Theodor Schimmelmann (right) discussing strategy on the Chir River Front.
(Author's Collection)

River was to some extent cleared up'.[63]

The 5th Mechanized Corps stabilized the situation by counter-attacking later that day and digging tanks into the ground around Surovikino.[64] Volkov and Romanenko scaled down the disaster in their reports on the battle. For example, Colonel Shaposhnikov, the 5th Mechanized Corps' chief-of-staff, reported:

> The enemy tanks and infantry, with air support, undertook attack after attack. However, our *tankists*, artillerymen, and motorized riflemen offered stubborn resistance to the enemy and managed to repel all of the attacks. . . . The enemy, having suffered significant losses in tanks and personnel, were forced to cease their attacks and go over to the defense.[65]

The 5th Tank Army's intelligence report also failed to mention the 5th Mechanized Corps' heavy losses:

The enemy on the army's front offered stubborn resistance, while launching counterattacks in separate sectors during the course of 19 December 1942. By day's end on 19 December, he [the enemy] was driven back from Sekretov, Staro-Derbenovskii, and Novo-Derbenovskii.[66]

On 20 December, heavy fighting continued south of Novo-Derbenovskii and north-west of Sovchos 79 as the 11th Panzer Division tried to push the 5th Mechanized Corps back across the Chir, even though Balck only had thirty-one operational panzers.[67] Henze's 110th Panzer Grenadier Regiment, supported by Schimmelmann's 15th Panzer regiment, moved north past Hills 149 and 137. Bosse's 111th Regiment meanwhile advanced 6 kilometres (3.7 miles) north of Sovchos 79. At 1300 h, at least thirty Soviet tanks attacked the 110th Regiment's right wing while two other Soviet tank groups with over thirty tanks attacked the 110th Regiment. These attacks forced Balck to withdraw his men south back to Hills 149 and 137, where they stabilized the front.[68] That day the *Wehrmacht* awarded Balck the Knight's Cross with Oak Leaves for his exceptional command of the 11th Panzer Division at the Chir.

Balck intended to destroy the remaining Red Army forces west of the Chir the next day, but in the evening a strong Russian counter-attack struck the division's right flank and advanced behind the 111th Panzer Grenadier Regiment. Although Schimmelmann's regiment saved their comrades and destroyed ten enemy tanks, Balck had been forced onto the defensive.

On 21 December in the pre-dawn darkness, the 5th Mechanized Corps attacked south toward Hills 149 and 137, striking the junction of 110th and 111th Panzer Grenadier Regiments. The 45th and 49th Mechanized Brigades, supported by the 165th and 168th Tank Regiments, captured the hills and forced the panzer grenadier regiments to withdraw.[69] Balck ordered a counter-attack to save his panzer grenadiers:

All hell had broken loose from all directions. The 110th Panzergrenadier Regiment had been penetrated and the 111th Panzergrenadier Regiment overrun. The 15th Panzer Regiment radioed that the situation was very critical. In the bright light of a full moon the Russians had attacked with tanks and infantry right at the seam between the two

Panzergrenadier regiments. . . . I immediately threw the tanks and Hauser's motorcycle riflemen into a hasty counterattack to close the gap between the two regiments.[70]

In the early afternoon, about twenty tanks from 15th Panzer Regiment and mounted infantry from 61st Motorcycle Battalion recaptured the lost ground south of Hill 149. By the end of the day, Balck had pushed the 5th Mechanized Corps' spearheads back 2 kilometres (1.2 miles), but his men suffered horrendous losses:

Russian tanks had crushed some of our wounded on the ground, who then froze in that position. When my troops saw what had happened they became uncontrollably mad, which is quite understandable. Our losses had been considerable. It was not an easy time to be a commander.[71]

The 11th Panzer Division had stabilized the front but attrition had seriously weakened the division; however, the Chir River battles had come to an end. Balck had devastated the 5th Tank Army by waiting for each enemy thrust to stop before swiftly counter-attacking: 'You had to wait for this moment and then counterattack them immediately. In the blink of an eye they'd be destroyed.'[72] He also added: 'If the Fifth Tank Army had attacked with all of its corps simultaneously across the Chir we could not have stopped them.'[73] Mellenthin recognized Balck's exceptional abilities demonstrated during these desperate battles:

I must pay tribute to General Balck, a born leader of armor. Throughout the fighting his panzer division had acted as the 'fire brigade,' moving behind the two infantry divisions to quell one dangerous conflagration after another. When the infantry found it impossible to deal with the larger Russian bridgeheads, Balck came tearing down on the enemy with the whole weight of his armor.[74]

The historian Dennis Showalter concluded that Balck's conduct at Chir River 'was an example of staff work, willpower, and tactical skill still legitimately cited as among the greatest divisional-level battles ever fought'.[75]

However, David Glantz explained that Balck's tactical success obscured the *Wehrmacht*'s larger operational disaster:

German writers such as Friedrich von Mellenthin give Western readers the impression that the skilful tactical performance of Balck's 11th Panzer Division thwarted 5th Tank Army's advance south of the Chir River time and again during the first three weeks of December. Although this is correct at the tactical level, the German were actually defeated operationally. . . . [The] 5th Tank Army's forces succeeded in overstretching and exhausting Knobelsdorff's panzer corps, preventing it from supporting Operation *Wintergewitter* [Winter Storm] in any manner. This not only fulfilled the mission assigned to Romanenko's tank army by the *Stavka* and Vatutin; it also led to an immediate Soviet victory at the operational level and a subsequent victory at the strategic level.[76]

Although Romanenko achieved his mission, General Vatutin, displeased by his failure to destroy the 11th Panzer Division, kept the *Stavka* informed of his shortcomings. On 28 December, Stalin informed Vatutin, 'If Romanenko is performing badly, we can replace him with General Popov.'[77] Vatutin replied:

Romanenko usually does not understand the general situation and quite frequently operates contrary to the general concept, in the best case, while trying to achieve individual interest to the detriment of the general. In addition, Romanenko organizes for combat poorly and, furthermore, is undisciplined since his reports clearly exaggerate information about the enemy and mislead, apparently so that he can receive this or another reinforcement. I believe it dangerous to have such a commander and request you replace him.[78]

Stalin ordered Vatutin to relieve Romanenko as commander of 5th Tank Army and place him at the disposal of the People's Commissariat of Defence. Despite being relieved of command, Romanenko later commanded the 2nd Tank Army in central Russia and the 48th Army until the end of 1944, fighting at Kursk and during Operational Bagration. After the war, he commanded the Eastern Siberian Military District before dying of a serious illness on 11 March 1949.

The Chir River front remained quiet, but further north Little Saturn had smashed the Italian 8th Army on the Don and Red Army tanks advanced deep into rear areas towards Morozovsk and Tatsinskaya, threating Rostov on the Black Sea.[79] If the Soviets liberated the city, they would cut off all German forces in the Caucasus. Manstein accordingly had little choice but to redeploy his forces to defeat Little Saturn, even though this meant abandoning the 6th Army in Stalingrad.

On 22 December, Manstein ordered the 48th Panzer Corps to leave the lower Chir region and move west to save Rostov. Although Balck could not rescue the German troops in Stalingrad, he now had orders to stop the Soviet offensive at Tatsinskaya, north-east of Rostov, before the Red Army reached the Black Sea and cut off Army Group A retreating from the Caucasus. As the 11th Panzer Division departed the region, the 5th Mechanized Corps left the Chir to rest and refit in order to support future 5th Tank Army operations east of Morozovsk.

CHAPTER ELEVEN
DISASTER AT STALINGRAD

TATSINSKAYA

As Balck fought the Soviet 5th Tank Army along the Chir River on 19 December 1942, Red Army forces assigned to Little Saturn overran the Italian 8th Army and advanced towards Rostov. The 24th and 25th Tank Corps and the 1st Guards Mechanized Corps thrust south toward the key airfields at Tatsinskaya and Morozovsk, which were supporting the *Luftwaffe*'s effort to resupply Stalingrad.

The 11th Panzer Division, after departing the Chir River sector, moved west towards Tatsinskaya, 145 kilometres (90 miles) away, as the Soviet 1st Guard Army advanced towards the Black Sea. Balck understood the seriousness of the situation:

> The Italians had been swept away and the Russians unopposed were thrusting south with multiple tank corps. . . . One Russian tank corps was advancing from the north toward the town, with our fire brigades in its path. The Russians also were feinting an encirclement of Tatsinskaya on the left. The situation was desperate and the only hope was my tired and worn-out division, which was arriving piecemeal.[1]

On Christmas Eve, Major General Vasily Mikhailovich Badanov's 24th

Tank Corps, with around eighty operational tanks, captured Tatsinskaya and destroyed fifty-six German transport aircraft on the airfield.[2] Badanov had delivered a critical blow against Stalingrad's lifeline, but the 11th Panzer Division arrived in the area, as Balck recalled:

> I drove closely behind the lead tank. We encountered no enemy forces short of Skasyrskaya. It was therefore clear that the Russians were farther along, at Tatsinskaya. Reports started to come in confirming this. We took Skasyrskaya in an intense fight against a Russian battalion supported by tanks.[3]

By this time, Colonel Theodor Graf Schimmelmann's 15th Panzer Regiment only had twenty operational tanks. Balck decided to attack the 24th Tank Corps after deploying his forces in a ring around Tatsinskaya and his headquarters intercepted a radio signal from Badanov to his subordinate units: 'Enemy tanks in our rear. All tanks assemble on me at Hill 175.'[4] Balck now planned to first surround and destroy this enemy concentration. In the afternoon, the panzer spearhead engaged fifteen Russian tanks on the road to Tatsinskaya near Hill 175. Schimmelmann destroyed five enemy tanks but lost four Panzer III medium tanks during the fighting.[5]

On Christmas Day, the 11th Panzer Division surrounded Tatsinskaya, but Balck failed to destroy the trapped 24th Tank Corps:

> We tangled with each other all day long in the pocket and pushed the Russians into Tatsinskaia, but in the end we could not crack the pocket. There apparently were many more Russians inside the pocket than there were Germans outside of it.[6]

The recent fighting had further eroded the 11th Panzer Division's strength and Balck only had eight operational tanks.[7] To reinforce the inadequate siege forces, Balck had been given operational control of one regiment and the assault gun battalion from the 6th Panzer Division. However, the next day, his division lacked the strength to break into the Soviet positions after the assault gun battalion failed to arrive. Balck instead tightened the ring around the 24th Tank Corps.

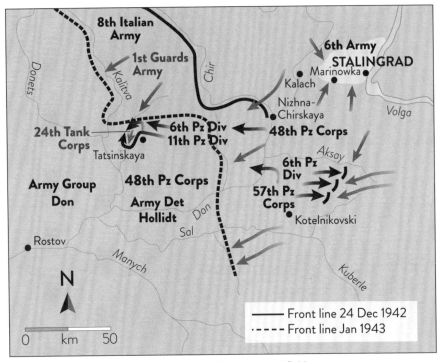

The 11th Panzer Division's counter-attack at Tatsinskaya airfield,
24–28 December 1942.

On 27 December, the 6th Panzer Division reinforced the German
position with thirty-one tanks and eight assault guns, and Balck attacked
Tatsinskaya from all directions, reducing the Red Army pocket:

> Our concentric attack on Tatsinskaya was starting to strangle the enemy,
> but his resistance was still significant. At least we were wearing him down
> significantly. We had destroyed twelve enemy tanks, but it was hard to
> estimate what they had left in the cauldron.[8]

News of the plight of Badanov's 24th Tank Corps at Tatsinskaya had reached
the highest Soviet levels. Stalin instructed Colonel General Nikolai Vatutin,
commander of the Southwestern Front: 'Your primary task is to prevent
the defeat of Badanov's corps.'[9] General Georgy Zhukov similar instructed
Vatutin: 'Keep Badanov in mind all the time. Rescue him at any cost.'[10]

On 28 December, the 11th Panzer Division finally captured Tatsinskaya as the shattered survivors of the 24th Tank Corps attempted a breakout. Balck's men looted the Red Army's supply depots in the village and threw chocolate, cigarettes and salami into Balck's *Kübelwagen*, shouting, 'We have to take care of our general too!'[11] The division soon received orders to withdraw and Balck noted: 'We left the area with a great deal of satisfaction. The 11th Panzer Division had the singular fortune to take on an enemy twice its strength and win a Cannae-like battle.'[12] However, Zhukov also felt a great deal of satisfaction with the conduct of the 24th Tank Corps:

> . . . the corps broke out of the encirclement thanks to the men's courage and Badanov's skilled guidance of the battle. They subsequently retreated in full fighting order to Ilyinka. Several days later this same formation successfully attacked Morozovsk. In token of its signal contribution to the enemy rout in the Volga-Don area, the 24th Corps was renamed the 2nd Guards Tatsinskaya Tank Corps, while its commander, Badanov, was the first in the USSR to be decorated with the Order of Suvorov, 2nd Class.[13]

After the 11th Panzer Division captured Tatsinskaya, Balck ordered his men to return to Skasyrskaya as the Soviet 266th Infantry Division had captured the village the previous night. The 15th Panzer Regiment and the mechanized infantry from the 110th Panzer Grenadier Regiment recaptured Skasyrskaya just before midday.

On 30 December, the Red Army cancelled Little Saturn, but the operation had forced Army Group Don to transfer the 48th Panzer Corps to the Morozovsk region, undermining the 4th Panzer Army's attempt to rescue the 6th Army in Stalingrad during Winter Storm.[14] That day, the 2nd Guards Mechanized Corps captured Chapurin and Aginov and headed north-west toward Tormosin while the 33rd Guards Rifle Division crossed the Don and advanced west after overcoming light resistance. The only hope of halting these Soviet offensives rested with the 11th Panzer Division.

On 31 December, Army Group Don ordered Balck to march south-east to Tsimlyansk on the Don to defend the western bank of the Tsimla River and halt the 2nd Guards Army's westward advance. The 11th Panzer Division, with twenty operational tanks, only succeeded in delaying the 2nd

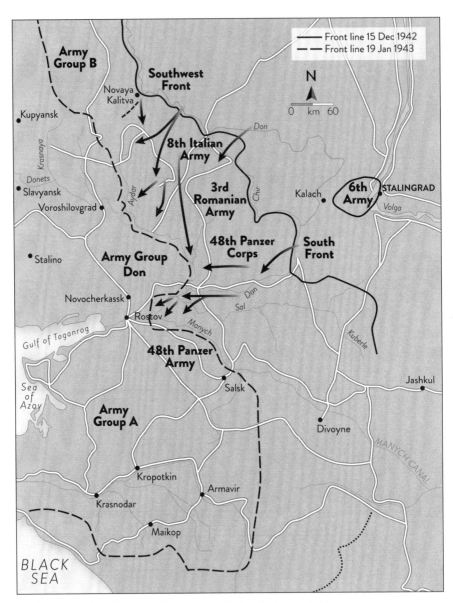

The Soviet threat to Rostov, 15 December 1942 to 19 January 1943.

Guards Army at the Tsimla River for three days.[15]

On New Year's Day, the High Command promoted Balck to lieutenant general. In January 1943, the 11th Panzer Division detached from the 48th

Panzer Corps and headed south from the Don to support 4th Panzer Army's defence of the Caucasus 'bottleneck', as Balck explained:

> Operations now focused on the control of Rostov. That was the bottleneck through which our withdrawing Army Group Caucasus had to pass. The Russians were closer to Rostov than was Army Group Caucasus. Even though some new units had arrived, the covering force near Rostov that was supposed to screen the withdrawal of Army Group Caucasus was pretty thin.[16]

The Soviet Southwestern and Southern Fronts continued to pressure Army Group Don, hoping to liberate Rostov and cut off Army Group A's withdrawal route from the Caucasus.[17] The Southwestern Front's 1st and 3rd Guards Army, the 5th Tank and the 5th Shock Army intended to exploit gains made during the Chir River battles and Little Saturn by wearing down German forces in the eastern Donbas region.[18]

On 8 January 1943, a Red Army breakthrough west of the 11th Panzer Division threatened to outflank the unit. Balck counter-attacked with Schimmelmann's 15th Panzer Regiment and Paul Freiherr von Hauser's 61st Motorcycle Battalion. The troops advanced 16 kilometres (10 miles), but Balck cancelled the attack after another nearby German division was at risk of being overrun. The counter-attack had nevertheless disrupted the Soviet thrust and the Red Army remained passive the next day.

On 10 January, the 61st Motorcycle Infantry Battalion, only fielding two companies, defended itself from an attack by a Red Army regiment. Hauser checked the assault with one company while the other flanked the attackers, causing the Russians to withdraw, and Balck noted in his journal: 'Hauser received a well-deserved Iron Cross Knight's Cross. It is impossible to reward such troops adequately.'[19] He also visited the weary battalion:

> I was able to assemble them in the forwardmost line and thank these faithful men personally. They looked audacious, unwashed, and unshaved. For days they had been sleeping outside in sub-zero Fahrenheit temperatures, but they were quite alive and feisty. With such soldiers and officers you could do anything. Hauser took good care of them. Behind

A German machine gunner and an anti-tank gun during the Russian winter.
(Sueddeutsche Zeitung Photo/Alamy Stock Photo)

the front he established warm-up trucks with iron stoves, and at regular
intervals everybody had an opportunity to thaw out for two hours.[20]

The 11th Panzer Division moved north behind the 1st Panzer Army and
Balck received orders to advance north to counter the 3rd Tank Corps and 4th
Guards Tank Corps. After the division approached Kramatorsk, the troops
engaged the 5th Shock Army in bitter fighting but failed to capture the town
over the next few days. Balck took personal responsibility for this defeat: 'I had
attacked before every one of my units was assembled. I did exactly what I had
so often criticized others of doing. The division's first failure was my fault.'[21]

Lieutenant General Markian Popov's 5th Shock Army attacked the
11th Panzer Division with his 4th Guards Tank Corps as the 10th Tank
Corps continued to resist from Kramatorsk. Balck again failed to capture
Kramatorsk, but he contained the 3rd and 10th Tank Corps in the town:

The Russians, meanwhile, were still interpreting our probing attacks as break-out attempts from the encirclement they thought they were forming around us, while we in fact were encircling them.[22]

Balck advocated bypassing Kramatorsk and advancing south into the rear of the 5th Shock Army and received permission to attempt the manoeuvre from the 1st Panzer Army. On 18 January, the 11th Panzer Division withdrew from Kramatorsk to prepare for the new operation.

The 11th Panzer Division advanced towards Novotroitsk on 19 January, using snowploughs to clear a path for the motorcycle troops and tanks. As the Germans entered the village, Balck parked his *Kübelwagen* next to Schimmelmann's tank and ordered Major Kaldrack to fetch the regimental commander. After Kaldrack returned, he announced, 'Sir, the Graf said that there is still heavy fighting going on in the village, and whether you would not rather join him in his tank.' Balck replied, 'Nonsense, you cannot see anything from a tank. I want Schimmelmann to come with me.' Kaldrack returned again and pleaded, 'I am supposed to report from the Graf that if the general does not behave and come forward with him in his tank, he will not go.'[23] Balck laughed before climbing on board Schimmelmann's panzer.

Balck's division attacked the 5th Shock Army from the rear, completely surprising Popov and shattering the 4th Guards Tank Corps:

By the time my division finally pivoted toward the north, there was no more fighting, only pursuit, during which we passed, cut off, and destroyed one Russian combat group after another.[24]

The 11th Panzer Division devastated the 5th Shock Army and captured Barvenkovo.

On 22 January, the 11th Panzer Division reached Rostov where the men spent the day resting. Field Marshal Erich von Manstein ordered the division to counter the Soviet offensive towards the Manych River, which had established a dangerous bridgehead on the south bank of the Don. The Red Army had pushed the 4th Panzer Army back to the Manych River, south-east of Rostov, and the 3rd Guards Tank Corps commanded by Major General Pavel Rotmistrov liberated Manychskaya village where the

Manych meets the Don, 20 kilometres (12 miles) north-east of Rostov. The 3rd Guards Tank Corps, previously the 7th Tank Corps, had fought Balck near Voronezh in July 1942 during the initial stage of Case Blue and later operated in the lower Chir as part of the 5th Shock Army.

On the morning of 23 January, the 11th Panzer Division advanced towards Manychskaya and overran weak Russian resistance before reaching the outskirts of the village. Balck attacked the Manychskaya bridgehead the next day, but the 3rd Guards Tank Corps, defending the village with dug-in tanks, repulsed three assaults. Balck explained his failure in an after-action report: 'An enemy tank force drove up and down the village street, constantly shifting superior forces into position at the right time and frustrating every attempt to break in.'[25]

On 25 January, Balck attacked again and, while his artillery concentrated its fire on the north-eastern sector, a small force of armoured cars and half-tracks conducted a feint attack under a smokescreen:

> The fake attack was staged to draw the Russian tanks to the northern end of the village, then to attack the southern end supported by strong artillery and Stuka preparations, and attack from the rear those Russian tanks that were drawn toward the northern end.[26]

After the Soviet tanks moved north to meet the perceived threat, the artillery suddenly bombarded the southern sector and Schimmelmann's 15th Panzer Regiment attacked. Balck observed his troops surge forward:

> Sitting up on a hill I observed how the dug-in Russian tanks came to life, left their positions, and drove toward the rear of the position of the ruse attack. Quickly, then, the fires of all available artillery were shifted to the location of the actual attack. Only one battery continued to fire smoke rounds in the direction of the feint attack. Then I launched my tanks.[27]

The attacking panzers assaulted the Red Army armour massed in the northern end of the village from the rear, destroying twenty-one tanks while only losing one panzer, shattering the 3rd Guards Tank Corps.[28] Only one soldier from the 11th Panzer Division had been killed while fourteen had been wounded.

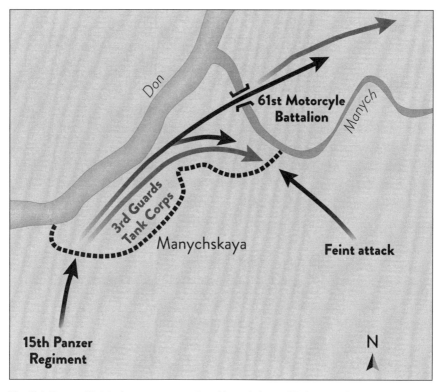

The 11th Panzer Division's counter-attack at Manychskaya, 25 January 1943.

Major General Pavel Rotmistrov survived the battle and would later command the 5th Guards Tank Army and become chief of Red Army armoured and mechanized forces.

After destroying the Manychskaya bridgehead, the 11th Panzer Division was pulled out of the front line, and Balck praised the endurance of his men who had prevailed despite weeks of near continuous operations:

> For weeks on end the division moved by night, and before dawn was at the very spot where the enemy was weakest, waiting to attack him an hour before he was ready to move. Such tactics called for unheard-of efforts, but saved lives, as the attack proper cost very few casualties, thanks to the Russians having been taken completely by surprise.[29]

Colonel Graf Theodor Schimmelmann.
(Author's Collection)

On 28 January, the 11th Panzer Division defended Rostov, which enabled the 1st Panzer Army to withdraw from the Caucasus. That night, Balck billeted in a village:

> I spent a cozy evening in the small house of a teacher. A clever device fed sunflower seeds into her stove, filling the room with a comfortable warmth. A balalaika hung on the wall. It had the most beautiful sound I ever heard. The people and the land here were different than in the North. The treeless countryside, showing all the contours in an even more pronounced way, had its own charm, especially when the setting winter sun covered everything in a violet light. The inhabitants were not excited about the approaching Reds. We were in the lands of the Don Cossacks.[30]

The 11th Panzer Division destroyed a Soviet anti-tank brigade near Kamenyi the next day before repulsing an attack by the 248th Rifle Division supported by two rifle brigades, which had attempted a breakout from an encirclement. On 30 January, Balck's troops completed their destruction:

> It turned out to be a successful day. We completely destroyed whatever was facing us or had already been encircled. The members of the enemy divisional staffs tore off their rank insignias or committed suicide.[31]

As Balck defended Rostov, Friedrich Paulus' 6th Army in Stalingrad disintegrated. On 16 January, the Red Army captured the main airfield at Pitomnik and, ten days later, the Soviets split the remaining pocket in half. Paulus, recently promoted to field marshal, surrendered on 31 January and the last German resistance was crushed two days later. The 6th Army had suffered 147,000 men killed and 91,000 became prisoners.[32] After Paulus surrendered, Balck wrote in his journal: 'The heroes of Stalingrad have given their lives to buy the time necessary to open up the new front.'[33]

In February, the 11th Panzer Division was pulled out of the line to rest and refit but soon deployed near Kharkov. On 20 February, the division attacked the Red Army near Nowa Alexandrowka in support of Manstein's counter-offensive towards Kharkov, causing the enemy to respond with fragmented and unplanned counter-attacks, resulting in fifteen Russian tanks destroyed with no panzer losses.[34] Balck used his 209th Pioneer Battalion to destroy a Red Army tank attack one week later, as he explained in an after-action report:

> The Battalion had laid a mine barrier during the night, guarded by an 8.8mm Flak gun. At dawn, five Russian tanks charged at high speed. Two ran onto mines; one was destroyed by the Flak gun. The other two broke into the village at high speed and were destroyed by close-combat teams.[35]

On 13 March 1943, Balck's tenure commanding the 11th Panzer Division ended, two days before German forces recaptured Kharkov. 'While in the Kharkov area my reassignment orders to the Leaders Reserve caught up with me,' he recalled. 'My time as a division commander was over. It was time to say farewell.'[36] He visited his regiments and thanked his men: 'I could with good conscience recommend all of my regimental commanders for divisional command.'[37] Balck ultimately attributed his success to the calibre of his men:

Well-trained, older Panzer crews are the decisive factor for success. Their experience, in addition to their calmness and self-assuredness gained through previous successes, is the basis for all of the great achievements.[38]

Balck also noted that the division's impressive performance 'was due mainly to the high morale of the troops, their determined will to fight, and the quality of their commanders'.[39] In particular, he praised an outstanding maintenance NCO, Kurt Reuschel, from the 15th Panzer Regiment who had played a critical role in keeping his tanks operational despite battle damage and strain caused by the winter weather.

During the Chir River battles and subsequent operations near Rostov, the 11th Panzer Division lost 215 men killed in action, 1019 wounded and 155 missing. Balck believed his division killed 30,700 Red Army soldiers and he also estimated enemy tank losses:

During the period from 28 June 1942 to 11 March 1943, the division knocked out 1000 tanks, of which 664 were knocked out by Panzer-Regiment 15 and 336 by other weapons. Of the latter, 65 were destroyed by tank-hunter teams in close combat. This compares to our own losses of 50 Panzers as total write-offs.[40]

The 11th Panzer Division continued to fight in the Kharkov area until June 1943. The division fought at Kursk in July, the greatest tank battle in history, and was later virtually destroyed in the Cherkassy Pocket in February 1944. The rebuilt division transferred to the Western Front in June and conducted delaying operations up the Rhone Valley the following month. The division later fought in the Ardennes during the battle of the Bulge and escaped being trapped in the Ruhr Pocket in 1945, only to surrender to the American 90th Infantry Division in Bavaria on 2 May.

Theodor Graf von Schimmelmann later became a general staff officer in Jutland. 'His ancestry, family connections, and language skills particularly suited him for that assignment,' Balck observed. 'I would have liked to see him as a divisional commander.'[41] Schimmelmann and Balck remained close after the war. Schimmelmann died on 19 November 1970.

On 2 March 1943, Albert Henze was awarded the German Cross in

A Red Army tank crew on the Eastern Front.
(Archive PL/Alamy Stock Photo)

Gold for his command of the 110th Panzer Grenadier Regiment during the Chir River battles. He later received the Knight's Cross with Oak Leaves and commanded the 30th and 60th Divisions on the Eastern Front and was eventually captured by the Red Army in the Courland Pocket towards the end of the war. After being held in Soviet custody until 1955, he died on 31 March 1979.

Alexander von Bosse later commanded the 1st Cossack Division, mostly comprised of Don Cossack volunteers who agreed to fight the Soviet Union. In 1945, he retreated to Austria with his Cossacks and surrendered to the British. Although the British transferred the Cossacks to Soviet custody, they released Bosse and he later died on 23 April 1978.

On 28 October 1944, Paul Graf von Hauser received the Knight's Cross with Oak Leaves for his command of the 901st Panzer Grenadier Regiment in France. He later commanded the *Panzerlehr* Division in April 1945. After surrendering to American soldiers, he lived in Vienna and died on 1 April 1999.

Nikolai Vatutin, still commanding the Southwest Front, expelled the *Wehrmacht* from the Eastern Ukraine until Manstein's counterstroke at Kharkov recaptured the city. Vatutin later commanded the Voronezh Front at Kursk and liberated Kiev in November 1943. In the following year,

A Panzer III medium tank and German soldiers struggling in the Russian winter.
(Bundesarchiv, Bild 146-2000-013-21A)

Vatutin's Voronezh Front inflicted heavy casualties on the Germans at the Korsun salient and the Cherkassy Pocket. However, on 28 February 1944, Ukrainian nationalists killed Vatutin in an ambush.

Markian Popov later commanded the Bryansk Front at Kursk and the 2nd Baltic Front until April 1944. However, after denouncing a commissar, he was demoted to chief-of-staff of the Leningrad Front but returned to favour after the Stalin era and was promoted to Chief of the General Staff of the Soviet Ground Forces.

Balck's command of the 11th Panzer Division, particularly during the Chir River battles, established his reputation as one of the finest armoured warfare leaders in the German Army. The High Command accordingly awarded him the Knight's Cross with Swords on 4 March 1943.

Although Little Saturn failed to capture Rostov, its true purpose had been to undermine Winter Storm and seal the fate of the 6th Army in Stalingrad. Although Balck had won outstanding tactical battles, these had occurred within the context of a larger strategic disaster, which turned the tide of war against Germany. Although the war continued until 1945, Balck would remain on the defensive, fighting at the operational level of war — as a corps, army and army group commander — against increasingly desperate odds, until the fall of the Third Reich.

EPILOGUE

Balck was a likable character because he did not take himself too seriously. He went on winning battles, just as Picasso went on painting pictures, without pretentiousness or pious talk. He won battles because the skill came to him naturally. He never said that battle-winning was a particularly noble or virtuous activity; it was simply his trade.

Freeman Dyson

GÖTTERDÄMMERUNG

After Balck left the 11th Panzer Division, he briefly commanded the *Grossdeutschland* Division before departing Russia. As his Berlin home had been destroyed in a bombing raid, he spent time with his family in Silesia where they lived in a castle.

Balck next commanded the 14th Panzer Corps in Italy in September 1943, opposing the Allied landing at Salerno. He counter-attacked the beachhead with the 16th Panzer Division and the *Hermann Göring* Panzer Division, forcing the Allies back towards Salerno while General Mark Clark's 5th Army faced the prospect of being pushed into the sea. Balck, however, failed to adequately reinforce the 16th Panzer Division — as he retained a large reserve to counter other potential landings — and his troops lacked the strength to destroy the beachhead. This decision historian David Zabecki assessed to be one of Balck's 'few battlefield mistakes'.

As Balck fought the western Allies in Italy, the Red Army launched a major offensive at the Dnieper River which liberated Kiev on 6 November

1943. Field Marshal Erich von Manstein planned to recapture the Ukrainian capital with the 48th Panzer Corps. Manstein placed Balck, who had been promoted to General of Panzer Troops on 12 November, in command: 'That's where the point of decision will be and that's where I need the best Panzer leader.' Balck also became reacquainted with Colonel Friedrich von Mellenthin, the 48th Panzer Corps' chief-of-staff, with whom he had worked closely during the Chir River battles: 'It was an extremely "happy marriage," which I now continued with this outstanding General Staff officer.'

As the 48th Panzer Corps contained the 1st Panzer Division, Balck had a bittersweet reunion with the 1st Motorized Regiment, the unit he commanded in France in 1940:

> I was able to greet by name quite a number of old acquaintances among the enlisted troops. The current regimental commander was Lieutenant Colonel von Seydlitz, who in France had been a senior lieutenant and company commander under me. But such moments brought home to me the unbelievable levels of attrition we had experienced. Very few officers of the old cadre were still with the unit; many of them had been killed.

Before advancing towards Kiev, Balck needed to first eliminate the Red Army around Zhitomir. The 48th Panzer Corps had advanced 30 kilometres (18.5 miles) into the First Ukrainian Front's flank and he captured the city on 17 November.

The Red Army responded with a large counter-attack launched by the 3rd Guards Tank Army at Brusilov. Balck contained the Soviet offensive and, by 15 December, he succeeded in stabilizing the front. He next attempted to envelop Soviet forces near Korosten but, as Mellenthin explained, 'the Russian resistance stiffened and on 21 December their forces in the pocket launched counterattacks on a scale which took our breath away'. Balck attempted to surround three armoured corps and four rifle corps but soon abandoned the encirclement given the vast size of the enemy force. On 23 December, the 48th Panzer Corps went on the defensive as Balck lacked the strength to recapture Kiev.

Mellenthin nevertheless noted the great tactical success Balck had achieved during the campaign:

... the conduct of operations was the most brilliant in my experience. General Balck handled his corps with masterly skill; he showed a complete understanding of the classic principles of maneuver and surprise, and he displayed a resourcefulness, a flexibility, and an insight into tactical problems, strongly reminiscent of the methods of the great captains of history.

Balck's troops had destroyed two Russian armies, crippled a third and knocked out 700 Soviet tanks.

On Christmas Day, the Red Army launched a massive offensive near Brusilov as the 1st Tank Army and 1st Guards Army advanced west from Kiev. After Balck spotted Red Army tank columns near Teterev at dawn, he immediately attacked an overwhelmingly superior force with no prospect of success, a decision his superior, General Erhard Raus — commander of the 3rd Panzer Army — understandably criticized:

General Balck could not resist the temptation and, instead of following his instructions, decided to make an immediate surprise attack against the open enemy flank. Unfortunately, this flank attack had no chance of succeeding, because 150 German panzers could neither combat nor even deflect the mass of Russian armor that had meanwhile grown to nearly 1,000 tanks.

However, over the next six days, Balck repulsed repeated Soviet attacks, which Raus praised: 'the Russians attempted to break through General Balck's lines, but the only visible results they achieved could be calculated by their mounting tank losses'. He continued: 'General Balck's blocking force formed the steel clamp that held together the isolated infantry corps and preserved the army from disintegration.'

On 14 July 1944, Balck attempted to repulse a Red Army offensive in the Galician region of the Ukraine by counter-attacking with the 1st Panzer Division at Oleyyov. The assault blunted the Russian advance, but the Soviets later overran the 48th Panzer Corps' left flank and, although he soon restored the front, the defence of southern Galicia had become untenable. As the Red Army entered Poland, the 48th Panzer Corps retreated into the Carpathian Mountains.

Hitler presents Hermann Balck with the Knight's Cross with Oak Leaves,
Swords and Diamonds.
(Author's Collection)

After departing the Ukraine, Balck took command of the 4th Panzer
Army in August 1944 and Mellenthin continued to serve as his chief-of-staff.
On 10 August, the 4th Panzer Army counter-attacked the Red Army at the
Sandomierz bridgehead in Poland. The 3rd Panzer Corps achieved initial
success before running out of steam, but Balck's counter-stroke stopped the
Russian offensive in the Vistula bend, earning him the Knight's Cross with
Oak Leaves, Swords and Diamonds.

In September 1944, Balck reported to Hitler's headquarters where the
dictator gave him command of Army Group G in France. After arriving in
Alsace with Mellenthin, Balck had orders to halt the American 3rd Army,
commanded by General George S. Patton, in Lorraine in order to buy
time for the upcoming winter offensive in the Ardennes, which would later
become known as the Battle of the Bulge.

Balck organized his inferior forces — a ragtag assortment of understrength
units — to fight an elastic defence centred on the Metz Fortress. He tied down
a significant number of Patton's troops at Metz while his mobile panzer forces

disrupted the American advance towards the West Wall. As Balck delayed Patton's troops in Alsace-Lorraine, his men also engaged the American 7th Army and the French 2nd Armoured Division in bitter fighting. Although the Americans captured the Metz Fortress on 21 November, Balck achieved his strategic objective, as Mellenthin explained:

> The whole front of Army Group G was under continuous pressure. The enemy was achieving important successes, but we were keeping our forces relatively intact and falling back slowly to the West Wall; I must emphasize that throughout these operations our object was to fight for time and so enable O.K.W. to assemble reserves for the great counteroffensive in Belgium.

By delaying the Allies around Metz, Strasbourg and Belfort, Balck successfully bought time for the Ardennes offensive, which commenced on 16 December 1944. Mellenthin departed Army Group G in December and never again served under Balck: 'It was a bitter experience for me to terminate my long and happy association with General Balck.'

Balck returned to the Eastern Front to command the German 6th Army in Hungary with orders to relieve the Soviet siege of Budapest. Operation Spring Awakening would be the *Wehrmacht*'s last major offensive. The 6th SS Panzer Army and Balck's troops planned to destroy the Red Army's 3rd Ukrainian Front between the Balaton and Velence lakes. The offensive commenced on 6 March 1945, and Balck's 6th Army initially made good progress but a Soviet counter-attack ten days later doomed Spring Awakening. As the Third Reich faced total collapse, Balck worried about the fate of his family in Silesia as he retreated towards Austria with his men. After arriving, they surrendered to Major General Horace McBride's American 80th Infantry Division on 8 May 1945. General Hermann Balck's war ended as the guns went silent on VE Day.

COMMAND PRINCIPLES

The foundation of Balck's outstanding success as a commander was his avoidance of dogma. He had learned that lesson in World War I after witnessing how the power of artillery, machine guns and barbed wire conferred an advantage to defenders only to see trench-mortars and tanks shift this advantage back to the attackers. Balck realized that nothing is permanent 'as every situation is different and subject to change'. He accordingly avoided fixed methods and always improvised solutions to planning problems:

> First and foremost, never follow a rigid scheme. Every situation is different — no two are the same. Even if they appear to be the same, in one case the troops will be fresh while in another they'll be fatigued. That difference will lead to different decisions. I'm against the school approach that says, 'In accordance with the ideas of the General Staff, in this situation you must do thus and such'. On the contrary, you must proceed as dictated by the personalities involved and the particulars of the situation.

Balck accepted the chaos of war and refused to follow doctrinal solutions, possessing what the German Army calls *fingerspitzengefuehl* (fingertip feeling), an instinctive sixth sense for terrain, tactics and the art of war. He understood that success leads to complacency, which encourages predicable planning, which in turn invites defeat: 'If you repeat yourself you end up playing with open cards and handing the advantage to the enemy.' Therefore, Balck cautioned against dogma in favour of creative thinking:

> Never do the same thing twice. Even if something works well for you once, by the second time the enemy will have adapted. So you have to think up something new. No one thinks of becoming a great painter simply by imitating Michelangelo. Similarly, you can't become a great military leader just by imitating so and so. It has to come from within. In the last analysis, military command is an art: one man can do it and most will never learn. After all, the world is not full of Raphaels either.

General Heinrich Gaedcke, who served as the 6th Army's chief-of-staff in Hungary in 1945, recalled how Balck taught him how to think creatively:

General Balck taught me to ask, 'Where is the enemy strong?' He'll be strong at the forward point of the bridgehead and at the two shoulders. The weak points are the two stretches between the point and each of the shoulders. And where is the enemy commander? His headquarters will be between those two weak stretches. So I cut through the weak stretches, slice open the bulge from two sides, grab the headquarters and the whole bridgehead will collapse by itself without exposing me to heavy defenses. That's what I call innovative leadership, far indeed from the standardized, rigid approach.

The *kampfgruppe* concept epitomized Balck's thinking on how to organize troops in battle. In France in May 1940, he realized the foolishness of organizing troops in rigid 'infantry regiments' and 'panzer regiments', which resulted in a near disaster at Sedan after his riflemen crossed the Meuse River without panzer support. Balck's solution to the traditional organization of soldiers was to form mission-orientated battlegroups consisting of the right balance of forces need to achieve the given objective. Balck personally perfected this combined arms approach in the mountains of Greece where he outmanoeuvred Australian and New Zealand troops in terrain ideally suited to defensive warfare. The soldiers of *Kampfgruppe Balck* — a mixed assortment of capabilities drawn from panzer, infantry, motorcycle, engineer and artillery units — consistently outperformed the Allied soldiers fighting in rigid World War I platoon, company and battalion formations.

Balck also distinguished himself with his forward presence on the battlefield, trusting his subordinates such as Mellenthin to keep everything under control at his headquarters. By giving up centralized control, Balck gained control of what was really important — fleeting opportunities at the front which he exploited to maximum effect. He would be at the *schwerpunkt*, the focal point, where a decisive decision can win a battle:

I commanded from the front by radio and could thus always be at the most critical point of action. I would transmit my commands to the Chief of Staff, and then it was up to him to make sure that they were passed on to the right units and that the right actions were taken. The result was to give us a fantastic superiority over the divisions facing us.

Mellenthin appreciated the wisdom of Balck's approach:

> General Balck and myself were very close. When he went to the front
> lines I stayed behind and kept all things under control while he was at the
> Schwerpunkt, or vice versa. I myself, every second or third day, went to the
> front. General Balck then sat at the desk at Corps or Army Headquarters.
> . . . I had complete freedom when he was away — to make my own
> decisions.

Balck's forward command style contrasted strongly with the Allied and Russian commanders, who usually commanded their soldiers over the telephone or radio from rear headquarters. 'The secret of modern armor leadership is that everything has to happen in the blink of an eye,' he explained. 'That can only be accomplished if the commander is right at the point of action.' Balck would give his subordinate commanders brief verbal orders which would be swiftly executed:

> The most important thing was that I gave all orders verbally. Even my
> largest and most important operations orders were verbal. . . . I always
> prized most highly those commanders that needed to be given the least
> orders — those you could discuss the matter with for five minutes and
> then not worry about them for the next eight days.

Balck's record of combat success also reflected his men who fought the hard battles and his subordinate commanders who enjoyed a great deal of command responsibility under the Prussian principle of *auftragstaktik* (mission tactics). He usually told his subordinate commanders what he wanted them to achieve but allowed their initiative to determine exactly how this would be done:

> Generally the German higher commander rarely or never reproached their
> subordinates unless they made a terrible blunder. They were fostering
> the individual's initiative. They left him room for initiative, and did not
> reprimand him unless he did something very wrong. This went down to
> the individual soldier, who was praised for developing initiative.

Balck realized that 'combat leadership is largely a matter of psychology. As much as possible, I tried not to tell my people what to do', he said. 'As long as I saw that a man was sound, I let him do things his way, even if I would have done them differently.' However, in rejecting fixed schemes, he also knew that less-talented subordinates could not be trusted with too much independence. 'It depended entirely on the subordinate,' Balck explained. 'If he was a stupid fellow, you had to go into much detail explaining the situation to him; if he was an intelligent officer, a word was sufficient for him.'

While Balck mastered the art of armoured warfare, he did not end the war with clean hands, although no evidence has come to light indicating that he participated in the Holocaust or murdered civilians. During the Lorraine campaign in November 1944, Balck discovered that Lieutenant Colonel Johann Schottke, the divisional artillery commander, was drunk in his bunker and unaware of where his batteries were located. Balck ordered Schottke's summary execution, which was duly carried out. In 1948, a civilian court in Stuttgart found that he had not acted within the framework of the German military justice and sentenced him to three years in prison and he served eighteen months.

In November 1944, while Balck opposed the American advance through Vosges, he ordered the civilian population of Gérardmer towards the Allied lines. In the subsequent fighting, his forces virtually destroyed the town. In 1950, a French military tribunal in Paris tried Balck in absentia with the war crime of destroying Gérardmer and sentenced him to twenty years in prison, a verdict he condemned as hypocritical: 'It was predictable that the French would show no understanding in this case, although they later did exactly the same sort of things in Indochina and Algeria.' However, the American occupation authorities and the West German government refused to extradite Balck so he never spent any time in a French prison.

On 19 September 1949, a West German Denazification Court cleared Balck, concluding, 'These proceedings have found no causal connection between this man and National Socialism.' However, Balck never really came to terms with having fought for the Nazi regime or the suffering the *Wehrmacht* caused. Although he acknowledged the crimes of the Nazis, he never acknowledged how his actions contributed to the suffering inside occupied counties.

After the conquest of Greece, German forces requisitioned food and medicine which resulted in the deaths of 100,000 Athenians. By the end of the war, over 500,000 Greek civilians had died from disease, starvation and reprisals while 59,000 Greek Jews were murdered during the Holocaust, leaving only 14,000 survivors. After Allied soldiers liberated the country in October 1944, they found a malnourished and exhausted population. Although Balck had played such a critical role during the German invasion of Greece, he never linked his actions with this level of death and suffering.

Balck never acknowledged that during Operation Barbarossa, the *Wehrmacht* was a willing participant in Hitler's criminal ideological war against 'Jewish Bolshevism' in Russia.[31] After the war, he remained vocal about Red Army war crimes, notably the massacre of German soldiers at Sovchos 79. However, he never spoke of the *Wehrmacht*'s crimes in Russia, such as the 'Commissar Order', which called for the immediate execution of all Soviet political officers, or its wilful support of the Holocaust, such as the massacre of Ukrainian Jews at Babi Yar in September 1941. Balck never acknowledged the *Wehrmacht*'s criminal nature and never fully came to terms with the evil cause that his extraordinary talents had served. Furthermore, his claim in *Order in Chaos* to be ignorant of the Holocaust's true nature is simply unconvincing.[32]

Balck also struggled to reconcile his mostly fond wartime memories of Hitler and post-war acceptance of the man's crimes. Balck certainly could have killed Hitler if he had wished: 'I was never required to surrender my pistol while visiting Hitler; and if I had decided to use it, nobody could have stopped me.'[33] During the war, he opposed Claus von Stauffenberg's assassination attempt, but he was also friends with the man:

I had known Stauffenberg well for a long time. We had been assigned to the same cavalry brigade. I often had many pleasant conversations with this intelligent man who was highly educated in history.[34]

When Balck became aware that Stauffenberg had become highly critical of the regime, he warned him: 'We are for better or for worse tied to Hitler.'[35] However, after the war, he acknowledged that Stauffenberg 'acted as he saw right' and that he 'will always hold Stauffenberg in honorable remembrance'.[36] Balck's final verdict on Hitler concluded:

> But despite all my conscious efforts to evaluate Hitler with complete
> objectivity, I cannot escape the final verdict — he was our downfall.
> Beware of strong men who do not know the limits of their power.[37]

Even with the benefit of post-war hindsight, Balck's analysis of Hitler cannot escape his memoirs from the time he had fallen under the dictator's spell.

BALCK'S LAST BATTLE

After being released from American custody in 1947, Balck worked in a warehouse in Germany and later represented well-known firms, living an obscure life. Mellenthin meanwhile immigrated to South Africa where he worked in the aviation industry and later became director of Lufthansa in Africa. Although Balck had refused to participate in the United States Army Historical Division's work while a prisoner of war, Mellenthin did and developed five monographs before finding fame with his bestselling book *Panzer Battles*. Mellenthin would again work with the American military and this time he convinced Balck to break his thirty-year silence.

After the United States experienced defeat in Vietnam, the American Army refocused on its traditional Cold War role — defeating a possible Red Army invasion of Western Europe — but it faced a dilemma in determining how this could be achieved given the numerical superiority of Warsaw Pact forces compared with NATO's. Balck had the perfect credentials to help solve this problem as David Zabecki and Dieter Biedekarken explained:

> . . . the U.S. Army's major challenge was to develop a tactical and
> operational doctrine for fighting outnumbered and winning against the
> overwhelming numerically superior tank forces of the Soviet Union and
> the Warsaw Pact. Balck, of course, was one of the undisputed masters of
> just that.[38]

The army's leadership accordingly invited Mellenthin and Balck to America, seeking their advice on how to fight while being outnumbered and win against overwhelming Soviet strength. Consequently, during the late 1970s and early 1980s, both men participated in interviews, seminars, conferences and wargames facilitated by the American Army's War College.[39] 'Balck and Mellenthin,' as Dennis Showalter explained, 'made virtual second careers in the late 1970s as think-tank consultants advising the US Army how to fight outnumbered against the Soviet Union in the Fulda Gap and win panzer-style.'[40]

General William E. DePuy understood that Balck and Mellenthin's combat experiences on the Eastern Front gave them tactical expertise the American Army lacked:

> . . . they achieved a virtually unmatched record of battlefield success, despite being greatly outnumbered, in terms of men and materiel, on many occasions. Indeed, toward the end of the war it became the normal condition. Of special significance for us today is the fact that while expecting to be outnumbered by as much as ten or more to one, they also expected to win — and often did.[41]

Balck provided authoritative advice to the American military on how to destroy Red Army tank formations and, in particular, his conduct during the Chir River battles impressed his audience.

In May 1980, Balck and Mellenthin participated in a conference and wargame on NATO tactics at the Army War College hosted by the BDM Corporation. DePuy arranged the event 'to examine twentieth century German military experience in battle against Russian forces' in order to develop 'insights useful in aiding our understanding of the challenges NATO faces today in Europe as it prepares to confront the Soviets in any future conflict'.[42] DePuy found himself in awe of Balck and noted in his report on the conference:

> General Balck tends to be a man of few words — somewhat brusque — almost laconic, but deeply thoughtful. He was, and is, clearly a man of iron will and iron nerves. He exudes a strong aura of confidence — confidence in himself, in the German Army and in the German soldier.[43]

The activities included a wargame in which Balck and Mellenthin assumed command of the 3rd Armoured Division to defend West Germany against a Warsaw Pact invasion in the Hunfeld–Lauterbach–Bad Hersfeld sector of the country, which included the Kassel–Frankfurt Autobahn. They were both astounded to discover that their division contained 325 main battle tanks.

Balck and Mellenthin had to deploy the division to defend as close as possible to the East German border to keep the Red Army out of the West German heartland. They were expected to slow the Warsaw Pact advance, locate its main effort and destroy the enemy force as far forward as possible. After conferring over the situation map, Mellenthin announced that they would not take long, adding that on the Eastern Front they normally decided upon a course of action in five minutes.[44]

Balck and Mellenthin's plan involved deploying three cavalry squadrons as a covering force to screen the battlefield between the border and the main battle position. Two brigades would defend the southern sector, supported by artillery, tactical airpower and attack helicopters with orders to defend the area. They left the north-western sector open to entice the Red Army to commit two tank divisions to advance along the Autobahn toward Alsfeld and Giessen, hoping to create an operational breakthrough. As these Soviet divisions advanced along the Autobahn, five American battalions would attack their flank just north of Lauterbach and destroy the entire force. After Warsaw Pact forces advanced beyond Alsfeld, a NATO counter-attack would strike the rear of the lead enemy division and the vanguard of the next division. Balck and Mellenthin added that such a manoeuvre would require a NATO commander with strong nerves.

American observers questioned Balck and Mellenthin on the wisdom of allowing a Russian tank division into the rear area near the population centre of Frankfurt. They replied that the deeper the enemy advances, the greater the opportunity to destroy the force; however, upon further reflection they decided it would be wiser to deploy a delaying force on the Autobahn to protect German civilians and Balck later added: 'We were very much hampered towards the end of the war in our mobility, because we could not let the Russians get into areas that were settled by Germans.'[45] DePuy considered Balck and Mellenthin's plan a risky gamble:

The boldness — indeed the audacity — of their plan might be regarded as irresponsible, had it been proposed by other parties. But their willingness to open up the battle was rooted in their highly successful experiences and cannot be dismissed. Presumably they had learned that the big pay-offs came under conditions in which they — not the Russians — shaped the battlefield and retained the initiative. They must also have believed that nothing less than big pay-offs could solve the problem with which they were faced.[46]

Lieutenant General Paul Gorman independently conducted the same wargame and his solution involved defending the northern sector and deploying a covering force to draw Warsaw Pact forces into a pocket near Fulda, where they would be destroyed in a counter-attack from the south. A brigade would defend the sector east of Fulda while two brigades with artillery support would conduct an 'active defence' in the rugged Hohe Rhoen region where some ground could be yielded to the Soviets without allowing a significant enemy advance. A large brigade of three tank and one mechanized battalions would form a mobile reserve south of Fulda and would either counter-attack the south flank of the Soviet main advance as its vanguard reached the defensive position near Fulda or against the Soviets near Alsfeld, if their main effort approached that region.

Balck and Mellenthin praised General Gorman's plan and noted that it conformed with their concept on how to fight the Red Army. Balck even declared to Gorman that they were 'brothers under the skin'.[47] DePuy also noted the convergence of American and German operational thinking:

The similarity between the two concepts — the German and American — was remarkable. In both cases, the larger part of the sector was held by the smallest part of the force. In both cases, the enemy was 'invited in' to a selected avenue or pocket. In both cases, a large reserve was held out for a decisive counterattack. The principal (and only significant) difference lay in the fact that the German generals wished to let the Russians go on — the farther the better — while General Gorman planned to stop them cold in front of Fulda.[48]

DePuy acknowledged the risky nature of the German plan and concluded that in 'the hands of average commanders it would probably be a disaster.

In the hands of a Balck, working with a von Mellenthin, it is an option with distinguished historical precedent.'[49] DePuy, pleased with the outcome of the wargame, believed that Balck and Mellenthin had helped demonstrate that a smaller well-led force could synchronize its operations and defeat a larger less-organized force, as the *Wehrmacht* had achieved on numerous occasions on the Eastern Front.[50] Balck's legacy became part of the way the American Army fights, influencing all western militaries, as David Zabecki and Dieter Biedekarken explained:

> German tactical doctrine, especially as it had been practiced by Balck against the Russians, had a clear influence on the development of the new American doctrine, called AirLand Battle. From the mid-1980s through the early 1990s the study of Balck's December 1942 battle on the Chir River as commander of the 11th Panzer Division was a standard element in the formal course of instruction at the U.S. Army Command and General Staff College. It was held up as one of the best historical examples of the tactical principles embodied in AirLand Battle.[51]

Balck had kept a detailed journal throughout World War I and World War II, and after being 'discovered' by the American military, he used this record as the basis to finally write his memoir, published as *Ordnung im Chaos* in German in 1981. The English version was only published in 2015. Earlier German memoirs, such as Guderian's *Panzer Leader*, Manstein's *Lost Victories* and Mellenthin's *Panzer Battles* — all published in the 1950s — tended to blame Germany's defeat solely on Hitler and avoided criticism of the *Wehrmacht*'s operational performance. For example, Guderian in *Panzer Leader* declared:

> I had repeated angry altercations with him [Hitler], because over and over again he would sabotage the taking of necessary military measures for the sake of the obscure political game he was playing. He would also attempt to interfere in matters that purely concerned the Army, always with unfortunate results.[52]

Manstein similarly announced in *Lost Victories* that Hitler became 'increasingly accustomed to interfering in the running of the army groups, armies and lower formations by issuing special orders which were not his concern at all'.[53] Mellenthin in *Panzer Battles* likewise concluded that 'Hitler's method of direct command hastened Germany's defeat. Orders to "fight for every foot" had disastrous effects. But apart from strategy, his methods of control affected the whole war machine.'[54]

Guderian, Manstein and Mellenthin's accounts, of course, have an agenda of inflating their own reputations and explaining away the *Wehrmacht*'s defeat. Balck's memoir, in contrast, refused to endorse the myth of Hitler's inflexible orders, giving a more balanced view:

> Hitler never interfered in the operations of my corps. I always had complete freedom of action. I was allowed to attack, defend, or withdraw as I thought appropriate. In the usual fashion, army and army group allocated the tasks and objectives without ever getting involved in details.[55]

Balck also explained that 'the number of Hitler's interventions was not nearly as high as popular legend now describes it.'[56] He nevertheless was critical of Hitler's leadership, but in a more balanced and measured manner:

> Operationally, Hitler had a clear and one might even say an exceptional understanding. He combined this with a rare ability to influence men. He was incapable, however, of judging what could be accomplished with the available forces and when the correlation of forces was completely against him. He believed that he could bridge any gaps with his iron will.[57]

As Balck did not blame the German defeat exclusively on Hitler, he acknowledged both the *Wehrmacht*'s failure and his own shortcomings with honest self-assessment:

> We lost Stalingrad, Africa, and the Caucasus campaign because these campaigns were conducted beyond secured supply lines, and when this error became apparent, we did not abort in time.[58]

Balck acknowledged that the Red Army counter-offensive during the winter of 1942–43 'was well planned, well prepared, and brilliantly executed'.[59] He also added, 'I also underestimated the Russians considerably.'[60] Balck's honesty makes his memoir a far more valuable resource for historians than the earlier accounts written by his contemporaries.

Although the German Army won spectacular tactical victories, its lack of operational perspective and strategic bankruptcy failed to translate its initial success into a victorious war. Balck understood this truth all too well and perfectly expressed this sentiment by comparing German conduct during World War II with the Punic Wars from ancient times:

> After Cannae, Hannibal did not march on to Rome, which caused his cavalry commander Marhabal to exclaim, 'Vincere scis, Hannibal, victoria uti nescis. [You know how to gain a victory, Hannibal, but you do not know how to make use of it.]' Did Hannibal lack military leadership greatness, or did he correctly know the limits of his power? He probably was right because he was vulnerable in human resources and space. Both of these factors were on the side of Rome, as well as decisive maritime dominance. Germany also achieved legendary victories but in the end succumbed to the human factor, space, and maritime domination, all of which were clearly on the side of Russia. Unfortunately, we did not have the sense of proportion and reality, like the great Carthaginian.[61]

On 29 November 1982, one year after the publication of *Ordnung im Chaos*, Hermann Balck, former commander of panzer troops, died in Erlenbach-Rockenan, West Germany, aged eighty-eight.

BIBLIOGRAPHY

Primary Sources and Monographs

1st Panzer Division War Diary (Kriegstagebuch), France June 1940, National Archives (United States) (T-315 Roll 15)

2nd Panzer Division War Diary (Kriegstagebuch), West October 1939 – July 1940, National Archives (United States) (T-315 Roll 88)

2nd Panzer Division War Diary (Kriegstagebuch), West May 1940 – March 1941, National Archives (United States) (T-315 Roll 89)

11th Panzer Division War Diary (Kriegstagebuch), Russia June – December 1942, National Archives (United States) (T-315 Roll 594)

11th Panzer Division War Diary (Kriegstagebuch), Russia December 1942, National Archives (United States) (T-315 Roll 595)

11th Panzer Division War Diary (Kriegstagebuch), Russia November 1942 – January 1943, National Archives (United States) (T-315 Roll 596)

16 Infantry Brigade, Australian War Memorial (AWM52, 8/2/16)

2/2nd Australian Infantry Battalion, Australian War Memorial (AWM52, 8/3/2)

2/3rd Australian Infantry Battalion, Australian War Memorial (AWM52, 8/3/3)

Armored Warfare in World War II: Conference Featuring F.W. Von Mellenthin, Battelle Columbus Laboratories, Columbus, 1979

Documents Relating to New Zealand's Participation in the Second World War 1939–45: Volume II, War History Branch, Wellington, 1951

Generals Balck and Von Mellenthin on Tactics: Implications for NATO Military Doctrine, BDM Corporation, McLean, 1980

German Army Documents on the Campaign in Greece, Australian War Memorial (AWM54, 534/2/27)

Small Unit Actions during the German Campaign in Russia, DA Pam 20-269, Center of Military History United States Army, Washington, 1953

The Balkan Campaign. The German invasion of Greece and Yugoslavia, Information obtained by Historical Section Australian Military Mission, Berlin, 1947, Australian War Memorial (AWM54, 624/7/2)

The German Campaigns in the Balkans (Spring 1941), DA Pam 20-260, Center of Military History United States Army, Washington, 1953

Translation of Taped Conversation with General Hermann Balck, 12 January 1979, Battelle Columbus Laboratories, Columbus, 1979

Translation of Taped Conversation with General Hermann Balck, 13 April 1979, Battelle Columbus Laboratories, Columbus, 1979

Translation of Taped Conversation with Lieutenant General Heinz Gaedcke, 12 April 1979, Battelle Columbus Laboratories, Columbus, 1979

Journal Articles

Carlson, Verner, 'Portrait of a German General Staff Officer', *Military Review*, Volume 70, Number 4 (April 1990)

Citino, Robert, 'New Gang in Town: The Rise of the German Panzer Division', *The Quarterly Journal of Military History*, Volume 28, Issue 2 (Winter 2016)

Citino, Robert, 'The War Hitler Won: The Battle for Europe, 1939–1941', *Journal of Military and Strategic Studies*, Volume 14, Issue 1 (Fall 2011)

Cook, Samuel, 'The German Breakthrough at Sedan', *Armor*, Volume 113, Issue 5 (Sep/Oct 2004)

Forster, Jurgen and Mawdsley, Evan, 'Hitler and Stalin in Perspective: Secret Speeches on the Eve of Barbarossa', *War in History*, Volume 11, Number 1 (Jan 2004)

Gat, Azar, 'British Influence and the Evolution of the Panzer Arm: Myth or Reality? Part I', *War in History*, Volume 4, Number 2 (Apr 1997)

Gat, Azar, 'British Influence and the Evolution of the Panzer Arm: Myth or Reality? Part II', *War in History*, Volume 4, Number 3 (Jul 1997)

Jovanovich, Leo M., 'The War in the Balkans in 1941', *East European Quarterly*, Volume 28, Number 1 (Spring 1994)

Matthew, Christopher A., 'The Strategy of the Thermopylae Artemisium Line in 480 BC', *Ancient History*, Volume 39, Issue 1 (2009)

Newland, Samuel J., 'Blitzkrieg in Retrospect', *Military Review*, Volume 84, Issue 4 (Jul/Aug 2004)

Newland, Samuel, 'German Panzers on the Offensive: Russian Front, North Africa, 1941–1942', *Parameters*, Volume 35, Issue 1 (Spring 2005)

Osborn, John. W, 'Greek Tragedy', *The Quarterly Journal of Military History*, Volume 21, Number 4 (Summer 2009)

Powaski, Ronald E., 'Cut of the Sickle', *World War II*, Volume 18, Issue 4 (Nov 2003)

Pryer, Douglas A., 'Growing Leaders Who Practice Mission Command and Win the Peace', *Military Review*, Volume 93, Issue 6 (Nov/Dec 2013)

Sadkovich, James J. 'Anglo-American Bias and the Italo-Greek War of 1940–1941', *The Journal of Military History*, Volume 58, Number 4 (Oct 1994)

Scott, Christopher J., 'The Battle for Sowchos 79', *Engineer*, Volume 41, Issue 2 (May–Aug 2011)

Stockings, Craig, 'The Battle of Pinios Gorge: A Study of a Broken Anzac Brigade', *Australian Army Journal*, Volume 7, Number 3 (Summer 2011)

Stockings, Craig, 'The Fairy Tale of the Panzers in Greece, April 1941', *Australian Defence Force Journal*, Number 185 (2011)

Strauss, Barry, 'Go Tell the Spartans', *The Quarterly Journal of Military History*, Volume 17, Number 1 (Autumn 2004)

Williamson, Murray and O'Leary, Thomas, 'Military Transformation and Legacy Forces', *Joint Force Quarterly*, JFQ 30 (Spring 2002)

Zabecki, David T., 'Hermann Balck — Germany's Forgotten Panzer Commander', *Military Review*, Volume 79, Number 6 (Nov/Dec 1999)

Books

Anderson, Thomas, *The History of the Panzerwaffe: Volume I: 1939–43*, Osprey Publishing (Kindle Edition), Oxford, 2015

Anderson, Thomas, *The History of the Panzerwaffe: Volume II: 1943–45*, Osprey Publishing (Kindle Edition), Oxford, 2017

Balck, Hermann, *Order in Chaos: The Memoirs of General of Panzer Troops Hermann Balck*, The University Press of Kentucky, Lexington, 2015

Borman, C.A., *Official History of New Zealand in the Second World War 1939–45: Divisional Signals*, War History Branch, Wellington, 1954

Carr, John, *The Defence and Fall of Greece, 1940–41*, Pen and Sword (Kindle Edition), South Yorkshire, 2013

Citino, Robert M., *The Path to Blitzkrieg: Doctrine and Training in the German Army, 1920–1939*, Lynne Rienner Publishers, London, 1999

Cody, J.F., *Official History of New Zealand in the Second World War 1939–45: 21 Battalion*, War History Branch, Wellington, 1953

Cole, Hugh M., *The Lorraine Campaign*, US Government Printing Office, Washington, 1950

Dawson, W.D., *Official History of New Zealand in the Second World War 1939–45: 18 Battalion and Armoured Regiment*, War History Branch, Wellington, 1961

Dennis, Peter and Grey, Jeffrey, eds., *Victory or Defeat: Armies in the Aftermath of Conflict*, Big Sky Publishing, Canberra, 2010

Doughty, Robert A., *The Breaking Point: Sedan and the Fall of France, 1940*, Stackpole Books (Kindle Edition), Mechanicsburg, 1990

Doughty, Robert Allan, *The Seeds of Disaster: The Development of French Army Doctrine, 1919–39*, Archon Books, Hamden, 1985

Dyson, Freeman, *Weapons and Hope*, Harper Colophon Books, New York, 1984

Ewer, Peter, *Forgotten Anzacs: The Campaign in Greece, 1941*, Scribe (Kindle Edition), Melbourne, 2008

Forczyk, Robert, *Tank Warfare on the Eastern Front 1941–1942: Schwerpunkt*, Pen and Sword (Kindle Edition), South Yorkshire, 2013

Forczyk, Robert, *Tank Warfare on the Eastern Front 1943–1945: Red Steamroller*, Pen and Sword (Kindle Edition), South Yorkshire, 2016

Frieser, Karl-Heinz, *The Blitzkrieg Legend: The 1940 Campaign in the West*, Naval Institute Press (Kindle Edition), Annapolis, 2005

Ganz, A. Harding, *Ghost Division: The 11th 'Gespenster' Panzer Division and the German Armored Force in World War II*, Stackpole Books, Mechanicsburg, 2016

Glantz, David M., *Companion to Endgame at Stalingrad*, University Press of Kansas, Lawrence, 2014

Glantz, David M., *When Titans Clashed: How the Red Army Stopped Hitler*, University Press of Kansas, Lawrence, 2015

Glantz, David M. and House, Jonathan M., *Endgame at Stalingrad Book Two: December 1942 – February 1943, Volume 3*, University Press of Kansas, Lawrence, 2014

Glantz, David M. and House, Jonathan M., *To the Gates of Stalingrad: Soviet-German Combat Operations, April–August 1942*, University Press of Kansas, Lawrence, 2009

Gole, Henry G., *General William E. DePuy: Preparing the Army for Modern War*, University Press of Kentucky (Kindle Edition), Lexington, 2008

Greentree, David, *New Zealand Infantryman vs German Motorcycle Soldier: Greece and Crete 1941*, Osprey Publishing, Oxford, 2017

Grehan, John and Mace, Martin, *Operations in North Africa and the Middle East 1939–1942: Tobruk, Crete, Syria and East Africa*, Pen and Sword (Kindle Edition), South Yorkshire, 2015

Guderian, Heinz, *Panzer Leader*, Penguin Books, London, 1952

Gudmundsson, Bruce I., *On Armor*, Praeger, Westport, 2004

Hall, D.O.W., *Prisoners of Germany*, War History Branch, Wellington, 1949

Hart, Russell, *Guderian: Panzer Pioneer or Myth Maker?*, Potomac Books (Kindle Edition), Dulles, 2006

Henderson, Jim, *Official History of New Zealand in the Second World War 1939–45: 22 Battalion*, War History Branch, Wellington, 1958

Holland, James, *The War in the West: Volume 1: The Rise of Germany 1939–1941*, Atlantic Monthly Press, New York, 2015

Horne, Alistair, *To Lose a Battle: France 1940*, Pan Macmillan UK (Kindle Edition), London, 2012

Jentz, Thomas L., *Panzertruppen: The Complete Guide to the Creation and Combat Employment of Germany's Tank Force, 1933–1942*, Schiffer, Atglen, 1996

Jentz, Thomas L., *Panzertruppen: The Complete Guide to the Creation and Combat Employment of Germany's Tank Force, 1943–1945*, Schiffer, Atglen, 1996

Keitel, Wilhelm, *The Memoirs of Field-Marshal Wilhelm Keitel*, Cooper Square Press, (Kindle Edition), New York, 2000

Lemay, Benoit, *Erich Von Manstein: Hitler's Master Strategist*, Casemate, Philadelphia, 2010

Liedtke, Gregory, *Enduring the Whirlwind: The German Army and the Russo-German War 1941–1943*, Helion and Company, (Kindle Edition), Solihull, 2016

Long, Gavin, *Australia in the War of 1939–1945: Series One: Army, Volume II: Greece, Crete and Syria*, Australian War Memorial, Canberra, 1953

Loughnan, R.J.M., *Official History of New Zealand in the Second World War 1939–45: Divisional Cavalry*, War History Branch, Wellington, 1963

Manstein, Erich von, *Lost Victories*, Greenhill Books, London, 1958

Mazower, Mark, *Inside Hitler's Greece: The Experience of Occupation*, Yale University Press, 1993

McCarthy, Peter and Syron, Mike, *Panzerkrieg: The Rise and Fall of Hitler's Tank Divisions*, Robinson (Kindle Edition), London, 2012

McClymont, W.G., *Official History of New Zealand in the Second World War 1939–45: To Greece*, War History Branch, Wellington, 1959

Mellenthin, F.W. von, *German Generals of World War II*, University of Oklahoma Press, Norman, 1977

Mellenthin, F.W. von, *Panzer Battles*, Spellmount, Gloucestershire, 1955

Mitcham, Samuel W., *Panzer Legions: A Guide to the German Army Tank Divisions of World War II and Their Commanders*, Stackpole (Kindle Edition), Mechanicsburg, 2000

Mitcham, Samuel W. and Mueller, Gene, *Hitler's Commanders: Officers of the Wehrmacht, the Luftwaffe, the Kriegsmarine, and the Waffen-SS*, Rowman & Littlefield Publishers (Kindle Edition), New York, 2012

Mosier, John, *Cross of Iron: The Rise and Fall of the German War Machine, 1918–1945*, Henry Holt and Co., New York, 2006

Mosier, John, *Deathride: Hitler vs. Stalin — The Eastern Front, 1941–1945*, Simon & Schuster, New York, 2010

Mosier, John, *The Blitzkrieg Myth: How Hitler and the Allies Misread the Strategic Realities of World War II*, HarperCollins, New York, 2003

Murphy, W.E., *Official History of New Zealand in the Second World War 1939–45: 2nd New Zealand Divisional Artillery*, Historical Publications Branch, Wellington, 1966

Naveh, Shimon, *In Pursuit of Military Excellence: The Evolution of Operational Theory*, Frank Cass, London, 1997

Plowman, Jeffrey, *War in the Balkans: The Battle for Greece and Crete 1940–1941*, Pen and Sword (Kindle Edition), South Yorkshire, 2013

Raus, Erhard, *Panzer Operations: The Eastern Front Memoir of General Raus, 1941–1945*, Da Capo Press (Kindle Edition), 2003

Showalter, Dennis, *Hitler's Panzers: The Lightning Attacks that Revolutionized Warfare*, Penguin, New York, 2009

Smelser, Ronald and Davies, Edward J., *The Myth of the Eastern Front: The Nazi-Soviet War in American Popular Culture*, Cambridge University Press, Cambridge, 2008

Stockings, Craig and Hancock, Eleanor, *Swastika over the Acropolis: Re-interpreting the Nazi Invasion of Greece in World War II*, Brill, Leiden, 2013

Stolfi, R.H.S., *German Panzers on the Offensive*, Schiffer Military History, Atglen, 2003

Tyquin, Michael, *Greece: February to April 1941*, Big Sky Publishing, Canberra, 2014

Walters, Robert G. *Order Out Of Chaos: A Case Study of the Application of Auftragstaktik by the 11th Panzer Division during the Chir River Battles 7–19 December 1942*, United States Military Academy, 1989

Wards, I. McL., *Official History of New Zealand in the Second World War 1939–45: Episodes and Studies Volume 2: The Other Side of the Hill I: Panzer Attack in Greece*, War History Branch, Wellington, 1952

Wette, Wolfram, *The Wehrmacht: History, Myth, Reality*, Harvard University Press, London, 2006

Williamson, Gordon, *German Mountain and Ski Troops 1939–45*, Osprey Publishing (Kindle Edition), Oxford, 1996

Wilmot, Chester, *The Struggle for Europe*, Lucknow Books (Kindle Edition), London, 1952

Wood, Peter William, *A Battle to Win: An Analysis of Combat Effectiveness through the Second World War Experience of the 21st (Auckland) Battalion*, Massey University, New Zealand, 2012

Zhukov, Georgy, *Marshal of Victory: The Autobiography of General Georgy Zhukov*, Pen and Sword (Kindle Edition), South Yorkshire, 2013

Websites

2/2nd Australian Infantry Battalion, Australian War Memorial
https://www.awm.gov.au/unit/U56045/

2/3rd Australian Infantry Battalion, Australian War Memorial
https://www.awm.gov.au/collection/U56046

Rutherford, Noel, 'In Their Own Words — The Battle of Tempe Gorge — Part 1', *ABC Open* (21 Apr 16),
https://open.abc.net.au/explore/127336

Rutherford, Noel, 'In Their Own Words — The Battle of Tempe Gorge — Part 2', *ABC Open* (21 Apr 16),
https://open.abc.net.au/explore/127334

Rutherford, Noel, 'In Their Own Words — The Battle of Tempe Gorge — Part 3', *ABC Open* (21 Apr 16),
https://open.abc.net.au/explore/127335

Showalter, Dennis E., 'A Dubious Heritage: The Military Legacy of the Russo-German War', *Air University Review* (March–April 1985), http://www.airpower.maxwell.af.mil/airchronicles/aureview/1985/mar-apr/showalter.html

NOTES

Introduction

1   D'Este, 'Foreword,' in Balck, *Order in Chaos*, p. vii
2   Dyson, *Weapons and Hope*, p. 151
3   *Translation of Taped Conversation with Lieutenant General Heinz Gaedcke*, p. 27
4   D'Este, 'Foreword,' in Balck, *Order in Chaos*, p. vii
5   D'Este, 'Foreword,' in Balck, *Order in Chaos*, p. vii
6   Cole, *The Lorraine Campaign*, p. 230
7   Cole, *The Lorraine Campaign*, p. 230
8   Wilmot, *The Struggle for Europe*, 10756/10758
9   Mellenthin, *Panzer Battles*, p. 306
10   Mellenthin, *Panzer Battles*, p. 247
11   Zabecki and Biedekarken, 'Preface' in Balck, *Order in Chaos*, p. ix
12   Pryer, 'Growing Leaders Who Practice Mission Command and Win the Peace,' pp. 32 and 40
13   Zabecki and Biedekarken, 'Preface' in Balck, *Order in Chaos*, p. xi
14   The original German version *Ordnung im Chaos* was published in 1981.
15   Balck, *Order in Chaos*, pp. 3–4
16   Balck, *Order in Chaos*, p. 4
17   Balck, *Order in Chaos*, p. 12
18   Balck, *Order in Chaos*, p. 17
19   Balck, *Order in Chaos*, p. 29
20   Balck, *Order in Chaos*, p. 34
21   Balck, *Order in Chaos*, p. 106
22   Mellenthin, *German Generals of World War II*, p. 192
23   Mellenthin, *German Generals of World War II*, pp.192–3
24   Balck, *Order in Chaos*, p. 471
25   Balck, *Order in Chaos*, p. 148
26   Balck, *Order in Chaos*, p. 86
27   Balck, *Order in Chaos*, p. 49
28   Balck, *Order in Chaos*, p. 55
29   Balck, *Order in Chaos*, p. 170
30   Dyson, *Weapons and Hope*, p. 155

Chapter One: Breakthrough at Sedan

1   Balck, *Order in Chaos*, p. 171
2   Balck, *Order in Chaos*, p. 171
3   Balck, *Order in Chaos*, p. 172
4   Citino, *The Path to Blitzkrieg*, p. 250
5   Frieser, *The Blitzkrieg Legend*, 2070/14003
6   Showalter, *Hitler's Panzers*, p. 105
7   Powaski, 'Cut of the sickle', p. 60
8   Frieser, *The Blitzkrieg Legend*, 3286/14003
9   Frieser, *The Blitzkrieg Legend*, 4211/14003
10   Holland, *The War in the West*, p. 203
11   Holland, *The War in the West*, pp. 202–3
12   Frieser, *The Blitzkrieg Legend*, 1979/14003
13   Powaski, 'Cut of the Sickle,' p. 62
14   Balck, *Order in Chaos*, p. 172
15   Balck, *Order in Chaos*, p. 172
16   Balck, *Order in Chaos*, p. 172
17   Balck, *Order in Chaos*, p. 174
18   Balck, *Order in Chaos*, p. 174
19   Cook, 'The German Breakthrough at Sedan', p. 11
20   Cook, 'The German Breakthrough at Sedan', p. 11
21   Mellenthin, *Panzer Battles*, p. 14
22   Doughty, *The Breaking Point*, 2909/7793

23 Powaski, 'Cut of the Sickle', p. 63
24 Doughty, *The Breaking Point*, 1961/7793
25 Balck, *Order in Chaos*, p. 172
26 Balck, *Order in Chaos*, p. 174
27 Balck, *Order in Chaos*, p. 174
28 Frieser, *The Blitzkrieg Legend*, 3434/14003
29 Frieser, *The Blitzkrieg Legend*, 3490/14003
30 Frieser, *The Blitzkrieg Legend*, 3490/14003
31 Frieser, *The Blitzkrieg Legend*, 3490/14003
32 *Translation of Taped Conversation with General Hermann Balck, 13 April 1979*, p. 4
33 Balck, *Order in Chaos*, p. 174
34 *Translation of Taped Conversation with General Hermann Balck, 13 April 1979*, p. 3
35 *Translation of Taped Conversation with General Hermann Balck, 13 April 1979*, p. 3
36 Balck, *Order in Chaos*, p. 175
37 Guderian, *Panzer Leader*, 2028/10570
38 Frieser, *The Blitzkrieg Legend*, 3577/14003
39 Balck, *Order in Chaos*, p. 175
40 Balck, *Order in Chaos*, p. 175
41 Balck, *Order in Chaos*, p. 175
42 Doughty, *The Breaking Point*, 2762/7793
43 Balck, *Order in Chaos*, p. 175
44 Frieser, *The Blitzkrieg Legend*, 3809/14003
45 Frieser, *The Blitzkrieg Legend*, 3831/14003
46 Balck, *Order in Chaos*, p. 84
47 Balck, *Order in Chaos*, p. 175
48 Balck, *Order in Chaos*, p. 175
49 Doughty, *The Breaking Point*, 3594/7793
50 Doughty, *The Breaking Point*, 3594/7793
51 Frieser, *The Blitzkrieg Legend*, 3632/14003
52 Frieser, *The Blitzkrieg Legend*, 3772/14003
53 Balck, *Order in Chaos*, p. 176
54 Balck, *Order in Chaos*, p. 176
55 Frieser, *The Blitzkrieg Legend*, 3910/14003
56 Frieser, *The Blitzkrieg Legend*, 4011/14003
57 Balck, *Order in Chaos*, p. 176
58 Balck, *Order in Chaos*, p. 176
59 Balck, *Order in Chaos*, p. 176
60 Balck, *Order in Chaos*, p. 177
61 Frieser, *The Blitzkrieg Legend*, 3957/14003
62 Balck, *Order in Chaos*, p. 177
63 Balck, *Order in Chaos*, p. 178

Chapter Two: The Fall of France

1 Showalter, *Hitler's Panzers*, p. 108
2 Frieser, *The Blitzkrieg Legend*, 5554/14003
3 *Translation of Taped Conversation with General Hermann Balck, 13 April 1979*, pp. 6–7
4 Mellenthin, *German Generals of World War II*, p. 197
5 Balck, *Order in Chaos*, p. 179
6 Balck, *Order in Chaos*, p. 179
7 Balck, *Order in Chaos*, p. 179
8 Mellenthin, *German Generals of World War II*, pp. 197–8
9 Balck, *Order in Chaos*, p. 179
10 Horne, *To Lose a Battle*, 6089/8138
11 Mellenthin, *German Generals of World War II*, p. 198
12 Guderian, *Panzer Leader*, 2122/10570
13 Balck, *Order in Chaos*, p. 180
14 Balck, *Order in Chaos*, p. 180
15 Balck, *Order in Chaos*, p. 180
16 Frieser, *The Blitzkrieg Legend*, 4300/14003
17 Horne, *To Lose a Battle*, 8132/8138
18 Balck, *Order in Chaos*, p. 182
19 Balck, *Order in Chaos*, p. 183
20 Balck, *Order in Chaos*, p. 185
21 Balck, *Order in Chaos*, p. 186
22 Balck, *Order in Chaos*, p. 191
23 Balck, *Order in Chaos*, p. 195
24 Doughty, *The Breaking Point*, 6113/7793
25 Horne, *To Lose a Battle*, 4976/4980
26 Mellenthin, *German Generals of World War II*, p. 197
27 Mosier, *Cross of Iron*, p. 212
28 Williamson and O'Leary, 'Military Transformation and Legacy Forces', p. 23

29   Williamson and O'Leary, 'Military
      Transformation and Legacy Forces',
      p. 22
30   Newland, 'Blitzkrieg in Retrospect',
      p. 86
31   *Translation of Taped Conversations with
      General Hermann Balck, 12 January
      1979*, p. 19
32   Citino, 'New Gang in Town', p. 26
33   Balck, *Order in Chaos*, p. 193
34   *Translation of Taped Conversations with
      General Hermann Balck, 12 January
      1979*, p. 20
35   Frieser, *The Blitzkrieg Legend*,
      3397/14003
36   Megargee, 'The German Army after the
      Great War,' in Dennis and Grey, *Victory
      or Defeat*, p. 110
37   Newland, 'Blitzkrieg in Retrospect',
      p. 87
38   Naveh, *In Pursuit of Military Excellence*,
      p. 117
39   Showalter, *Hitler's Panzers*, p. 108
40   *Translation of Taped Conversation with
      General Hermann Balck, 13 April 1979*,
      p. 13
41   Mellenthin, *Panzer Battles*, p. 17
42   *Translation of Taped Conversation with
      General Hermann Balck, 13 April 1979*,
      p. 14
43   Mellenthin, *German Generals of World
      War II*, p. 196
44   Mellenthin, *Panzer Battles*, p. 17
45   Newland, 'German Panzers on the
      Offensive', p. 145
46   Gat, 'British Influence and the Evolution
      of the Panzer Arm: Myth or Reality?
      Part II', p. 336
47   Hart, *Guderian*, 1254/3067
48   Gudmundsson, *On Armor*, p. 132
49   Gudmundsson, *On Armor*, pp. 105–6

Chapter Three: Intervention in the Balkans
1   Balck, *Order in Chaos*, p. 199
2   Mitcham, *Panzer Legions*, 1037/5468
3   Balck, *Order in Chaos*, p. 199
4   Balck, *Order in Chaos*, p. 199
5   *The German Campaigns in the Balkans*,
      p. 3
6   McClymont, *To Greece*, p. 88
7   Osborn, 'Greek Tragedy', p. 78
8   Osborn, 'Greek Tragedy', p. 78

9   Osborn, 'Greek Tragedy', p. 79
10   Holland, *The War in the West*, p. 406
11   Mosier, *Cross of Iron*, p. 149
12   Osborn, 'Greek Tragedy', p. 79
13   Keitel, *The Memoirs of Field-Marshal
      Wilhelm Keitel*, 1788/4185
14   McClymont, *To Greece*, p. 88
15   Jovanovich, 'The War in the Balkans in
      1941', pp. 105–29
16   Osborn, 'Greek Tragedy', p. 80
17   Jovanovich, 'The War in the Balkans in
      1941', pp. 105–29
18   Osborn, 'Greek Tragedy', p. 82
19   Stockings and Hancock, *Swastika Over
      the Acropolis*, p. 65
20   Sadkovich, 'Anglo-American Bias and
      the Italo-Greek War of 1940–1941', p.
      617
21   Stockings and Hancock, *Swastika Over
      the Acropolis*, pp. 46–7
22   Stockings and Hancock, *Swastika Over
      the Acropolis*, p. 67
23   Jovanovich, 'The War in the Balkans in
      1941', pp. 105–29
24   Osborn, 'Greek Tragedy', p. 83
25   Tyquin, *Greece*, p. 16
26   Stockings and Hancock, *Swastika Over
      the Acropolis*, p. 50
27   Grehan and Mace, *Operations in North
      Africa and the Middle East 1939–1942*,
      1254/7540
28   W Force was also known as Lustreforce.
29   McClymont, *To Greece*, p. 100
30   Grehan and Mace, *Operations in North
      Africa and the Middle East 1939–1942*,
      1366/7540
31   McClymont, *To Greece*, p. 101
32   *The German Campaigns in the Balkans*,
      p. 18
33   Stockings and Hancock, *Swastika Over
      the Acropolis*, p. 69
34   Balck, *Order in Chaos*, p. 200
35   Balck, *Order in Chaos*, p. 200
36   Balck, *Order in Chaos*, p. 200
37   Balck, *Order in Chaos*, p. 200
38   Balck, *Order in Chaos*, p. 201
39   Stockings and Hancock, *Swastika Over
      the Acropolis*, p. 102
40   Borman, *Divisional Signals*, p. 79
41   Osborn, 'Greek Tragedy', p. 84
42   Osborn, 'Greek Tragedy', p. 84
43   Tyquin, *Greece*, p. 16

44 Stockings and Hancock, *Swastika Over the Acropolis*, p. 118
45 Balck, *Order in Chaos*, p. 205
46 *The German Campaigns in the Balkans*, p. 21
47 Jovanovich, 'The War in the Balkans in 1941', 105-129
48 Stockings and Hancock, *Swastika Over the Acropolis*, p. 128
49 Stockings and Hancock, *Swastika Over the Acropolis*, p. 129
50 Stockings and Hancock, *Swastika Over the Acropolis*, p. 129
51 *The German Campaigns in the Balkans*, p. 22
52 The 12th Army also included the 50th Corps which remained in Romania as a reserve and the 16th Panzer Division which defended the Turkish-Bulgarian border.
53 Balck, *Order in Chaos*, p. 202
54 Tyquin, *Greece*, p. 35
55 Balck, *Order in Chaos*, p. 202
56 Balck, *Order in Chaos*, p. 202

Chapter Four: The Shadow of Olympus
1 Stockings and Hancock, *Swastika Over the Acropolis*, p. 152
2 Stockings and Hancock, *Swastika Over the Acropolis*, p. 157
3 Stockings and Hancock, *Swastika Over the Acropolis*, p. 154
4 Balck, *Order in Chaos*, p. 207
5 Balck, *Order in Chaos*, p. 202
6 Balck, *Order in Chaos*, p. 202
7 Balck, *Order in Chaos*, p. 202
8 Anderson, *The History of the Panzerwaffe: Volume I*, 2545/3061
9 Anderson, *The History of the Panzerwaffe: Volume I*, 2556/3061
10 Stockings and Hancock, *Swastika Over the Acropolis*, p. 158
11 Carr, *The Defence and Fall of Greece*, 4440/5813
12 McClymont, *To Greece*, p. 161
13 Anderson, *The History of the Panzerwaffe: Volume I*, 2556/3061
14 Balck, *Order in Chaos*, p. 203
15 Balck, *Order in Chaos*, p. 203
16 Plowman, *War in the Balkans*, 401/1190
17 Stockings and Hancock, *Swastika Over the Acropolis*, p. 167
18 Stockings and Hancock, *Swastika Over the Acropolis*, p. 168
19 Carr, *The Defence and Fall of Greece*, 4719/5813
20 Balck, *Order in Chaos*, p. 203
21 Stockings and Hancock, *Swastika Over the Acropolis*, p. 181
22 Carr, *The Defence and Fall of Greece*, 4721/5813
23 Balck, *Order in Chaos*, p. 204
24 Anderson, *The History of the Panzerwaffe: Volume I*, 2556/3061
25 *The German invasion of Greece and Yugoslavia* (AWM54, 624/7/2)
26 Balck, *Order in Chaos*, p. 204
27 Balck, *Order in Chaos*, p. 204
28 Long, *Greece, Crete and Syria*, p. 45
29 Balck, *Order in Chaos*, p. 204
30 Stockings and Hancock, *Swastika Over the Acropolis*, p. 194
31 McClymont, *To Greece*, p. 137
32 Long, *Greece, Crete and Syria*, p. 35
33 Stockings and Hancock, *Swastika Over the Acropolis*, p. 161
34 Stockings and Hancock, *Swastika Over the Acropolis*, p. 186
35 Stockings and Hancock, *Swastika Over the Acropolis*, p. 189
36 Balck, *Order in Chaos*, pp. 205-6
37 McClymont, *To Greece*, p. 173
38 Balck, *Order in Chaos*, p. 207
39 Stockings and Hancock, *Swastika Over the Acropolis*, p. 196
40 *German Army Documents on the Campaign in Greece* (AWM54, 534/2/27)
41 McClymont, *To Greece*, p. 205
42 Stockings and Hancock, *Swastika Over the Acropolis*, p. 238
43 Stockings and Hancock, *Swastika Over the Acropolis*, p. 245
44 Stockings and Hancock, *Swastika Over the Acropolis*, p. 252
45 Stockings and Hancock, *Swastika Over the Acropolis*, p. 253
46 Stockings and Hancock, *Swastika Over the Acropolis*, p. 262
47 McClymont, *To Greece*, p. 203
48 Balck, *Order in Chaos*, p. 207
49 Ewer, *Forgotten Anzacs*, 2216/6692

50   Translation of Taped Conversation with
     General Hermann Balck, 13 April 1979,
     p. 11
51   Stockings and Hancock, Swastika Over
     the Acropolis, p. 275
52   Balck, Order in Chaos, p. 204
53   Balck, Order in Chaos, p. 207
54   The German Campaigns in the Balkans,
     p. 98
55   Stockings and Hancock, Swastika Over
     the Acropolis, p. 249
56   German Army Documents on the
     Campaign in Greece (AWM54,
     534/2/27)
57   Balck, Order in Chaos, p. 207

**Chapter Five: The Battle of Platamon
Ridge**
1   McClymont, To Greece, p. 175
2   McClymont, To Greece, p. 175
3   Wood, A Battle to Win, p. 81
4   Cody, 21 Battalion, p. 45
5   Cody, 21 Battalion, p. 45
6   Cody, 21 Battalion, p. 46
7   Cody, 21 Battalion, p. 46
8   McClymont, To Greece, p. 176
9   Cody, 21 Battalion, p. 2
10   Stockings and Hancock, Swastika Over
     the Acropolis, p. 217
11   Wood, A Battle to Win, p. 80
12   Wood, A Battle to Win, p. 81
13   German Army Documents on the
     Campaign in Greece (AWM54,
     534/2/27)
14   Stollbrock had fought as an infantry
     officer in World War I and was
     wounded in France in May 1940.
     Greentree, New Zealand Infantryman vs
     German Motorcycle Soldier, p. 53
15   Translation of Taped Conversations with
     General Hermann Balck, 12 January
     1979, p. 28
16   Cody, 21 Battalion, p. 51
17   Cody, 21 Battalion, p. 50
18   Wards, Panzer Attack in Greece, p. 4
19   Wood, A Battle to Win, p. 83
20   Cody, 21 Battalion, p. 51
21   Cody, 21 Battalion, p. 51
22   German Army Documents on the
     Campaign in Greece (AWM54,
     534/2/27)

23   German Army Documents on the
     Campaign in Greece (AWM54,
     534/2/27)
24   McClymont, To Greece, p. 246
25   Greentree, New Zealand Infantryman vs
     German Motorcycle Soldier, p. 46
26   Wards, Panzer Attack in Greece, p. 4
27   Wards, Panzer Attack in Greece, p. 4
28   Wood, A Battle to Win, p. 85
29   Stollbrock was later appointed
     commander of the NCO school for
     armoured reconnaissance troops at
     Sternberg in October 1941 and he
     served in this capacity until March 1944.
     In April 1944 he was made a regimental
     commander and later commanded
     the 2nd Panzer Division in April 1945.
     Greentree, New Zealand Infantryman vs
     German Motorcycle Soldier, p. 53
30   German Army Documents on the
     Campaign in Greece (AWM54,
     534/2/27)
31   Wood, A Battle to Win, p. 106
32   Jentz, Panzertruppen: 1933–1942, p. 53
33   Mellenthin, Panzer Battles, p. 33
34   Wards, Panzer Attack in Greece, p. 5
35   Cody, 21 Battalion, p. 247
36   Jentz, Panzertruppen: 1933–1942,
     p. 153
37   Stockings and Hancock, Swastika Over
     the Acropolis, p. 296
38   Jentz, Panzertruppen: 1933–1942,
     p. 153
39   Wood, A Battle to Win, p. 87
40   Balck, Order in Chaos, p. 209
41   McClymont, To Greece, p. 248
42   Jentz, Panzertruppen: 1933–1942,
     p. 153
43   Wards, Panzer Attack in Greece, p. 5
44   Wards, Panzer Attack in Greece, p. 5
45   Balck, Order in Chaos, p. 209
46   Translation of Taped Conversation with
     General Hermann Balck, 13 April 1979,
     p. 12
47   Murphy, 2nd New Zealand Divisional
     Artillery, p. 39
48   Cody, 21 Battalion, p. 55
49   Wood, A Battle to Win, p. 88
50   Balck, Order in Chaos, p. 209
51   Borman, Divisional Signals, p. 101
52   Cody, 21 Battalion, p. 58
53   Wood, A Battle to Win, pp. 100–1

54   Balck, *Order in Chaos*, p. 209
55   Jentz, *Panzertruppen: 1933–1942*,
      p. 153
56   Wards, *Panzer Attack in Greece*, p. 5
57   Cody, *21 Battalion*, p. 56
58   Mellenthin, *Panzer Battles*, p. 33
59   McClymont, *To Greece*, p. 249
60   *Translation of Taped Conversation with
      General Hermann Balck, 13 April 1979*,
      p. 12
61   McClymont, *To Greece*, p. 250
62   Cody, *21 Battalion*, p. 57
63   Wood, *A Battle to Win*, p. 91
64   Borman, *Divisional Signals*, p. 101
65   Murphy, *2nd New Zealand Divisional
      Artillery*, p. 40
66   Wood, *A Battle to Win*, p. 90
67   Anderson, *The History of the
      Panzerwaffe: Volume I*, 2571/3061
68   Jentz, *Panzertruppen: 1933–1942*, p.
      153
69   Ewer, *Forgotten Anzacs*, 2802/6692
70   Mellenthin, *Panzer Battles*, p. 35
71   Wood, *A Battle to Win*, p. 94
72   Wood, *A Battle to Win*, pp. 113–14
73   Greentree, *New Zealand Infantryman vs
      German Motorcycle Soldier*, p. 28
74   Wood, *A Battle to Win*, p. 114
75   Balck, *Order in Chaos*, p. 209
76   *German Army Documents on the
      Campaign in Greece* (AWM54,
      534/2/27)
77   *German Army Documents on the
      Campaign in Greece* (AWM54,
      534/2/27)

Chapter Six: The Race to Larissa
1   Stockings and Hancock, *Swastika Over
      the Acropolis*, p. 290
2   Stockings and Hancock, *Swastika Over
      the Acropolis*, p. 292
3   McClymont, *To Greece*, p. 280
4   Stockings and Hancock, *Swastika Over
      the Acropolis*, p. 313
5   Stockings and Hancock, *Swastika Over
      the Acropolis*, p. 323
6   *The German Campaigns in The Balkans*,
      p. 100
7   McClymont, *To Greece*, p. 251
8   Strauss, 'Go Tell the Spartans', p. 20

9   Matthew, 'The Strategy of the
      Thermopylae Artemisium Line in
      480 BC', p. 8
10   Stockings and Hancock, *Swastika Over
      the Acropolis*, p. 305
11   Plowman, *War in the Balkans*, 520/1190
12   Stockings and Hancock, *Swastika Over
      the Acropolis*, p. 320
13   McClymont, *To Greece*, p. 252
14   Stockings and Hancock, *Swastika Over
      the Acropolis*, p. 318
15   McClymont, *To Greece*, p. 251
16   Cody, *21 Battalion*, p. 62
17   *16 Infantry Brigade* (AWM52, 8/2/16)
18   Ewer, *Forgotten Anzacs*, 2892/6692
19   McClymont, *To Greece*, p. 318
20   Cody, *21 Battalion*, p. 64
21   McClymont, *To Greece*, p. 319
22   Long, *Greece, Crete and Syria*, p. 107
23   Murphy, *2nd New Zealand Divisional
      Artillery*, p. 60
24   Cody, *21 Battalion*, p. 63
25   Stockings, 'The Battle of Pinios Gorge',
      p. 146
26   Long, *Greece, Crete and Syria*, p. 108
27   *16 Infantry Brigade* (AWM52, 8/2/16)
28   McClymont, *To Greece*, p. 320
29   Wards, *Panzer Attack in Greece*, p. 6
30   *German Army Documents on the
      Campaign in Greece* (AWM54,
      534/2/27)
31   Balck, *Order in Chaos*, p. 209
32   Wards, *Panzer Attack in Greece*, p. 7
33   *German Army Documents on the
      Campaign in Greece* (AWM54,
      534/2/27)
34   *German Army Documents on the
      Campaign in Greece* (AWM54,
      534/2/27)
35   *German Army Documents on the
      Campaign in Greece* (AWM54,
      534/2/27)
36   Stockings, 'The Battle of Pinios Gorge',
      p. 144
37   *German Army Documents on the
      Campaign in Greece* (AWM54,
      534/2/27)
38   *German Army Documents on the
      Campaign in Greece* (AWM54,
      534/2/27)

39   German Army Documents on the
      Campaign in Greece (AWM54,
      534/2/27)
40   Translation of Taped Conversation with
      General Hermann Balck, 13 April 1979,
      p. 11
41   Balck, Order in Chaos, p. 209
42   German Army Documents on the
      Campaign in Greece (AWM54,
      534/2/27)
43   Stockings and Hancock, Swastika Over
      the Acropolis, p. 330
44   Balck, Order in Chaos, p. 210
45   Long, Greece, Crete and Syria, p. 108
46   Cody, 21 Battalion, p. 65
47   Cody, 21 Battalion, p. 65
48   German Army Documents on the
      Campaign in Greece (AWM54,
      534/2/27)
49   German Army Documents on the
      Campaign in Greece (AWM54,
      534/2/27)
50   16 Infantry Brigade (AWM52, 8/2/16)
51   Cody, 21 Battalion, p. 66
52   German Army Documents on the
      Campaign in Greece (AWM54,
      534/2/27)
53   Jentz, Panzertruppen: 1933–1942,
      p. 155
54   German Army Documents on the
      Campaign in Greece (AWM54,
      534/2/27)
55   German Army Documents on the
      Campaign in Greece (AWM54,
      534/2/27)
56   Long, Greece, Crete and Syria, p. 108
57   Stockings, 'The Battle of Pinios Gorge',
      p. 147
58   16 Infantry Brigade (AWM52, 8/2/16)
59   Balck, Order in Chaos, p. 210
60   German Army Documents on the
      Campaign in Greece (AWM54,
      534/2/27)
61   Wood, A Battle to Win, p. 136

Chapter Seven: The Battle of Tempe Gorge
1   German Army Documents on the
      Campaign in Greece (AWM54,
      534/2/27)
2   Murphy, 2nd New Zealand Divisional
      Artillery, p. 60

3   Long, Greece, Crete and Syria, p. 113
4   German Army Documents on the
      Campaign in Greece (AWM54,
      534/2/27)
5   German Army Documents on the
      Campaign in Greece (AWM54,
      534/2/27)
6   Stockings, 'The Battle of Pinios Gorge',
      p. 148
7   2/2nd Australian Infantry Battalion
      (AWM52, 8/3/2)
8   McClymont, To Greece, p. 330
9   Stockings, 'The Battle of Pinios Gorge',
      p. 148
10   German Army Documents on the
      Campaign in Greece (AWM54,
      534/2/27)
11   German Army Documents on the
      Campaign in Greece (AWM54,
      534/2/27)
12   Murphy, 2nd New Zealand Divisional
      Artillery, p. 63
13   German Army Documents on the
      Campaign in Greece (AWM54,
      534/2/27)
14   German Army Documents on the
      Campaign in Greece (AWM54,
      534/2/27)
15   German Army Documents on the
      Campaign in Greece (AWM54,
      534/2/27)
16   Rutherford, 'In Their Own Words — The
      Battle of Tempe Gorge' (online)
17   Rutherford, 'In Their Own Words — The
      Battle of Tempe Gorge' (online)
18   Rutherford, 'In Their Own Words — The
      Battle of Tempe Gorge' (online)
19   German Army Documents on the
      Campaign in Greece (AWM54,
      534/2/27)
20   Long, Greece, Crete and Syria, p. 127
21   Wood, A Battle to Win, p. 118
22   German Army Documents on the
      Campaign in Greece (AWM54,
      534/2/27)
23   Jentz, Panzertruppen: 1933–1942,
      p. 155
24   Wood, A Battle to Win, p. 127
25   McClymont, To Greece, p. 324
26   McClymont, To Greece, p. 324
27   Jentz, Panzertruppen: 1933–1942,
      p. 155

28 German Army Documents on the Campaign in Greece (AWM54, 534/2/27)

29 German Army Documents on the Campaign in Greece (AWM54, 534/2/27)

30 German Army Documents on the Campaign in Greece (AWM54, 534/2/27)

31 Wood, A Battle to Win, p. 138

32 Wood, A Battle to Win, pp. 127–8

33 Balck, Order in Chaos, p. 211

34 Wood, A Battle to Win, p. 135

35 Jentz, Panzertruppen: 1933–1942, p. 155

36 Murphy, New Zealand Divisional Artillery, p. 62

37 Jentz, Panzertruppen: 1933–1942, p. 155

38 German Army Documents on the Campaign in Greece (AWM54, 534/2/27)

39 German Army Documents on the Campaign in Greece (AWM54, 534/2/27)

40 Murphy, 2nd New Zealand Divisional Artillery, p. 62

41 Jentz, Panzertruppen: 1933–1942, p. 155

42 McClymont, To Greece, p. 327

43 Wood, A Battle to Win, p. 130

44 Ewer, Forgotten Anzacs, 3042/6692

45 Cody, 21 Battalion, p. 69

46 Wood, A Battle to Win, p. 143

47 16 Infantry Brigade (AWM52, 8/2/16)

48 Note: Major Paul Cullen was born Paul Cohen. AWM52 2/2 Inf Bn 8/3/2

49 16 Infantry Brigade (AWM52, 8/2/16)

50 German Army Documents on the Campaign in Greece (AWM54, 534/2/27)

51 German Army Documents on the Campaign in Greece (AWM54, 534/2/27)

52 Long, Greece, Crete and Syria, p. 115

53 2/2nd Australian Infantry Battalion (AWM52, 8/3/2)

54 16 Infantry Brigade (AWM52, 8/2/16)

55 16 Infantry Brigade (AWM52, 8/2/16)

56 16 Infantry Brigade (AWM52, 8/2/16)

57 Long, Greece, Crete and Syria, p. 115

58 Long, Greece, Crete and Syria, p. 117

59 Long, Greece, Crete and Syria, p. 116

60 Long, Greece, Crete and Syria, p. 116

61 16 Infantry Brigade (AWM52, 8/2/16)

62 German Army Documents on the Campaign in Greece (AWM54, 534/2/27)

63 2/2nd Australian Infantry Battalion (AWM52, 8/3/2)

64 2/2nd Australian Infantry Battalion (AWM52, 8/3/2)

65 McClymont, To Greece, p. 335

66 German Army Documents on the Campaign in Greece (AWM54, 534/2/27)

67 German Army Documents on the Campaign in Greece (AWM54, 534/2/27)

68 German Army Documents on the Campaign in Greece (AWM54, 534/2/27)

69 16 Infantry Brigade (AWM52, 8/2/16)

70 2/2nd Australian Infantry Battalion (AWM52, 8/3/2)

71 Balck, Order in Chaos, p. 211

72 Ewer, Forgotten Anzacs, 3179/6692

73 Long, Greece, Crete and Syria, p. 119

74 German Army Documents on the Campaign in Greece (AWM54, 534/2/27)

Chapter Eight: Athens and Escape

1 Stockings and Hancock, Swastika Over the Acropolis, p. 329

2 Henderson, 22 Battalion, p. 31

3 Stockings and Hancock, Swastika Over the Acropolis, p. 329

4 Dawson, 18 Battalion and Armoured Regiment, p. 106

5 Stockings and Hancock, Swastika Over the Acropolis, p. 387

6 Long, Greece, Crete and Syria, p. 122

7 Stockings and Hancock, Swastika Over the Acropolis, p. 344

8 16 Infantry Brigade (AWM52, 8/2/16)

9 McClymont, To Greece, p. 337

10 McClymont, To Greece, p. 338

11 16 Infantry Brigade (AWM52, 8/2/16)

12 Translation of Taped Conversation with General Hermann Balck, 13 April 1979, p. 10

13 McClymont, To Greece, p. 339

14   *2/3rd Australian Infantry Battalion* (AWM52, 8/3/3)
15   Long, *Greece, Crete and Syria*, p. 120
16   Ewer, *Forgotten Anzacs*, 3176/6692
17   Ewer, *Forgotten Anzacs*, 3167/6692
18   *16 Infantry Brigade* (AWM52, 8/2/16)
19   Stockings and Hancock, *Swastika Over the Acropolis*, p. 345
20   Balck, *Order in Chaos*, p. 211
21   Jentz, *Panzertruppen: 1933–1942*, p. 156
22   Jentz, *Panzertruppen: 1933–1942*, p. 156
23   Ewer, *Forgotten Anzacs*, 3191/6692
24   Long, *Greece, Crete and Syria*, pp. 120–1
25   Long, *Greece, Crete and Syria*, p. 121
26   *Translation of Taped Conversation with General Hermann Balck, 13 April 1979*, p. 25
27   *Translation of Taped Conversation with General Hermann Balck, 13 April 1979*, p. 25
28   *German Army Documents on the Campaign in Greece* (AWM54, 534/2/27)
29   Long, *Greece, Crete and Syria*, p. 121
30   *German Army Documents on the Campaign in Greece* (AWM54, 534/2/27)
31   *German Army Documents on the Campaign in Greece* (AWM54, 534/2/27)
32   *German Army Documents on the Campaign in Greece* (AWM54, 534/2/27)
33   *German Army Documents on the Campaign in Greece* (AWM54, 534/2/27)
34   *German Army Documents on the Campaign in Greece* (AWM54, 534/2/27)
35   Long, *Greece, Crete and Syria*, p. 121
36   *German Army Documents on the Campaign in Greece* (AWM54, 534/2/27)
37   Stockings and Hancock, *Swastika Over the Acropolis*, p. 348
38   Stockings and Hancock, *Swastika Over the Acropolis*, p. 366
39   Long, *Greece, Crete and Syria*, p. 379
40   Grehan and Mace, *Operations in North Africa and the Middle East*, 1628/7540
41   *German Army Documents on the Campaign in Greece* (AWM54, 534/2/27)
42   *German Army Documents on the Campaign in Greece* (AWM54, 534/2/27)
43   Balck, *Order in Chaos*, p. 211
44   *German Army Documents on the Campaign in Greece* (AWM54, 534/2/27)
45   Balck, *Order in Chaos*, p. 212
46   *German Army Documents on the Campaign in Greece* (AWM54, 534/2/27)
47   *German Army Documents on the Campaign in Greece* (AWM54, 534/2/27)
48   *German Army Documents on the Campaign in Greece* (AWM54, 534/2/27)
49   Cody, *21 Battalion*, p. 72
50   Cody, *21 Battalion*, p. 73
51   Long, *Greece, Crete and Syria*, p. 131
52   Cody, *21 Battalion*, p. 73
53   Carr, *The Defence and Fall of Greece*, 5244/5813
54   Osborn, 'Greek Tragedy', p. 86
55   Stockings and Hancock, *Swastika Over the Acropolis*, p. 452
56   Stockings and Hancock, *Swastika Over the Acropolis*, p. 463
57   Stockings and Hancock, *Swastika Over the Acropolis*, p. 477
58   *2/3nd Australian Infantry Battalion* (AWM52, 8/3/3)
59   Stockings and Hancock, *Swastika Over the Acropolis*, p. 479
60   Stockings and Hancock, *Swastika Over the Acropolis*, p. 489
61   Stockings and Hancock, *Swastika Over the Acropolis*, p. 499
62   Stockings and Hancock, *Swastika Over the Acropolis*, p. 500
63   *16 Infantry Brigade* (AWM52, 8/2/16)
64   Long, *Greece, Crete and Syria*, pp. 185–6
65   Long, *Greece, Crete and Syria*, p. 186
66   Ewer, *Forgotten Anzacs*, 3249/6692
67   Balck, *Order in Chaos*, p. 212
68   Balck, *Order in Chaos*, p. 212

69 Balck, *Order in Chaos*, p. 212
70 Balck, *Order in Chaos*, p. 213
71 Stockings and Hancock, *Swastika Over the Acropolis*, p. 589
72 Mitcham and Mueller, *Hitler's Commanders*, p. 175
73 Mitcham, *Panzer Legions*, 1093/5468
74 Williamson, *German Mountain & Ski Troops*, 633/1186
75 Ewer, *Forgotten Anzacs*, 5561/6692
76 Cody, *21 Battalion*, p. 69
77 *2/2nd Australian Infantry Battalion*, Australian War Memorial
78 *2/2nd Australian Infantry Battalion*, Australian War Memorial
79 *Translation of Taped Conversation with General Hermann Balck, 13 April 1979*, p. 3
80 Wood, *A Battle to Win*, p. 109
81 Ewer, *Forgotten Anzacs*, 3303/6692
82 Stockings and Hancock, *Swastika Over the Acropolis*, p. 365
83 Stockings and Hancock, *Swastika Over the Acropolis*, p. 354
84 Stockings, 'The Fairy Tale of the Panzers in Greece, April 1941', p. 22
85 Stockings and Hancock, *Swastika Over the Acropolis*, p. 298
86 *Documents Relating to New Zealand's Participation in the Second World War 1939–45: Volume II*, p. 17
87 Stockings, 'The Fairy Tale of the Panzers in Greece, April 1941', p. 21
88 *German Army Documents on the Campaign in Greece* (AWM54, 534/2/27)
89 Balck, *Order in Chaos*, p. 211
90 Wards, *Panzer Attack in Greece*, p. 8
91 Stockings and Hancock, *Swastika Over the Acropolis*, p. 594
92 *The German invasion of Greece and Yugoslavia* (AWM54, 624/7/2)
93 *Translation of Taped Conversations with General Hermann Balck, 12 January 1979*, pp. 49–50

Chapter Nine: Case Blue
1 Balck, *Order in Chaos*, p. 219
2 *Translation of Taped Conversation with General Hermann Balck, 12 January 1979*, p. 50
3 Balck, *Order in Chaos*, p. 223
4 Zabecki, 'Hermann Balck — Germany's Forgotten Panzer Commander', p. 78
5 Balck, *Order in Chaos*, p. 236
6 Balck, *Order in Chaos*, p. 225
7 Balck, *Order in Chaos*, p. 227
8 Balck, *Order in Chaos*, p. 228
9 Balck, *Order in Chaos*, p. 228
10 Balck, *Order in Chaos*, p. 229
11 Balck, *Order in Chaos*, p. 230
12 Balck, *Order in Chaos*, p. 227
13 *Translation of Taped Conversation with General Hermann Balck, 12 January 1979*, p. 36
14 *Translation of Taped Conversation with General Hermann Balck, 12 January 1979*, p. 36
15 *Translation of Taped Conversation with General Hermann Balck, 12 January 1979*, p. 36
16 Balck, *Order in Chaos*, p. 231
17 Balck, *Order in Chaos*, p. 231
18 Balck, *Order in Chaos*, p. 246
19 Balck, *Order in Chaos*, p. 246
20 Balck, *Order in Chaos*, p. 247
21 *Translation of Taped Conversation with General Hermann Balck, 12 January 1979*, pp. 39–40
22 Balck, *Order in Chaos*, p. 327
23 Glantz, *When Titans Clashed*, p. 133
24 Glantz and House, *To the Gates of Stalingrad*, p. 126
25 Glantz and House, *To the Gates of Stalingrad*, pp. 126–8
26 Glantz and House, *To the Gates of Stalingrad*, p. 117
27 Balck, *Order in Chaos*, p. 248
28 Balck, *Order in Chaos*, p. 248
29 Balck, *Order in Chaos*, p. 248
30 Balck, *Order in Chaos*, p. 248
31 Balck, *Order in Chaos*, p. 249
32 Glantz, *When Titans Clashed*, p. 138
33 Balck, *Order in Chaos*, p. 250
34 Glantz and House, *To the Gates of Stalingrad*, p. 131
35 Glantz and House, *To the Gates of Stalingrad*, p. 133
36 Glantz and House, *To the Gates of Stalingrad*, p. 136
37 Glantz and House, *To the Gates of Stalingrad*, p. 132
38 Glantz, *When Titans Clashed*, p. 138
39 Balck, *Order in Chaos*, p. 250

40 Balck, *Order in Chaos*, p. 251
41 Balck, *Order in Chaos*, p. 250
42 Balck, *Order in Chaos*, pp. 250–1
43 Forczyk, *Tank Warfare on the Eastern Front 1941–1942*, 5253/7229
44 Glantz and House, *To the Gates of Stalingrad*, p. 143
45 Glantz, *When Titans Clashed*, p. 138
46 Glantz and House, *To the Gates of Stalingrad*, p. 149
47 Glantz and House, *To the Gates of Stalingrad*, p. 149
48 Glantz and House, *To the Gates of Stalingrad*, p. 149
49 Glantz and House, *To the Gates of Stalingrad*, pp. 149–51
50 Glantz and House, *To the Gates of Stalingrad*, p. 152
51 Glantz and House, *To the Gates of Stalingrad*, p. 153
52 Glantz and House, *To the Gates of Stalingrad*, p. 136
53 Glantz, *When Titans Clashed*, p. 141
54 Balck, *Order in Chaos*, p. 252
55 *Small Unit Actions during the German Campaign in Russia*, pp. 122–3
56 Anderson, *The History of the Panzerwaffe: Volume II*, p. 75
57 Balck, *Order in Chaos*, p. 252
58 Ganz, *The 11th 'Gespenster' Panzer Division*, p. 108
59 Ganz, *The 11th 'Gespenster' Panzer Division*, p. 112
60 Ganz, *The 11th 'Gespenster' Panzer Division*, p. 112
61 Ganz, *The 11th 'Gespenster' Panzer Division*, p. 113
62 Balck, *Order in Chaos*, p. 253
63 Balck, *Order in Chaos*, p. 253
64 Balck, *Order in Chaos*, p. 253
65 Ganz, *The 11th 'Gespenster' Panzer Division*, p. 113
66 Balck, *Order in Chaos*, p. 254
67 Balck, *Order in Chaos*, p. 254
68 Balck, *Order in Chaos*, p. 255
69 Balck, *Order in Chaos*, p. 256
70 Balck, *Order in Chaos*, p. 256
71 *Small Unit Actions during the German Campaign in Russia*, p. 113
72 Balck, *Order in Chaos*, pp. 256–7
73 Balck, *Order in Chaos*, p. 258
74 Balck, *Order in Chaos*, pp. 257–8

75 Glantz, *When Titans Clashed*, p. 172
76 Zhukov, *Marshal of Victory*, 9640/9644
77 Glantz, *When Titans Clashed*, p. 174
78 Glantz, *When Titans Clashed*, p. 176
79 Balck, *Order in Chaos*, p. 261
80 *Armored Warfare in World War II: Conference Featuring F.W. Von Mellenthin, May 10, 1979*, p. 75
81 Balck, *Order in Chaos*, p. 263

Chapter Ten: The Chir River Battles

1 *Armored Warfare in World War II: Conference Featuring F.W. Von Mellenthin, May 10, 1979*, p. 77
2 Glantz and House, *Endgame at Stalingrad*, p. 41
3 Glantz and House, *Endgame at Stalingrad*, p. 47
4 Glantz and House, *Endgame at Stalingrad*, p. 47
5 Glantz and House, *Endgame at Stalingrad*, p. 46
6 Glantz, *Companion to Endgame at Stalingrad*, pp. 283–4
7 Glantz and House, *Endgame at Stalingrad*, p. 615
8 Glantz and House, *Endgame at Stalingrad*, p. 51
9 Walters, *Order Out Of Chaos*, p. 19
10 *Armored Warfare in World War II: Conference Featuring F.W. Von Mellenthin, May 10, 1979*, p. 77
11 Glantz and House, *Endgame at Stalingrad*, p. 52
12 Glantz and House, *Endgame at Stalingrad*, p. 53
13 Glantz and House, *Endgame at Stalingrad*, p. 54
14 Balck, *Order in Chaos*, p. 267
15 Glantz and House, *Endgame at Stalingrad*, p. 53
16 Scott, 'The Battle for Sowchos 79', p. 58
17 Balck, *Order in Chaos*, p. 265
18 Balck, *Order in Chaos*, p. 264
19 Glantz and House, *Endgame at Stalingrad*, p. 55
20 Balck, *Order in Chaos*, p. 265
21 Glant and House, *Endgame at Stalingrad*, p. 56
22 Walters, *Order Out Of Chaos*, pp. 28–9

23   Glantz, *Companion to Endgame at Stalingrad*, p. 284
24   Balck, *Order in Chaos*, pp. 265–6
25   Glantz and House, *Endgame at Stalingrad*, p. 58
26   Lieutenant General Markian Popov is often confused with Major General Aleksei Popov (commander of the 11th Tank Corps).
27   Glantz, *Companion to Endgame at Stalingrad*, p. 272
28   Glantz and House, *Endgame at Stalingrad*, p. 62
29   Glantz and House, *Endgame at Stalingrad*, pp. 62–3
30   Glantz and House, *Endgame at Stalingrad*, p. 63
31   Mellenthin, *Panzer Battles*, p. 174
32   Walters, *Order Out Of Chaos*, p. 32
33   Balck, *Order in Chaos*, p. 269
34   Glantz, *Companion to Endgame at Stalingrad*, p. 289
35   Liedtke, *Enduring the Whirlwind*, 7302/9543
36   Balck, *Order in Chaos*, p. 269
37   Glantz and House, *Endgame at Stalingrad*, p. 68
38   Mellenthin, *Panzer Battles*, p. 174
39   Balck, *Order in Chaos*, p. 270
40   Glantz and House, *Endgame at Stalingrad*, p. 69
41   Glantz and House, *Endgame at Stalingrad*, p. 77
42   Balck, *Order in Chaos*, p. 269
43   Balck, *Order in Chaos*, pp. 269-70
44   Balck, *Order in Chaos*, p. 264
45   Carlson, 'Portrait of a German General Staff Officer', p. 76
46   Glantz, *Companion to Endgame at Stalingrad*, p. 293
47   Glantz, *Companion to Endgame at Stalingrad*, p. 294
48   Glantz, *Companion to Endgame at Stalingrad*, p. 295
49   Glantz and House, *Endgame at Stalingrad*, p. 74
50   Zhukov, *Marshal of Victory*, 10032/10037
51   Glantz, *When Titans Clashed*, p. 182
52   Mellenthin, *Panzer Battles*, p. 176
53   Glantz and House, *Endgame at Stalingrad*, p. 247
54   Glantz and House, *Endgame at Stalingrad*, p. 248
55   *Armored Warfare in World War II: Conference Featuring F.W. Von Mellenthin, May 10, 1979*, p. 81
56   Balck, *Order in Chaos*, p. 270
57   Walters, *Order Out Of Chaos*, p. 47
58   Balck, *Order in Chaos*, p. 271
59   Walters, *Order Out Of Chaos*, pp. 47–8
60   Walters, *Order Out Of Chaos*, p. 48
61   Balck, *Order in Chaos*, pp. 271–2
62   Jentz, *Panzertruppen: 1943–1945*, p. 30
63   Mellenthin, *German Generals of World War II*, p. 204
64   Glantz and House, *Endgame at Stalingrad*, p. 253
65   Glantz, *Companion to Endgame at Stalingrad*, p. 398
66   Glantz and House, *Endgame at Stalingrad*, p. 252
67   Glantz and House, *Endgame at Stalingrad*, p. 69
68   Glantz and House, *Endgame at Stalingrad*, p. 253
69   Glantz and House, *Endgame at Stalingrad*, p. 255
70   Balck, *Order in Chaos*, p. 272
71   Balck, *Order in Chaos*, p. 272
72   *Translation of Taped Conversation with General Hermann Balck 13 April 1979*, p. 16
73   Balck, *Order in Chaos*, p. 272
74   Mellenthin, *Panzer Battles*, p. 178
75   Showalter, *Hitler's Panzers*, p. 215
76   Glantz and House, *Endgame at Stalingrad*, pp. 256–8
77   Glantz and House, *Endgame at Stalingrad*, pp. 271–2
78   Glantz and House, *Endgame at Stalingrad*, pp. 271–2
79   Liedtke, *Enduring the Whirlwind*, 7313/9543

Chapter Eleven: Disaster at Stalingrad
1   Balck, *Order in Chaos*, p. 273
2   Glantz, *When Titans Clashed*, p. 182
3   Balck, *Order in Chaos*, p. 273
4   Balck, *Order in Chaos*, p. 273
5   Walters, *Order Out Of Chaos*, p. 56
6   Balck, *Order in Chaos*, p. 274
7   Jentz, *Panzertruppen: 1943–1945*, p. 30
8   Balck, *Order in Chaos*, p. 274

9   Zhukov, *Marshal of Victory*, 10056/10062
10   Zhukov, *Marshal of Victory*, 10063/10068
11   Balck, *Order in Chaos*, p. 275
12   Balck, *Order in Chaos*, p. 275
13   Zhukov, *Marshal of Victory*, 10075/10078
14   Glantz and House, *Endgame at Stalingrad*, p. 284
15   Glantz and House, *Endgame at Stalingrad*, p. 285
16   Balck, *Order in Chaos*, p. 279
17   Glantz, *When Titans Clashed*, pp. 185-6
18   Glantz, *When Titans Clashed*, p. 188
19   Balck, *Order in Chaos*, p. 278
20   Balck, *Order in Chaos*, p. 279
21   Balck, *Order in Chaos*, p. 288
22   Balck, *Order in Chaos*, p. 288
23   Balck, *Order in Chaos*, p. 289
24   Balck, *Order in Chaos*, p. 289
25   Jentz, *Panzertruppen: 1943–1945*, p. 30
26   Jentz, *Panzertruppen: 1943–1945*, p. 30
27   Balck, *Order in Chaos*, p. 280
28   Jentz, *Panzertruppen: 1943–1945*, p. 30
29   Mellenthin, *Panzer Battles*, p. 179
30   Balck, *Order in Chaos*, p. 281
31   Balck, *Order in Chaos*, p. 282
32   Glantz, *When Titans Clashed*, p. 185
33   Balck, *Order in Chaos*, p. 283
34   Jentz, *Panzertruppen: 1943–1945*, p. 30
35   Jentz, *Panzertruppen: 1943–1945*, p. 30
36   Balck, *Order in Chaos*, p. 292
37   Balck, *Order in Chaos*, 293
38   Jentz, *Panzertruppen: 1943–1945*, pp. 28–9
39   Jentz, *Panzertruppen: 1943–1945*, p. 29
40   Jentz, *Panzertruppen: 1943–1945*, p. 29
41   Balck, *Order in Chaos*, p. 293

Epilogue
1   Dyson, *Weapons and Hope*, p. 156
2   Zabecki, 'Hermann Balck — Germany's Forgotten Panzer Commander', p. 80
3   Balck, *Order in Chaos*, p. 312
4   Balck, *Order in Chaos*, p. 312
5   Balck, *Order in Chaos*, p. 314
6   Mellenthin, *Panzer Battles*, p. 258
7   Mellenthin, *Panzer Battles*, p. 259
8   McCarthy and Syron, *Panzerkrieg*, 3938/7755
9   Glantz, *When Titans Clashed*, p. 227

10   Raus, *Panzer Operations*, 5364/5367
11   Raus, *Panzer Operations*, 5386/5391
12   Raus, *Panzer Operations*, 5451/5455
13   Mellenthin, *Panzer Battles*, p. 325
14   Mellenthin, *Panzer Battles*, p. 326
15   Balck, *Order in Chaos*, p. 80
16   *Translation of Taped Conversation with General Hermann Balck, 13 April 1979*, p. 16
17   Balck, *Order in Chaos*, p. 433
18   *Translation of Taped Conversation with General Hermann Balck, 13 April 1979*, p. 42
19   *Translation of Taped Conversation with Lieutenant General Heinz Gaedcke, 12 April 1979*, p. 29
20   *Translation of Taped Conversations with General Hermann Balck, 12 January 1979*, p. 21
21   *Generals Balck and Von Mellenthin on Tactics*, p. 11
22   *Translation of Taped Conversation with General Hermann Balck, 12 January 1979*, p. 58
23   *Translation of Taped Conversation with General Hermann Balck 13 April 1979*, p. 26
24   *Generals Balck and Von Mellenthin on Tactics*, p. 17
25   *Translation of Taped Conversation with General Hermann Balck, 13 April 1979*, p. 20
26   *Generals Balck and Von Mellenthin on Tactics*, pp. 18–19
27   Balck, *Order in Chaos*, p. 396
28   Zabecki and Biedekarken, 'Preface', in Balck, *Order in Chaos*, p. x
29   Osborn, 'Greek Tragedy', p. 87
30   Mazower, *Inside Hitler's Greece*, p. xii
31   On 30 March 1941, shortly before Balck's panzer's invaded Greece, Hitler summoned senior military leaders to the Reich Chancellery to ensure they understood the ideological nature of Operation Barbarossa — the German invasion of Russia. Hitler explained that commissars and the intelligentsia would be liquidated, requiring German soldiers to 'forget the concept of comradeship between soldiers'. As Barbarossa would be an ideological struggle between two worldviews represented by two

opposing races, the *Wehrmacht* needed to be ideologically committed to the destruction of 'Jewish Bolshevism. Wette, *The Wehrmacht*, p. 91 and Forster and Mawdsley, 'Hitler and Stalin in Perspective', pp. 63–4

32 Balck stated: 'One officer had been to Galicia and told us there were no more Jews there. To my question as to where they had gone, he stated that they had been moved and eliminated. I answered skeptically, "Well you better win the war, otherwise Lord help us." I did not put much weight on his statement, because from my time in Frankfurt I knew what sort of misinformation was going around. Sometime later another officer traveled through. He had been to Auschwitz and had seen the camps. He described enthusiastically how the Jews there were being prepared for their resettlement. He described the barns, the agriculture, schools, and such. I interjected, "I thought the Galician Jews had all been killed." "But no, nobody harmed them; they are all well taken care of in Auschwitz." Balck, *Order in Chaos*, pp. 327–8

33 Balck, *Order in Chaos*, p. 369
34 Balck, *Order in Chaos*, p. 360
35 Balck, *Order in Chaos*, p. 360
36 Balck, *Order in Chaos*, p. 361
37 Balck, *Order in Chaos*, p. 436
38 Zabecki and Biedekarken, 'Preface', in Balck, *Order in Chaos*, p. xi
39 Smelser and Davies, *The Myth of the Eastern Front*, p. 122
40 Showalter, *Hitler's Panzers*, p. 373
41 *Generals Balck and Von Mellenthin on Tactics*, p. 2
42 *Generals Balck and Von Mellenthin on Tactics*, p. 1
43 *Generals Balck and Von Mellenthin on Tactics*, p. 10
44 *Generals Balck and Von Mellenthin on Tactics*, p. 25
45 *Generals Balck and Von Mellenthin on Tactics*, p. 31
46 *Generals Balck and Von Mellenthin on Tactics*, pp. 31–2
47 *Generals Balck and Von Mellenthin on Tactics*, p. 33

48 *Generals Balck and Von Mellenthin on Tactics*, p. 39
49 *Generals Balck and Von Mellenthin on Tactics*, p. 39
50 Gole, *General William E. DePuy*, 3629/4758
51 Zabecki and Biedekarken, 'Preface', in Balck, *Order in Chaos*, p. xi
52 Guderian, *Panzer Leader*, p. 449
53 Manstein, *Lost Victories*, p. 284
54 Mellenthin, *Panzer Battles*, p. 348
55 Balck, *Order in Chaos*, p. 327
56 Balck, *Order in Chaos*, p. 359
57 Balck, *Order in Chaos*, p. 432
58 Balck, *Order in Chaos*, p. 448
59 Balck, *Order in Chaos*, pp. 291–2
60 Balck, *Order in Chaos*, p. 292
61 Balck, *Order in Chaos*, p. 374

INDEX